"This is the book that the field of Equine Assist
ing for! Integrating theory, research, and pract
the foundation for the future professional de\
approach. This book is essential for anyone working in this field. It offers a
vital contribution to the compassionate equestrian movement that I teach.
Read it and be of benefit to all beings."
Allen M. Schoen, DVM, MS, PhD (hon.), *author of Kindred Spirits:
How the Remarkable Bond Between Humans and Animals Can Change the
Way We Live and co-author of "The Compassionate Equestrian, 25 Principles
to Live by When Caring for and Working With Horses" (Trafalgar Books,
2015)*

"This book tells the truth about where the Equine-Assisted industry is
today in a completely honest manner using scientific methodology. While
it is a book that can be enjoyably read from cover to cover, it also should
be a required reference for every person involved in the industry, especially
students, practitioners, patients, and researchers."
C. Mike Tomlinson, DVM, MBA, *president of the Horses & Humans
Research Foundation and FEI/USET Team Veterinarian*

"Leif Hallberg provides us with an extensive review of the literature within
the field of Equine Assisted Therapy in the US, and reminds us how much
more is needed. Acceptance of use of the terminology presented here would
standardize the description of our work, erase the confusion that remains
so prevalent and promote growth in our fields. This is recommended reading for all professionals incorporating equine-assisted interactions."
Carol Huegel, PT, *HPCS Chair, American Hippotherapy Certification
Board (AHCB)*

"Leif Hallberg succeeds in giving our industry an exceptional and unique
textbook about the history and current state of EAT in the United States.
Her critical analysis based on an impressive compilation of reference literature is spot on and offers EAT practitioners much food for thought.
Her 'Vision for the Future' examines all the important areas that this
relatively new industry needs to address and provides suggestions about
how to improve international collaboration, such as creating a unified terminology, defining the scope of practice and protecting the needs of the
equines."
Gisela Heimsath-Rhodes, *executive director of the Horses in Education
and Therapy International Federation (HETI)*

The Clinical Practice of Equine-Assisted Therapy

The Clinical Practice of Equine-Assisted Therapy bridges theory, research, and practical methods to fill a rapidly developing gap for physical, occupational, speech, and mental health professionals interested in incorporating horses in therapy. Extensively researched and citing over 300 peer-reviewed journal articles, it examines core issues such as terminology, scope of practice, competency recommendations, horse care ethics, and clinical practice considerations. This book is an essential resource for professionals who wish to use a best-practices approach to equine-assisted therapy.

Leif Hallberg, MA, LPC, LCPC, is an internationally acclaimed author, consultant, licensed mental health professional, and educator whose career has centered on the practice of equine-assisted activities and therapies. She is the author of *Walking the Way of the Horse: Exploring the Power of the Horse-Human Relationship*. Leif provides consultation services, offers individual sessions, teaches courses, and leads professional development trainings and workshops both nationally and internationally. She can be reached at http://www.leifhallberg.com.

The Clinical Practice of Equine-Assisted Therapy
Including Horses in Human Healthcare

Leif Hallberg

Routledge
Taylor & Francis Group

NEW YORK AND LONDON

First published 2018
by Routledge
711 Third Avenue, New York, NY 10017

and by Routledge
2 Park Square, Milton Park, Abingdon, Oxon, OX14 4RN

Routledge is an imprint of the Taylor & Francis Group, an informa business

Library of Congress Cataloging-in-Publication Data
Names: Hallberg, Leif, 1976– author.
Title: The clinical practice of equine-assisted therapy : including horses in
    human healthcare / Leif Hallberg.
Description: New York : Routledge, 2018. | Includes bibliographical
    references and index.
Identifiers: LCCN 2017036085 | ISBN 9781138674622 (hardcover : alk.
    paper) | ISBN 9781138674639 (pbk. : alk. paper) | ISBN 9781315545905
    (e-book)
Subjects: MESH: Equine-Assisted Therapy—methods | Horses—psychology |
    Professional Practice
Classification: LCC RM931.H6 | NLM WB 460 | DDC 615.8/51581—dc23
LC record available at https://lccn.loc.gov/2017036085

ISBN: 978-1-138-67462-2 (hbk)
ISBN: 978-1-138-67463-9 (pbk)
ISBN: 978-1-315-54590-5 (ebk)

Typeset in Garamond
by Apex CoVantage, LLC

Cover image: © "Grazing" by Laurie Pace, www.lauriepace.com

Dedicated to Ann Kern-Godal (May 1943–May 2017)

Contents

Acknowledgements

Special thanks to Ian McNairy, without whom there would be no book; to John and Nancy Hallberg for their dedication and tireless support; and to Dr. Daniel Stroud, Dr. Leslie Stewart, Dr. Allen Schoen, Ann Kern-Godal, Jacqueline Tiley, Dr. Heather Ajzenman, Steve McKenzie, Tina Rocco, Donna Latella, Becky Cook, Laura Brinckerhoff, Tanya Bailey, Kali Welch, and Jama Rice for their help and expertise as subject matter experts and reviewers. Thank you to artist Laurie Pace for granting me permission to use her beautiful art as the cover for the book. An important thanks is also in order for all the professionals who responded to the 2016 Oregon State University Professional Practice of Equine-Assisted Therapy survey, your comments helped to shape this book. Finally, thank you to Anna Moore and the team at Routledge for making this project possible.

About the Author

Leif Hallberg, MA, LPC, LCPC, is an internationally acclaimed author, consultant, licensed mental health professional, educator, and avid lover of nature and animals. Her professional career and life's work have centered around researching the human-equine bond, and studying the industry of equine-assisted activities and therapies. As a leading expert, innovator, and pioneer, she has developed a reputation over the past 20 years for her broad-reaching and objective study of the industry and dissemination of information. It has been Leif's goal to clarify, define, and objectively describe the complexity and diversity of the human-equine relationship and the professional applications of this relationship.

A horseback riding instructor and horse trainer turned mental health professional and educator, Leif relies both upon practical equine knowledge and her clinical experience to design innovative programs for a wide range of populations. Leif designs curricula and teaches courses and workshops at both an undergraduate and graduate level, and provides continuing education opportunities for professionals, presenting both nationally and internationally. Leif's books are used by colleges and universities around the world as teaching texts, and professionals consider them essential resources for research and clinical practice. It is used by colleges and universities around the world as a teaching text, and has been purchased by thousands of professionals as a reference to guide their practices.

Today, Leif provides consultation services, offers individual sessions, teaches courses, and leads professional development trainings and workshops both nationally and internationally. She can be reached at www.leifhallberg.com.

Acronyms

ACA	The American Counseling Association
ADD/ADHD	Attention Deficient Disorder/Attention Deficient Hyperactivity Disorder
AHA	The American Hippotherapy Association, Inc.
AHCB	The American Hippotherapy Certification Board
AIA	Adventures in Awareness™
AOTA	The American Occupational Therapy Association
APA	The American Psychology Association
ASHA	The American Speech-Language-Hearing Association
APTA	The American Physical Therapy Association
CBEIP	The Certification Board for Equine Interaction Professionals
EAAT	Equine-assisted activities and therapies
EAGALA	The Equine Assisted Growth and Learning Association
EAL	Equine-assisted learning
EAMH	Equine-assisted mental health
EAP	Equine-assisted psychotherapy
EFMHA	The Equine Facilitated Mental Health Association
EFP/L	Equine-facilitated psychotherapy and learning
EPI	The Equine Psychotherapy Institute
GEIR	The Gestalt Equine Institute of the Rockies
HEAL	The Human-Equine Alliances for Learning
HERD	The Human-Equine Relational Development Institute
HETI	The Federation of Horses in Education and Therapy International
HHRF	The Horses and Humans Research Foundation
HT or HPOT	Hippotherapy
ICE	The Institute for Credentialing Excellence
NARHA	The North American Riding for the Handicapped Association
NASW	The National Association of Social Workers
NBCC	The National Board for Certified Counselors
NEHA	The National Environmental Health Association

NL	Natural Lifemanship
PATH Intl.	The Professional Association of Therapeutic Horsemanship International
PTSD	Post-traumatic stress disorder
SAMHSA	The Substance Abuse and Mental Health Services Administration
TF-EAP	Trauma-focused equine-assisted psychotherapy
TR or THR	Therapeutic riding

Foreword

Leif Hallberg and I have known each other for many years. We met through our work with PATH Intl. (Professional Association of Therapeutic Horsemanship, International), then the North American Riding for the Handicapped Association (NARHA). We worked closely together on board and committee tasks, helping to grow this industry we are both so passionate about.

Over the years Leif and I have had a number of discussions about the need for articulation in terminology, and the importance of defining the differences between equine-assisted therapy and equine-assisted activities. Confusion between therapy and non-therapy services continues to cause challenges for those seeking services, those providing services, and those looking to fund services, specifically third-party payers, and affects the industry as a whole.

The Clinical Practice of Equine-Assisted Therapy: Including Horses in Human Healthcare supports those providing equine-assisted therapy by differentiating between therapy and non-therapy services, defining key terminology use, and addressing scope of practice issues.

Ms. Hallberg has done extensive research across disciplines, and this book offers tools for licensed physical, occupational, speech-language, and mental health professionals to better clarify and define the services they provide. Ms. Hallberg has made appropriate comparisons to show how the medical model of equine-assisted therapy should function. She addresses competency, education and training, credentialing, clinical practice issues, and healthcare business models. It is my belief this book will be able to not only guide new practitioners but also offer clarity to those currently practicing, the partnering equine programs these professionals may contract and work with, and even medical professionals interested in referring patients.

As the Executive Director of the American Hippotherapy Association, Inc., I felt most drawn to this book because of Ms. Hallberg's insights into the future of this industry. It is clear that both national and international organizations need to work together, and I am happy to share that the American Hippotherapy Association, Inc. is working towards this goal by meeting with many of the organizations Leif speaks of as regularly as possible. The ultimate goal of all those providing service whether it be equine-assisted activities or equine-assisted therapies is to see improvements in our riders and patients, to raise the bar on professionalism by obtaining the necessary education and credentials, and to grow the body of knowledge through more rigorous research. As Ms. Hallberg points out, as professionals in this industry it is our job to be part of the change that will set our industry on course for a long-lasting and sustainable future.

Thank you, Leif, for bringing us all together under the umbrella of equine-assisted therapy. We are stronger as one undivided group, and we can work together to increase awareness and guide the industry into its next stage of growth. I look forward to collaborating with those of you reading this book, and have great faith in the future of this industry.

Jacqueline Rae Tiley
Executive Director
American Hippotherapy Association, Inc.

Preface

Until just a few years ago, horses shaped nearly every aspect of my daily life. They were my friends, my family, and my community. I spent most of my time in their company, learning from them as I observed their behaviors and engaged in their daily lives.

My love affair with horses began at 3 years of age, and continued without ceasing through high school, undergraduate college, and graduate school. Horses permeated every aspect of my life and that of my family's. My parents became avid supporters of all things horse, and even turned into competent horse people themselves. We had many horses over the years, and most of them lived with us. My parents helped with every equine endeavor I was a part of, and eventually transitioned into helping me run the non-profit equine-assisted mental health and learning organization, Esperanza, I founded and directed for over 10 years. When I met my husband, he moved out west to live on the farm, and he too became a competent horseperson and soon began helping with Esperanza's services. To say our lives were deeply interconnected with horses would be an understatement.

I started Esperanza because of what I learned from horses. I came to believe that if people could learn a non-verbal interspecies form of communication and way of being that was based on concepts of respect, sensitivity, awareness, and compassion, they might change how they treated each other and the natural world. My motivation was centered around my concern for the environment and for the wellbeing of all who could not protect themselves from harm (animals, children, the poor, and the disenfranchised).

My transition away from horses began slowly 5 years ago. Of our long-time herd, three horses passed away, and one moved to a new home. That left only Suzy Q. When she passed away 3 years later at the age of 35, we had been together for 30 years. To lose Suzy was like losing an older sister. She taught me how to be in relationship, how to communicate, how to lead, and when to follow. The adventures we had and the lessons I learned are innumerable. Losing her was heartbreaking in a way I still have not recovered from.

I share all of this with you because as you read this book, there may be times when you wonder if I am a supporter of equine-assisted therapy. I am. However, after Suzy Q's death, I thought a great deal about what she taught me, and how I might honor her. One of the most important lessons I learned from Suzy was to bravely question the status quo, leading fearlessly forward towards new horizons.

This book is a tribute to Suzy, to her indomitable spirit and her tenacious, thoughtful, and strong leadership style that guided her herd (horses and humans alike) toward safer and more fertile pastures.

Leif Hallberg
February, 2017

Introduction

Including horses in physical, occupational, speech, and mental health professionals has been a part of human healthcare since the 1950s (Wang, et al., 2015). Many attest to the therapeutic qualities of horses, and believe passionately in the horse's ability to help humans heal.

Equine-assisted therapy broadly refers to any type of therapy or treatment that includes equine interactions, activities, or treatment strategies, and the equine milieu. Services are regulated by healthcare laws and provided by appropriately educated, trained, and credentialed (licensed or registered) healthcare professionals. Equine-assisted therapy includes equine-assisted mental health (sometimes also known as equine-assisted psychotherapy), equine-assisted physical therapy, equine-assisted occupational therapy, and equine-assisted speech therapy.

This book provides an overview of equine-assisted therapy and is applicable for physical therapists, occupational therapists, speech therapists, mental health professionals, nurses, and other healthcare professionals, as well as researchers, or educators interested in equine-assisted therapy. Parents, patients, referents, and the general public may also find this book enlightening when considering equine-assisted therapy.

Over the years, equine-assisted therapy has become increasingly recognized by consumers and referents alike. Medical doctors refer patients for equine-assisted physical, occupational, or speech therapy, mental health professionals see their patients at the farm, and consumers report improvement across a broad spectrum of conditions. This surge in popularity has established equine-assisted therapy as a viable treatment option in the eyes of the public. However, there is a notable gap between the outcomes of scholarly research and the personal passions, beliefs, opinions, and practice patterns prevalent in the accessible literature.

Many providers of equine-assisted therapy report inadequate access to peer-reviewed journals (Stroud & Hallberg, 2016), which are the primary source for documenting current research and practice trends. This phenomenon is called the "science to service gap" (National Implementation Science Research Network, 2016). Common across most healthcare disciplines, the results of scientific study are not always accessible to those in clinical practice. When professionals do not have access to current research, healthcare strategies may be provided that are ineffective, outdated, or lack conclusive research results (International Council of Nurses, 2012). The field of implementation science is attempting to help remedy this gap by studying the integration of research findings and evidence into healthcare policies and practices, and identifying common bottle necks or road blocks (National Institutes of Health, 2016).

When contemplating the foundation for this book, it was clear an approach was needed that would help bridge the gap between scientific research and the personal beliefs, opinions, and practices prevalent in mainstream literature and promoted by membership or training organizations. To achieve this goal, a comprehensive review of research articles on equine-assisted therapy published between 1985–2016 was conducted using 14 databases including PsycINFO, PsycARTICLES, PubMed, CAB Abstracts, Psychiatric Online, Psychological and Behavioral Sciences Collection, the Social Sciences Citation Index, Nursing & Allied Health Collection, Physical Therapy and Sports Medicine Collection, EBSCO Academic Search, EBSCO SPORTDiscus, EBSCO Educational Research Complete, EBSCO HealthSource, and VetMed.

Key words used for the search were equine-assisted therapy, hippotherapy, therapeutic riding, adaptive riding, equine-assisted psychotherapy, equine-facilitated psychotherapy, equine-assisted counseling, equine-assisted learning, and equine-facilitated learning. Additional search terms were used in conjunction with those key words including: autism, addictions, amputations, anxiety, at-risk youth, ADD/ADHD, cancer, cerebral palsy, chemical dependency, children and adolescents, depression, Down syndrome, eating disorders, elderly, intellectual disability, learning disability, multiple sclerosis, physical abuse, psychiatric condition, PTSD, severe mental illness, sexual assault or abuse, stroke, spine injury, trauma, traumatic brain injury, veterans. Bibliographies from the retrieved articles were also examined and the Equine Interventions Repository was searched to make sure not to miss any additional articles.

The following inclusion criteria were used to select the final papers:

1. Peer-reviewed (refereed) papers
2. Primary source
3. Written in English
4. Published between 1985–2016
5. Directly relevant to equine-assisted therapy, but includes papers on the following related topics:

   a. Robo (or mechanical horse simulator use as it relates to equine-assisted therapy)
   b. Practice patterns, reviews, and perspectives related to equine-assisted interventions

c. Horse care and welfare, ethics, and selection criteria related to equine-assisted therapy
d. Horse ethology (including communication, behavior, psychology)
e. Safety and accident data related to working with horses

A total of 354 papers were identified that met the inclusion criteria. These articles were coded and sorted into categories by population or condition addressed by an equine-assisted intervention, or by the topic of research inquiry. The outcome of this process is the foundation on which this book was written.

As Dr. Steven Novella, a clinical neurologist and professor at Yale's School of Medicine states, "The most compelling stories are our own. When we believe we have experienced something directly, it is difficult to impossible to convince us otherwise" (Novella, 2008, para. 5). In many ways, those providing equine-assisted therapy may be able to relate. Once one has experienced the power of working with horses, it can be difficult to take an objective look at one's own practices, and the treatment strategy as a whole.

Although at times, information presented in this book may be hard to read for those passionately involved in providing equine-assisted therapy, the purpose of the book is not to diminish the healing potential of the horse-human relationship. Rather, it serves as a resource to examine the professional practice of equine-assisted therapy through an objective, scholarly lens.

☐ Internationalism and Equine-Assisted Therapy

Equine-assisted therapy is provided in over 50 countries around the world (HETI, 2016; PATH Intl., 2016; EAGALA, 2016). At the conception of this book, it was the intention of the author to create a text that would be inclusive of the many ways people practice in these different countries. However, it became obvious that due to the differences between countries, such a level of specification would be nearly impossible to achieve. Therefore, detailed information provided in this book related to healthcare laws and practices is specific to the United States, and may or may not transfer to other countries.

That being said, the international nature of equine-assisted therapy is represented by the voices of researchers from all over the world, and echoed by professionals from many countries who responded to the professional practice survey conducted by Stroud & Hallberg (2016). It is hoped readers from other countries will find use in the concepts provided in this book, and will apply the material within the context of their own laws, ethics, and standards of practice.

☐ How to Use This Book

The book provides an overview of equine-assisted therapy and addresses important themes prevalent in the industry today. The outcomes of a cross-sectional international research project (Stroud & Hallberg, 2016) identified topics of interest or concern to current-day providers of equine-assisted therapy, and helped to guide and shape much of the content. Terminology, scope of practice, ethics, and professional competencies emerged as important topics to investigate and discuss within the context of this book.

The book is accompanied by *The Equine-Assisted Therapy Workbook: A Learning Guide for Professionals and Students*. This workbook offers an opportunity for continued learning, personal exploration, and professional development, and includes hands-on learning activities, self-assessments, practical scenarios, ethics questions, and journal assignments. Using the book and workbook together is highly recommended.

☐ Future Editions

Given the ever-evolving nature of equine-assisted therapy, some of the information included in this book may be outdated or eclipsed even by its publication. Therefore, future editions of this book will update and rectify any outdated information, and continue to keep readers as informed as possible about the state of the industry, current research results, and practice trends related to equine-assisted therapy.

☐ Relevant Terminology

Inconsistent use of terminology and an over-abundance of terms has caused challenges in both practice and research for those interested in, or studying, equine-assisted activities and therapies. In many cases, terms are changed or adapted from their conventional uses by individuals or organizations who are not familiar with the standard (and sometimes legal) applications of the terms.

The following is a list of relevant terms and their definitions that will be presented throughout the book. Added to these definitions are terms that could be used synonymously as well as additional information to help researchers and providers better understand and correctly utilize the term.

Readers are encouraged to remember that many different types of professionals from around the world will be using this book. In order to be as relevant as possible to this diverse group, terms will be defined as broadly and inclusively as possible.

Adaptive Riding: Adaptive riding is a type of equine-assisted activity that is a non-therapy skills-based service in which specially trained instructors teach horseback riding and horsemanship skills to students with disabilities or special needs. This term can be used synonymously with "therapeutic riding", however, "adaptive riding" is recommended to help further differentiate between therapy and non-therapy services.

Animal-Assisted Activities: Animal-assisted activities refers to the non-therapy services that include animals and focus on teaching skills and enhancing quality of life. Although these services are not regulated by healthcare laws, ethics, competency requirements, or standards of practice in the United States, and thus are not considered a form of "therapy", they are usually provided by specialty trained professionals, paraprofessionals, and/or volunteers. The animals who typically work in animal-assisted activities programs are also specialty-trained and sometimes certified by industry associations.

Animal-Assisted Therapy: Animal-assisted therapy broadly refers to including animals in clinical services that are provided by licensed healthcare professionals. Services are regulated by healthcare laws and commonly offered by physicians, occupational therapists, physical therapists, speech therapists, certified therapeutic recreation specialists, nurses, or mental health professionals. The term "animal-assisted interventions" can be used synonymously.

Certificate of Completion: A certificate of completion marks the successful completion of a trade or method-specific training program. These "certificates" are given out at the complication of a professional development workshop or course to indicate the attendee has completed the necessary requirements for the training. A certificate of completion or "certificate program" that is offered through the same organization that provides the education should not be confused with a credential or a certification that is the outcome of a credentialing process.

Conventional Therapy: Forms of therapy that are widely accepted and commonly used by most professionals. Although the term "traditional" therapy can be used synonymously, it is avoided in this book due to the indigenous connotations related to ancient knowledge or wisdom handed down through the generations.

Credential: Credentialing is a process by which a third party validates the education, experience, qualifications, and competency of a professional. Credentialing requires a separation between the education source (i.e. a college degree program or a trade-specific certificate program) and the credentialing body in order to promote non-biased, ethical evaluation. Credentialing bodies do not provide training or education. Rather, these entities support the broad acquisition of knowledge from diverse sources. Credentialing bodies do not align with, require, or assess for specific methodological knowledge. The outcome of a credentialing process is either a state issued license or an industry-approved "certification".

EAGALA Model of Equine-Assisted Psychotherapy: An approach to equine-assisted mental health provided by a licensed mental health professional that is methodologically-specific and activities-based. Only those who have been certified by the Equine Assisted Growth and Learning Association (EAGALA) and who adhere to the manualized approach may state they practice the EAGALA Model of equine-assisted psychotherapy. It is important to note there are many other ways to provide equine-assisted mental health or psychotherapy that do not follow the EAGALA model.

Education: Systemic instruction that takes place within institutions of education, as in traditional or alternative learning environments such as schools, colleges, or universities. The desired outcome of education is that the student finishes the program with an increased knowledge base that is demonstrated through the tangible application of information (i.e. written or practical exams, or other forms of competency testing).

Equine-Assisted Activities: Equine-assisted activities refers to the non-therapy services that include horses and focus on teaching skills and enhancing quality of life. Consumers and referring professionals should be aware these services are not regulated by healthcare laws, ethics, competency requirements, or standards of practice in the United States, and thus not considered a form of "therapy". The most common forms of equine-assisted activities are adaptive (or "therapeutic") riding and equine-assisted learning which includes life or professional development coaching.

Equine-Assisted Activities & Therapies or "EAAT": EAAT services are organized as either non-therapy "activities" such as adaptive riding or equine-assisted learning, or "therapies" in which the horse is included in physical therapy, occupational therapy, speech therapy, or mental health services provided by licensed professionals. "EAAT" should be used ONLY as an umbrella term to describe the larger industry that includes both therapy and non-therapy equine interactions, while the terms "equine-assisted activities" or "equine-assisted therapy" should be used specifically to distinguish between a therapy or non-therapy service.

Equine-Assisted Counseling: A type of equine-assisted mental health in which a licensed mental health professional uses practical, skills-based, problem-solving, and present-moment-focused equine and farm-based activities to address treatment goals. It aligns closely with the principles of choice and reality therapies.

Equine-Assisted Learning: Equine-assisted learning (EAL) is a type of equine-assisted activity that broadly refers to non-therapy, skills-based services that focus on teaching life skills, social skills, communication skills, relationship skills, or leadership skills while facilitating personal growth and increased self-awareness through both mounted and non-mounted interactions with horses. Services are provided by educators, riding instructors, or life/professional development coaches. EAL providers may teach horsemanship skills, and even use riding and other mounted activities as a means to foster skills. Providers practice using a variety of approaches or theoretical beliefs. The terms "equine-facilitated learning", "equine-facilitated experiential learning", "equine experiential education", "equine-guided education", or "equine-assisted coaching" are all used synonymously.

Equine-Assisted Mental Health: A term that used to describe any type of mental health service (psychology, counseling, psychotherapy, social work, etc.) that includes horses or the farm milieu. Mental health services are provided by professionals who have graduated from an accredited education program and are allowed by law to include mental health treatment as a part of their scope of practice. These licensed professionals may choose between a variety of different approaches (see below) when providing equine-assisted mental health. Equine-assisted mental health is sometimes used synonymously with "equine-assisted psychotherapy". Equine-assisted mental health is a type of equine-assisted therapy.

Equine-Assisted Occupational Therapy: This term describes the inclusion of horses in an occupational therapy service. Occupational therapy addresses physical, psychological, and cognitive aspects of well-being. Occupational therapy is provided by professionals who have graduated from an accredited occupational therapy education program and are licensed to practice occupational therapy. Equine-assisted occupational therapy is a type of equine-assisted therapy.

Equine-Assisted Physical Therapy: This term describes the inclusion of horses in a physical therapy service. Physical therapy uses treatment techniques to promote the ability to move, reduce pain, restore function, and prevent disability. Physical therapy is provided by professionals who have graduated from an accredited physical therapy education program and are licensed to practice physical therapy. Equine-assisted physical therapy is a type of equine-assisted therapy.

Equine-Assisted Psychotherapy: This term is usually used to speak broadly about the inclusion of horses in mental health services. At present, there is no specific method or model associated with this term. The term is commonly used synonymously with "equine-assisted mental health".

Equine-Assisted Speech Therapy: This term describes the inclusion of horses in a speech, language, or hearing therapy service. Speech-language pathologists treat speech, language, social communication, cognitive-communication, and swallowing disorders. Speech therapy is provided by professionals who have graduated from an accredited speech-language-hearing education program and are licensed to practice speech therapy. Equine-assisted speech therapy is a type of equine-assisted therapy.

Equine-Assisted Therapy: Equine-assisted therapy broadly refers to any type of therapy or treatment that includes equine interactions, activities, or treatment strategies, and the equine milieu. Services are regulated by healthcare laws and provided by appropriately educated, trained and credentialed (licensed or registered) healthcare professionals. Providers and researchers should indicate which type of professional is incorporating the equine interaction by using the following specific terms: Equine-assisted physical therapy, equine-assisted occupational therapy, equine-assisted speech therapy, or equine-assisted mental health. The term "equine-assisted interventions" can also be used to describe the clinical application of including horses in human healthcare while terms like "equine-assisted activities", "therapeutic riding", or "equine-assisted learning" should not be used interchangeably with equine-assisted therapy.

Equine-Facilitated Psychotherapy: An approach to equine-assisted mental health in which a licensed mental health professional views the horse as a sentient co-facilitator. Activities are steeped in mindfulness-based practices and include the creative arts. This approach is depth and insight-oriented, and is usually considered long-term in nature.

Ethology: The scientific and objective study of animal behavior, especially under natural conditions.

Farm: This term will be used to describe the equine environment or milieu and may be used interchangeably with "barn". The intention behind using this term is to encourage providers of equine-assisted therapy to consider ways to enhance the equine environment by including other farm animals, horticulture, and other experiences that typically take place at a farm.

Hippotherapy: Refers to how occupational, physical, and speech therapists incorporate equine movement and the farm milieu in a patient's treatment plan, using clinical reasoning in the purposeful manipulation of equine movement to engage sensory, neuromotor, and cognitive systems to achieve functional outcomes. Researchers and providers should specify the type of therapy provided when using hippotherapy, for example physical, occupational, or speech therapy.

Horse: This term will be used synonymously with "equine" for purposes of international use and simplicity, and is meant to broadly include all equids.

Industry: A commercial endeavor that combines similar businesses and embraces both licensed professionals as well as business owners, technicians, paraprofessionals, and support staff. The term "industry" is used throughout this book in place of "field", which is typically used to indicate a specific area of professional practice or study.

Learning: The process of gaining knowledge or skills, synthesizing information, or altering behaviors. Learning can occur anywhere, and is not limited to academic (or educational) settings.

Licensed: The term 'licensed' indicates a professional has met the credentialing requirements (including education, experience, and knowledge) necessary to provide a regulated healthcare service. Licensing is managed by individual states, and each state may require a different credentialing process. Only people with the appropriate state-mandated education and experience who have passed a national exam, and applied for, and been granted a state license are allowed by law to use the term "licensed".

Mental Health: This term describes emotional, psychological, and social well-being, the disorders, illnesses, or conditions that impact these aspects of human function, and how people think, feel, and act. By law, the treatment of mental health conditions or mental illness is only conducted by licensed professionals whose scope of practice includes mental health treatment.

Milieu: The environment (physical or social) in which something takes place.

Patient: A person receiving medical treatment. This term is used in place of "client" to help further differentiate equine-assisted therapy from non-therapy approaches like life or professional development coaching, riding lessons, or experiential learning services in which a participant may be called a "client".

Physical Therapy: For the purposes of this book, the terms "physical therapist" or "physical therapy" will be used broadly to include physiotherapy and physiotherapists.

Regulated: This term refers to state mandated laws set in place to regulate or govern a healthcare practice. Most common types of state regulation include professional licensure, scope of practice, term and title protection, or specific types of certifications required by the state. Any healthcare provider who offers a regulated service must adhere to specific state and federal laws and standards of practice. Examples of healthcare services that are regulated in all 50 states include physical therapy, occupational therapy, speech therapy, counseling, social work, and psychology.

Service: This word is used in a few different ways throughout this book. In some cases, "service" is used generically, as in "work that is done for others as an occupation or business" or "work done for others, usually for pay". However, in the case of licensed healthcare professionals, whatever profession they are licensed to provide is usually considered the service. For example, the service licensed physical therapists provide is physical therapy, not hippotherapy. For insurance billing purposes, licensed professionals are urged make this distinction.

Scope of Practice: The procedures, processes, and actions a licensed healthcare provider is permitted to undertake by law in keeping with the terms of their professional license. Individuals who are not licensed healthcare professionals do not have a "scope of practice". Instead, by law, these non-licensed individuals must provide services that are distinctly different than those which fall within the scope of practice of any type of licensed healthcare provider.

Specialty Area of Practice: An advanced or additional level of practice beyond the typical scope of knowledge included in a licensed professional's education and training.

Speech Therapist: In this book, the terms "speech therapy" and "speech therapists" will be used in place of "speech-language pathology" and "speech-language pathologists".

Therapy: A protected term used to describe the treatment of physical or mental illnesses, disorders or diseases that are regulated or sanctioned by healthcare laws and provided only by credentialed (licensed or registered) healthcare professionals.

Treatment: Medical (or mental health) care administered to a patient for an illness or injury and provided by licensed healthcare professionals. The term "treatment" is a protected term used by licensed healthcare professionals.

Treatment Approach: A broad way of dealing with a clinical concern or problem. This term may be used interchangeably with "treatment method" or "treatment model".

☐ References

Equine Assisted Growth and Learning Association (EAGALA). (2016). *Find a Program.* Retrieved from: http://home.eagala.org/find

Federation of Horses in Therapy and Education International (HETI). (2016). *Current Members.* Retrieved from: www.frdi.net/membership_list.html

International Council of Nurses. (2012). *Closing the Gap: From Evidence to Action.* Retrieved from: www.icn.ch/publications/2012-closing-the-gap-from-evidence-to-action/

National Implementation Science Research Network (NIRN). (2016). *Implementation Science Defined.* Retrieved from: http://nirn.fpg.unc.edu/learn-implementation/implementation-science-defined

National Institutes of Health (NIH). (2016). *Dissemination and Implementation Science.* Retrieved from: www.nlm.nih.gov/hsrinfo/implementation_science.html

Novella, S. (2008). *The Role of Anecdotes in Science-Based Medicine.* Retrieved from: https://sciencebasedmedicine.org/the-role-of-anecdotes-in-science-based-medicine/

Professional Association of Therapeutic Horsemanship International (PATH Intl.). (2016). *Find a Center.* Retrieved from: www.pathintl.org/path-intl-centers/find-center

Stroud, D., & Hallberg, L. (2016). [Horses in healthcare: An international assessment of the professional practice of equine-assisted therapy]. Unpublished raw data.

Wang, G., Ma, R., Qiao, G., et al. (2015). The effect of riding as an alternative treatment for children with cerebral palsy: A systematic review and meta-analysis. *Integrative Medicine International, 1*(4), 211–222.

1 Foundations of Equine-Assisted Therapy

☐ The History of Including Horses in Human Healthcare

Myth, magic, mystery, and metaphor have surrounded the topic of horses and human healthcare for centuries. Sources suggest horses were viewed as healing or therapeutic for humans since the time of the early Greeks (DePauw, 1986; Brudvig, 1988; Meregillano, 2004; Snider, et al., 2007; Bachi, et al., 2011; Burgon, 2011; Lanning & Krenek, 2013).

Legend tells us of the centaur Chiron, half-man, half-horse, who was shot while instructing a young man in the art of hunting and nearly died. He cured himself of the grievous wound, and through that experience discovered the healing arts. He went on to care for others, and is known in Greek mythology as the creator of medicine and surgery (Howey, 1923). Chiron's story is representative of our modern-day "wounded healer" archetype.

Horses are thought to have been domesticated around 4000 BC, on the Eurasian steppes of the Ukraine (McGreevy, 2012), and very early in history were viewed both as the terrifying tools of destruction, warfare and death, and as messengers of the Divine, capable of bringing humans into contact with the ethereal realms of the spirit world. The Hindus and the Celts believed horses traversed the space between heaven and earth, carrying their riders on the journey between life and death (McCormick & McCormick, 1997; Howey, 1923; Kohanov, 2007; Hallberg, 2008). Biblical stories of Zechariah tell of God using horses and the men who rode them to spread His message, in one instance stating "These are the four spirits of heaven, going out from standing in the presence of the Lord of the whole world" (Zechariah 6:5, New American Standard Bible). The role of horse as messenger between humans and the spirit world continues today, as many find peace and solace in their powerful presence, and use the quiet time spent with horses to pray or mediate, seeking answers to life's challenges (Dell, et al., 2011; Wach, 2014).

Hippocrates believed horseback riding was a universal language with a healing rhythm, and physicians prescribed riding to address mental, physical, and emotional issues (Granados & Agís, 2011). Medical literature from the 15th–18th centuries gives accounts of physicians from France, Italy, and Germany documenting both the psychological and physiological benefits of riding horses (Tissot, 1964; Bain, 1965; DePauw, 1986; Willis, 1997; All, et al., 1999; Snider, et al., 2007; Berryman, 2010; Berg & Causey, 2014).

In 1870, Chassignac published the first reported study on the effects of horseback riding for human health (DePauw, 1986; Bertoti, 1988; Lanning & Krenek, 2013). In the same year a Scottish physician suggested, "Riding a spirited horse should be recognized as a treatment for depression" (Kendall, et al., 2014: 82). Eight years later, Ghislani Durant published a book on the benefits of horseback riding from a medical perspective (Berg & Causey, 2014).

During the First World War, it is reported that returning British soldiers were paired with cavalry horses for rehabilitation purposes (Brudvig, 1988; Berg & Causey, 2014; Kendall, et al., 2014). There is also an account of a Miss Olive Sands, a physiotherapist, who brought her own horses to the Oxford Hospital and provided riding for the returning soldiers (CARD, 2016).

In 1943, Lis Hartel of Denmark contracted polio and became wheelchair bound. A competitive dressage rider before her illness, Lis rehabilitated herself through riding to not only become the first woman to ride for an Olympic equestrian team and medal, but the first person with a major physical disability to accomplish such a feat. Lis Hartel was paralyzed from the knees down, but according to reports, few people were aware of her disability as she rode to victory, claiming second place at the 1947 Scandinavian Riding Championships (Jackson, 2014). Lis went on to represent Denmark in the 1952 Helsinki Olympics, winning the silver medal. Lis lived out the rest of her life without the use of her legs, but her tenacity and courage sparked new interest in the potential of riding for rehabilitative purposes (DePauw, 1986; Ungermann & Gras, 2011; Gabriels, et al., 2012; Berg & Causey, 2014; Wanneberg, 2014).

Sources suggest that although Lis is most commonly credited with the modern advent of rehabilitative riding, it was in fact a Norwegian physical therapist, Eilset Bodther, who first organized riding as an activity for children with disabilities (Bain, 1965; DePauw, 1986; Bertoti, 1988). Shortly thereafter, Lis and Ulla Harpoth, a physical therapist from Copenhagen, went on to form the first riding center for people with disabilities in Europe (Steiger & Steigner, 2004; Jackson, 2014).

Following in the footsteps of Bodther, Hartel, and Harpoth, other rehabilitative riding programs and organizations formed throughout the United Kingdom, Scandinavia, the Netherlands, and Belgium during the 1950s and 1960s (DePauw, 1986; Granados & Agís, 2011).

In 1969, the concept that horses could be helpful for humans migrated from Europe to North America. Dr. Reginald Renaud and Mr. Joseph Bauer founded the Community Association for Riders with Disabilities (CARD) in Canada, and the North American Riding for the Handicapped Association (NARHA) was established in the United States (DePauw, 1986; Bond, 2007; Granados & Agís, 2011; CARD, 2016; PATH Intl., 2016b).

Since that time the number of therapy practices that include horses in human healthcare has grown by the thousands, with representation from over 50 countries around the world (DePauw, 1986; All, et al., 1999; PATH Intl., 2016a; HETI, 2016; EAGALA, 2016).

☐ Why Horses?

Although history clearly demonstrates the propensity for humans to be drawn to horses, believing in their healing qualities, surprisingly little is known from a research perspective about the role of the horse as a determining factor in human change (Bachi, 2012; Kern-Godal, et al., 2015).

This may be due in part to what researchers call a "novelty effect," which means it is hard to separate the individual factors that contribute to human change when providing therapy in a unique setting (such as a farm) with so many stimuli (Macauley & Gutierrez, 2004; Holmes, et al., 2012; Anestis, et al., 2014; Borgi, et al., 2016).

The following section organizes existing theories and corresponding research into categories that begin to address the question of "why horses?"

The Movement of the Horse

The movement of the horse is probably the most well documented of all possible theories answering the question "why horses?" (Bertoti, 1988; Debuse, et al., 2009; Honkavaara & Rintala, 2010; Kang, et al., 2012; Baik, et al., 2014; Krejčí, et al., 2015; Garner & Rigby, 2015). Specific research has been conducted to better understand the movement of the horse, its similarity to the human gait, and the possible benefits to the human body (Janura, et al., 2009; Uchiyama, et al., 2011; Garner & Rigby, 2015). Commonly, it is physical, occupational, and speech therapists who incorporate equine movement during therapy sessions.

Uchiyama, et al. (2011) demonstrated that riding a horse at the walk closely mirrors the human gait. Even though they found the acceleration of human walking was not completely consistent with that of a horse, they felt the benefits to the human were significant, stating:

> Our results indicate that horse riding at a walking gait provides the stimulation of a walking exercise more easily and effectively than does human walking. Thus, horse riding is even more efficient in providing motor and sensory inputs in the treatment of individuals with physical disabilities, as well as in achieving cardiorespiratory fitness and weight control.
>
> (p. 276)

Honkavaara & Rintala (2010) state:

> In hippotherapy the horse's walking (gait) is the basic component used to produce neurophysiologic therapeutic effects on the rider. The client has to adapt him- or herself to the altering physical forces. Horse's swinging movements are producing three-dimensional dynamic and rhythmic impulses that are transmitted to the rider. These impulses are exposing the rider to forward and backward movements, shifts sideways, and rotations.
>
> (p. 30)

Other researchers suggest that riding provides sensory input and stimulates both hemispheres of the human cerebrum as well as the vestibular system (Granados & Agís, 2011; Hession, et al., 2014).

Horseback riding simulators have been used because of cost and space efficiency to treat similar conditions as those addressed in hippotherapy (Sung, et al., 2013; Kim, et al., 2013; Park, et al., 2014; Lee, et al., 2014; Temcharoensuk, et al., 2015). Interestingly, Temcharoensuk, et al. (2015) found that the movement of a living horse could not be exactly replicated by the simulator, and that riding a living horse was more effective than riding the simulator for the populations they examined. They report: "The variety in horse direction and movement are believed to induce more signals from proprioceptive and vestibular receptors through various postural challenges" (p. 276). This research suggests the movement of the horse is unique, and its impact on the human body difficult to replicate in other known settings (Giagazoglou, et al., 2013; Temcharoensuk, et al., 2015).

It is important to note that these results are achieved when a trained physical, occupational, or speech therapist is providing the service who can manipulate the person's body position, the gait of the horse, and even the selection of specific types of horses to obtain greater therapeutic benefit (Snider, et al., 2007). Along with a knowledgeable therapist who understands the biomechanics of the horse's movement, the condition and training of the horse plays a vital role in outcome of treatment including horses. Ajzenman (2012), states, "Effective therapy occurs when a horse achieves appropriate balance. Using horses with quality training is important in order for the therapist and handler to influence the horse's movement" (p. 2). She goes on to report:

> Movement quality is influenced through the horse actively seeking the horse handler's hands (reins, long lines). The handler promotes a flexible neck and jaw by sending the horse forward into the contact with active engagement of the hindquarters and swinging of the back.
>
> (p. 2)

This level of training and conditioning allows horses to have the flexibility, adjustability, and focus necessary to be effective partners in helping patients to achieve their health goals.

Equine Movement and Sexual Assault Survivors

Although no empirical research exists, anecdotal reports of practitioners suggest the movement of the horse may also trigger memories and emotions, especially related to sexual assault or trauma (Kohanov, 2001; Hallberg, 2008; Brandt, 2013). A number of research articles suggest mounted work should be considered in the treatment of trauma and sexual abuse (Porter-Wenzlaff, 2007; Meinersmann, et al., 2008; Yorke, et al., 2008; Guerino, et al., 2015). These studies make note of the physicality of riding, but do not mention the possible effects related to memory recall that such close contact with a horse might have on participants who have been sexually assaulted. For example, Yorke, et al. (2008) state, "Few other companion animals can be ridden, offering the opportunity for such close and broad body-to-body contact" (p. 19).

Guerino, et al. (2015) published a study about the effects of hippotherapy on survivors of sexual assault and emotional stress, but did not investigate the act of riding as a possible stimulator for traumatic memories. They did note, "Changes of direction and speeds used in the course of animal gait evoked pelvic displacement and pelvic rotation, increasing the value of the horse as an instrument of kinesiotherapy" (p. 961). They also suggested that hippotherapy increased the participants' "affective capacities, excited their interest and aroused their curiosity, and improved their acceptance of physical contact and allowed their emotions to show" (p. 961).

The power of the horse's movement should not go underestimated or undervalued. There is much more to be learned, and the psychological effects and benefits of mounted work deserve more rigorous study.

Ethological Characteristics of Equines

Anecdotal reports from research participants and from the observations of mental health professionals providing equine-assisted therapy suggest the size of a horse, its strength, use of "congruent" non-verbal communication, instinctual prey animal nature, herd dynamics, and sensitivity are reasons why horses may be helpful to humans (Porter-Wenzlaff, 2007; Trotter, et al., 2008; Bachi, et al., 2011; Ford, 2013; Waite & Bourke, 2013; Kern-Godal, et al., 2015). Other such material states the ability of the horse to "mirror" human emotion, evoke archetypal imagery, and to bond with humans is a part of their therapeutic value (Vidrine, et al., 2002; Frewin & Gardiner, 2005; Rothe, et al., 2005; Porter-Wenzlaff, 2007; Johansen, et al., 2014).

Ford (2013) notes the participants involved in her study commented on "how the nonverbal nature of a horse's communication, and the large size of the animal, creates a nonverbal focus, and seems to evoke greater embodiment in clients" (p. 102).

Porter-Wenzlaff (2007) states, "That sensitivity [of the horse] extends to the humans with whom they interact. They have been called our mirrors, as their response to us reflects what our presence tells them" (p. 530).

Bachi, et al. (2011) suggests, "Horses are highly suitable for therapeutic work due to their being herd animals, for which cooperation is as important as competition, and the bonding among members is very strong" (p. 3).

Dr. Leslie Steward speaks of a time when early humans stuck close by prey species, relying upon their sensitivity for safety (Steward, 2017). She suggests as the human brain evolved, our acute senses diminished, leaving us less aware of potential threats. She notes that even today this phenomenon can be observed in primates who stay close to deer and antelope, watching their behaviors to predict danger. Just as humans watch animals to predict danger, humans may also be soothed by a calm animal. Dr. Steward says, "When we observe a calm animal, our brains tell our bodies we are safe" (Steward, 2017). Although the bulk of research cited by Dr. Steward involves mostly companion animals, it is reasonable to assume since horses are also prey animals, humans may experience similar reactions when in their presence.

Given that much of what is written about the effects of equine ethological characteristics on human wellbeing is anecdotal, the next step for researchers is to focus on conducting empirical study about the role equine nature, behavior, and physiology plays in the process of human change. This information will inform the practice of equine-assisted therapy, and help guide the development of more targeted clinical interventions.

Motivation and Equine-Assisted Therapy

The role of motivation created by including horses in human healthcare has been examined at some depth by physical, occupational, and speech therapists, as well as by mental health professionals (Macauley & Gutierrez, 2004; Cherng, et al., 2004; Trotter, et al., 2008; Debuse, et al., 2009; Taylor, et al., 2009; Frank, et al., 2011; Giagazoglou, et al., 2013; Kern-Godal, et al., 2015).

Lack of motivation due to pain avoidance is a considerable barrier to treatment for physical, occupational, and speech therapists who work with clients suffering from painful conditions. Cherng, et al. (2004) state, "It is often a challenge for professionals who provide therapeutic exercises and adapted activities to maintain the children's interest and enthusiasm for the therapeutic activities because of the difficulty and discomfort that these activities presented to them" (p. 104). Researchers suggest that equine-assisted therapy may offer a unique, exciting, and fun treatment intervention that can motivate patients to push themselves more than they would in an office setting (Debuse, et al., 2009; Frank, et al., 2011; Giagazoglou, et al., 2013).

Treatment avoidance and lack of compliance can also be significant issues when working with certain populations. In some cases, patients may develop negative associations with the treatment environment, or become bored with the same approaches used over and over with seemingly little success (Macauley & Gutierrez, 2004). Kern-Godal, et al. (2015) conducted one of the first studies specifically designed to understand the role of equine-assisted therapy on the retention and motivation of patients hospitalized for substance abuse. The results of their study suggest that patients spent more time in treatment and were more likely to complete treatment if they participated in equine-assisted therapy.

Authenticity, Horses, and the Patient-Therapist Relationship

Certainly in mental health therapy, and possibly in other forms of therapy as well, authenticity or "realness" is considered an important therapeutic component (Yalom, 2003; Gullo, et al., 2012) leading to increased patient engagement, especially with youth and other populations who may be hard to engage in a therapeutic process (Hurleya, et al., 2013).

When patients come to the farm to participate in equine-assisted therapy, they are likely to experience the therapist differently than they would in a clinic setting (Carlsson, et al., 2014). From the outside, the therapist may wear casual clothing and appear more approachable. Interpersonally, the therapist engages with other staff, volunteers, and the horses, and through these interactions the therapist may show emotion or disclose feelings. This allows the patient to view the therapist from a more human or "real" perspective (Carlsson, et al., 2014).

Through this experience of authenticity, the patient may come to establish a closer relationship with the therapist, trusting him/her and the treatment process more readily (Selby & Smith-Osborne, 2013; Lac, 2016). The ability of the therapist to align with the patient, form a meaningful, positive relationship, demonstrate their understanding of the clinical need, and engage with respect, empathy, and unfailing positive regard is critical to the success of treatment (Rogers, 1951; Del Re, et al., 2012).

Carlsson, et al. (2014) report, "The relationship between the staff and the clients in the presence of the horse was less strict and based more on mutual respect" (p. 28). They also note it seemed easier to communicate with their research participants in the presence of horses. Ajzenman (2012) agrees, reporting that treatment using the more comfortable and less formal farm environment can have many positive effects for both patients and their families, including a deeper sense of relationship, social engagement, and increased collaboration in the treatment process.

Dr. Leslie Steward references the "oxytocin boost" humans get through calming and safe interactions with animals. She suggests this change in neurochemistry effects not only the human's response to the animal, but also the way in which the human interacts with other people in the immediate vicinity. She calls this the "area of effect" (Steward, 2017). Although similar research has yet to be conducted with horses, it seems safe to assume this experience may be, in part, why patients appear to build stronger bonds with therapists when in the presence of horses.

Similarly to other theories about "why horses?", empirical research is needed to better understand the mechanisms by which horses encourage authenticity and help in the development of the patient-therapeutic relationship.

The Farm Milieu

Although not as well researched or documented as the other theories of "why horses?", providers of equine-assisted therapy have begun to recognize the potential benefits associated with the farm milieu (Vidrine, et al., 2002; Bizub, et al., 2003; Chardonnens, 2009; Bachi, et al., 2011).

The farm milieu is not a typical treatment environment. It is dynamic and unpredictable, lacking the sterility of a clinic setting (Vidrine, et al., 2002). While at the farm, patients are exposed to all types of sensory stimulation through their interactions with the natural world (Bachi, et al., 2011; Elkholm Fry, 2013).

The farm milieu also provides broader opportunities for human-animal bonding, and naturally encourages interactions with cattle, sheep, pigs, goats, and cats who are likely barn dwellers. These encounters provide wonderful opportunities for interspecies communication, social interactions, and relationship development (Berget & Braastad, 2011).

The benefits of being in nature are well documented by an ever-growing body of research (Selhub & Logan, 2012; Louv, 2008; Louv, 2012). When patients come to the farm, they inevitably experience these benefits simply by being outdoors and in a natural setting. Of course, these benefits can be enhanced by intentionally designed human-animal-nature activities that can be incorporated into the patient's treatment plan.

☐ The Human-Animal Bond

The relationship between humans and animals is ancient, stretching back at least 15,000 years when dogs are thought to have been domesticated (Larson, et al., 2012). Davis & Valla (1978) document the findings of a 12,000-year-old human skeleton with its hand resting on the bones of a wolf or dog puppy. This discovery is considered the first evidence of the human-animal bond.

From that time forward, animals have been included in our lives in many different ways. The bond between humans and animals is well documented in research and in popular works (Anderson, 2004). Like horses, this bond has been used in human healthcare throughout time. From ancient Greece, medieval Europe, and post-First World War America, to the current day, animals have been considered helpful for a myriad of health conditions (Bustad, 1995; Salotto, 2001; Ormerod, et al., 2005; Serpell, 2006; Morrison, 2007).

Both Dr. Sigmund Freud and Dr. Boris Levinson included dogs in their psychotherapy sessions (Levinson, 1962; Eggiman, 2006). Their observations about animal awareness and sensitivity corresponded with the beliefs of Konrad Lorenz, whose unique approach to the study of animal behavior resulted in our modern understanding of ethology and the human-animal bond. Lorenz believed it was best to study animals in their natural habitat, rather than in a laboratory. His unorthodox approach involved empathizing with animals, often anthropomorphizing their mental states. He believed that animals could experience the same or similar emotions to those of humans (Allen & Bekoff, 1999). His work, and the observations of Freud and Levinson, were foundational in the human-animal bond movement (Hines, 2003; Eggiman, 2006).

Beginning in the 1970s with the leadership of veterinarians and the field of veterinary medicine, the human-animal bond initiative grew and flourished through increased public awareness and the development of human-animal bond curriculum taught at universities around the world (Hines, 2003). This led to the creation of human-animal bond centers housed at major universities, research articles published in scientific journals, books written for the public, and associations founded to support the human-animal bond and its applications for human healthcare (Hines, 2003; Anderson, 2004).

As research demonstrates, the presence of companion animals in the lives of humans is attributed to lowered blood pressure, decreased risk of cardiovascular disease, increased motivation to exercise, decreased doctor visits, increased tolerance for pain, and increased social interactions, among a variety of different populations (Friedmann, et al., 1980; Friedmann & Thomas, 1995; Allen, et al., 2001; Heady, et al., 2002; Sobo, et al., 2006; Levine, et al., 2013; Bernabei, et al., 2013; O'Haire, et al., 2013; Maujean, et al., 2015; Maber-Aleksandrowicz, et al., 2016).

In 1977 the Delta Society (now called Pet Partners) was founded to support the inclusion of companion animals in therapeutic settings. Today, Pet Partners registers the handlers of multiple species and evaluates the animals themselves for appropriateness and compliance with safety training standards. In most cases, Pet Partners teams visit facilities such as nursing homes, schools, hospitals, or mental health clinics to provide animal-assisted therapy in partnership with licensed healthcare providers (Pet Partners, 2016).

Although the Pet Partners model of companion animal-assisted therapy is probably the most common in the United States, there are other ways to provide animal-assisted therapy. Beginning with the York Retreat (circa

1700s), interactions with farm animals and time spent working on the farm have also been included in the treatment of mental health issues, intellectual disabilities, learning disabilities, incarcerated populations, and young people (Eggiman, 2006; Berget & Braastad, 2011; Pedersen, et al., 2011). Today, care farming is a popular therapeutic approach commonly used in Europe (Leck, et al., 2014). Vulnerable populations are introduced to the farm environment and taught important life and vocational skills. Animals who live on care farms are not usually considered "therapy animals." Instead, participants learn to interact with them as a part of daily farm life. The therapeutic value is derived from the normalizing effects of being given responsibility, having important tasks to accomplish, and being part of a community (Sempik, et al., 2010; Granerud & Eriksson, 2014).

Green Chimneys, located in New York, is one of the few programs to combine the principles of care farming with equine-assisted therapy and animal-assisted therapy. Participants in Green Chimneys' therapeutic programming have the opportunity to interact with many species of animal, including farm animals and wildlife. The nature of these interactions ranges from learning the skills necessary to care for and tend to the animals to engaging in deep psychotherapeutic work (Green Chimneys, 2016).

The ways in which the human-animal bond manifests in our lives and in healthcare settings are diverse. There is much to be gained from a deeper understanding of this bond, and from increased collaboration between all those who include animals as a part of their therapeutic services.

☐ The Role of Nature

As research reminds us, little is truly known about the factors contributing to change when a patient engages in equine-assisted therapy. Is it the horse? Is it the physical exercise associated with being around horses and the farm? Is it the farm milieu and the other animals a patient might encounter? Is it being outdoors and experiencing all that nature has to offer? Or, is it a complex intersection of all these factors?

Since the answer is elusive at present, it seems advisable to assume all these factors may play a role in the potential effectiveness of the intervention. Therefore, understanding the contributions of nature to the wellbeing of humans is an important foundation for all those providing equine-assisted therapy.

The human connection to nature is timeless, universal, and innate, according to scientists Kellert & Wilson (1993). Human beings need nature to remain healthy, and our increasing separation from nature has led to both human suffering and environmental degradation (Van Haaften & Van De Vijver, 1996; Selhub & Logan, 2012). A growing body of research helps to explain the healing power of nature and its effects on attention and concentration, stress, anger, frustration, depression, anxiety, and physical health (Ulrich, 1979; Kaplan & Kaplan, 1989; Ulrich, et al.,

1991; Kaplan, 1995; Hartig, et al., 2003; Groenewegen, et al., 2006; Han, 2009; Taylor & Kuo, 2009; Barton & Pretty, 2010; van den Berg, et al., 2010; Bratman, et al., 2012; Thompson, et al., 2012; Cervinka, et al., 2012). Much of this research is directed towards two major themes: attention restoration and stress reduction.

Attention restoration theory suggests that nature can have a restorative effect on the brain's ability to focus (Kaplan & Kaplan, 1989; Han, 2009; Bratman, et al., 2012). In our fast-paced world, humans are inundated with a massive amount of stimuli, especially coming from technology sources. The human brain is constantly asked to sort information between what to pay attention to, and what to ignore. This process fatigues the brain and leads to irritation, frustration, inflexibility, giving up, stress, depression, and anxiety. Time spent in nature and away from the typical activities and stimuli of daily living can help the brain rest and replenish. This immersion can be effective in both small doses like viewing nature out of a window or a quick walk through a park, or with longer excursions like a day spent in a natural setting (Kaplan, 1995).

Stress reduction theory was formulated and repeatedly tested by pioneering researcher Roger Ulrich. During his experiments, he showed research participants photos and videos of peaceful nature scenes, and of stressful, urban landscapes. Participants were constantly monitored for levels of physiological stress through heart rate, blood pressure, and muscle tension measures (Bratman, et al., 2012). The outcomes of his studies showed that people recovered more quickly from stress, demonstrated lowered anger or aggression responses, and reported a greater sense of happiness when they were viewing nature scenery (Ulrich, 1979; Ulrich, et al., 1991).

Since stress and distraction are common concerns for many in today's fast-paced world (Louv, 2012), it would seem that providers of equine-assisted therapy are positioned nicely to purposefully utilize the restorative qualities of nature.

☐ Conclusion

Although science cannot yet tell us exactly how horses help humans, our rich history assures us there is a reason why horses have been included in healthcare for centuries. Our deep connection to the natural world also informs and supports our innate sense that healing comes when we are in relationship with other living beings, human and non-human alike. There is no doubt that humans have something to learn from animals and nature, and a responsibility to give back as much as we receive.

Although we still have much to learn, a growing body of research brings a new level of understanding to these foundational beliefs. As we tease apart the various factors contributing to change, we are reminded that nothing happens in a vacuum. While it is essential for learning that we identify the individual parts of the whole, at the end of the day it is probably the complexity and dynamic nature of the *whole* that brings about change.

☐ References

Ajzenman, H. (2012). [Hippotherapy practice model: Promoting occupational performance and participation for children with physical and developmental disabilities]. Unpublished manuscript.

All, A.C., Loving, G.L., & Crane, L.L. (1999). Animals, horseback riding, and the implications for rehabilitation therapy. *The Journal of Rehabilitation, 65,* 49–57.

Allen, C., & Bekoff, M. (1999). *Species of mind: The philosophy and biology of cognitive ethology.* Cambridge, MA: MIT Press.

Allen, K., Shykoff, B.E., Joseph, L., & Izzo, J. (2001). Pet ownership, but not ACE inhibitor therapy, blunts home blood pressure responses to mental stress. *Hypertension, 38,* 815–820.

Anderson, D.C. (2004). The human-companion animal bond. *The Reference Librarian, 41*(86), 7–23.

Anestis, M.D., Anestis, J.C., Zawilinski, L.L., Hopkins, T.A., & Lilienfeld, S.O. (2014). Equine-related treatments for mental disorders lack empirical support: A systematic review of empirical investigations. *Journal of Clinical Psychology,* 1–18. http://doi.org/10.1002/jclp.22113

Bachi, K. (2012). Equine-facilitated psychotherapy: The gap between practice and knowledge. *Society & Animals, 20,* 364–380.

Bachi, K., Terkel, J., & Teichman, M. (2011). Equine-facilitated psychotherapy for at-risk adolescents: The influence on self-image, self-control and trust. *Journal of Contemporary Psychotherapy, 17*(2), 298–312.

Baik, K., Byeun, J.K., & Baek, J.K. (2014). The effects of horseback riding participation on the muscle tone and range of motion for children with spastic cerebral palsy. *Journal of Exercise Rehabilitation, 10*(5), 265–270.

Bain, A. (1965). Pony riding for the disabled. *Physiotherapy, 51,* 263–265.

Barton, J., & Pretty, J. (2010). What is the best dose of nature and green exercise for improving mental health? A multi-study analysis. *Environmental Science Technology, 44,* 3947–3955.

Berg, E., & Causey, A. (2014). The life-changing power of the horse: Equine-assisted activities and therapies in the U.S. *Animal Frontiers, 4,* 72–75.

Berget, B., & Braastad, B.O. (2011). Animal-assisted therapy with farm animals for persons with psychiatric disorders. *Ann Ist Super Sanità, 47*(4), 384–390.

Bernabei, V., De Ronchi, D., La Ferla, T., Moretti, F., Tonelli, L., Ferrari, B., Forlani, M., & Atti, A.R. (2013). Animal-assisted interventions for elderly patients affected by dementia or psychiatric disorders: A review. *Journal of Psychiatric Research, 47*(6), 762–773.

Berryman, J. (2010). Exercise is medicine: A historical perspective. *Current Sports Medicine Reports, 9*(4), 195–201.

Bertoti, D. (1988). Effect of therapeutic horseback riding on posture in children with cerebral palsy. *Physical Therapy, 68*(10), 1505–1512.

Bizub, A., Joy, A., & Davidson, L. (2003). "It's like being in another world": Demonstrating the benefits of therapeutic horseback riding for individuals with psychiatric disability. *Psychiatric Rehabilitation Journal, 26*(4), 377–384.

Bond, M. (2007). Horseback riding as therapy for children with cerebral palsy: Is there evidence of its effectiveness? *Physical & Occupational Therapy in Pediatrics, 27*(2), 5–23.

Borgi, M., Loliva, D., Cerino, S., Chiarotti, F., Venerosi, A., & Bramini, M. (2016). Effectiveness of a standardized equine-assisted therapy program for children with autism spectrum disorder. *Journal of Autism and Developmental Disorders, 46*(1), 1–9.

Brandt, C. (2013). Equine-facilitated psychotherapy as a complementary treatment intervention. *Practitioner Scholar: Journal of Counseling & Professional Psychology, 2*(1), 23–42.

Bratman, G.N., Hamilton, P.J., & Daily, G.C. (2012). The impacts of nature experience on human cognitive function and mental health. *Annals of the New York Academy of Sciences, 1249*(1), 118–136.

Brudvig, T.J. (1988). Therapeutic horseback riding on a military base: One PT's experience. *Clinical Management, 8*(3), 30–32.

Burgon, H.L. (2011). "Queen of the world": Experiences of "at-risk" young people participating in equine-assisted learning/therapy. *Journal of Social Work Practice, 25*(2), 165–183.

Bustad, L. (1995). The role of pets in therapeutic programmes, historic perspectives. In I. Robinson (Ed.), *The Waltham book of human-animal interaction: Benefits and responsibility of pet ownership* (pp. 55–57). Oxford, UK: Pergamon Press.

Carlsson, C., Ranta, D.N., & Traeen, B. (2014). Equine assisted social work as a mean for authentic relations between clients and staff. *Human-Animal Interaction Bulletin, 2*(1), 19–38.

Cervinka, R., Roderer, K., & Hefler, E. (2012). Are nature lovers happy? On various indicators of well-being and connectedness with nature. *Journal of Health Psychology, 17*(3), 379–388.

Chardonnens, E. (2009). The use of animals as co-therapists on a farm: The child-horse bond in person-centred equine-assisted psychotherapy. *Person-Centered & Experiential Psychotherapies, 8*(4), 319–332.

Cherng, R.J., Liao, H.F., Leung, H.W.C., & Hwang, A.W. (2004). The effectiveness of therapeutic horseback riding in children with spastic cerebral palsy. *Adapted Physical Activity Quarterly, 21*(2), 103–121.

Community Association for Riders with Disabilities (CARD). (2016). *History*. Retrieved from: http://card.ca/about/history/

Davis, S.J.M., & Valla, F.R. (1978). Evidence for domestication of the dog 12,000 years ago in the Natufian of Israel. *Nature, 276*, 608.

Debuse, D., Gibb, C., & Chandler, C. (2009). Effects of hippotherapy on people with cerebral palsy from the users' perspective: A qualitative study. *Physiotherapy Theory and Practice, 25*(3), 174–192.

Dell, C.A., Chalmers, D., Bresette, N., Swain, S., Rankin, D., & Hopkins, C. (2011). A healing space: The experiences of First Nations and Inuit youth with equine-assisted learning (EAL). *Child and Youth Care Forum, 40*(4), 319–336.

Del Re, A.C., Flückiger, C., Horvath, A.O., Symonds, D., & Wampold, B.E. (2012). Therapist effects in the therapeutic alliance—Outcome relationship: A restricted-maximum likelihood meta-analysis. *Clinical Psychology Review, 32*, 642–649.

DePauw, K. (1986). Horseback riding for individuals with disabilities: Programs, philosophy, and research. *Adapted Physical Activity Quarterly, 3*(3), 217–226.

Durant, G. (1878). Horse-back riding, from a medical point of view. New York, NY: Cassell, Petter and Galpin.

Eggiman, J. (2006). Cognitive-behavioral therapy: A case report—Animal-assisted therapy. *Topics in Advances Practice Nursing, 6*(3), 7–13.

Elkholm Fry, N. (2013). Equine-assisted therapy: An overview. In M. Grassberger, R.A. Sherma, O.S. Gileva, C.M.H. Kim, & K.Y. Mumcuoglu (Eds.), *Biotherapy: History, principles, and practice* (pp. 255–258). Netherlands: Springer.

Equine Assisted Growth and Learning Association (EAGALA). (2016). *Find a Program*. Retrieved from: http://home.eagala.org/find

Federation of Horses in Education and Therapy International (HETI). (2016). *Current Members*. Retrieved from: www.frdi.net/membership_list.html

Ford, C. (2013). Dancing with horses: Combining dance/movement therapy and equine facilitated psychotherapy. *American Journal of Dance Therapy, 35*(2), 93–117.

Frank, A., Mccloskey, S., & Dole, R.L. (2011). Effect of hippotherapy on perceived self-competence and participation in a child with cerebral palsy. *Pediatric Physical Therapy, 23*, 301–308.

Frewin, K., & Gardiner, B. (2005). New age or old sage? A review of equine assisted psychotherapy. *The Australian Journal of Counselling Psychology, 6*, 13–17.

Friedmann, E., Katcher, A.H., Lynch, J.J., & Thomas, S.A. (1980). Animal companions and one-year survival of patients after discharge from a coronary care unit. *Public Health Reports, 95*(4), 307–312.

Friedmann, E., & Thomas, S.A. (1995). Pet ownership, social support, and one-year survival after acute myocardial infarction in the Cardiac Arrhythmia Suppression Trial (CAST). *The American Journal of Cardiology, 76*(17), 1213–1217.

Gabriels, R.L., Agnew, J.A., Holt, K.D., et al. (2012). Pilot study measuring the effects of therapeutic horseback riding on school-age children and adolescents with autism spectrum disorders. *Research in Autism Spectrum Disorders, 6*(2), 578–588.

Garner, B.A., & Rigby, B.R. (2015). Human pelvis motions when walking and when riding a therapeutic horse. *Human Movement Science, 39*, 121–137.

Giagazoglou, P., Arabatzi, F., Kellis, E., Liga, M., Karra, C., & Amiridis, I. (2013). Muscle reaction function of individuals with intellectual disabilities may be improved through therapeutic use of a horse. *Research in Developmental Disabilities, 34*(9), 2442–2448.

Granados, A.C., & Agís, I. (2011). Why children with special needs feel better with hippotherapy sessions: A conceptual review. *Journal of Alternative and Complementary Medicine, 17*(3), 191–197.

Granerud, A., & Eriksson, B. (2014). Mental health problems, recovery and the impact of green care services: A qualitative, participant-focused approach. *Occupational Therapy in Mental Health, 30*, 317–336.

Green Chimneys. (2016). Retrieved from: www.greenchimneys.org/

Groenewegen, P., van den Berg, A.E., de Vries, S., & Verheij, R. (2006). Vitamin G: Effects of green space on health, well-being, and social safety. *BMC Public Health, 6*, 1–9.

Guerino, M.R., Briel, A.F., & Araújo, M.G.R. (2015). Hippotherapy as a treatment for socialization after sexual abuse and emotional stress. *Journal of Physical Therapy Science, 27*(3), 959–962.

Gullo, S., Lo Coco, G., & Gelso, C. (2012). Early and later predictors of outcome in brief therapy: The role of real relationship. *Journal of Clinical Psychology, 68*(6), 614–619.

Hallberg, L. (2008). *Walking the way of the horse: Exploring the power of the horse-human relationship*. Bloomington, IN: iUniverse.

Han, K.T. (2009). An exploration of relationships among the responses to natural scenes: Scenic beauty, preference, and restoration. *Environment and Behavior, 42*(2), 243–270.

Hartig, T., Evans, G.W., Jamner, L.D., Davis, D.S., & Garling, T. (2003). Tracking restoration in natural and urban field settings. *Journal of Environmental Psychology, 23*, 109–123.

Heady, B., Grabka, M., Kelley, J., Reddy, P., & Tseng, Y.P. (2002). Pet ownership is good for your health and saves public expenditure too: Australian and German longitudinal evidence. *Australian Social Monitor, 5*, 93–99.

Hession, C.E., Eastwood, B., Watterson, D., Lehane, C.M., Oxley, N., & Murphy, B.A. (2014). Therapeutic horse riding improves cognition, mood arousal, and ambulation in children with dyspraxia. *Journal of Alternative and Complementary Medicine, 20*(1), 19–23.

Hines, L. (2003). Historical perspectives on the human-animal bond. *American Behavioral Scientist, 47*(1), 7–15.

Holmes, C.M.P., Goodwin, D., Redhead, E.S., & Goymour, K.L. (2012). The benefits of equine-assisted activities: An exploratory study. *Child and Adolescent Social Work Journal, 29*(2), 111–122.

Honkavaara, M., & Rintala, P. (2010). The influence of short term, intensive hippotherapy on gait in children with cerebral palsy. *European Journal of Adapted Physical Activity, 3*(2), 29–36.

Howey, M.O. (1923). *The horse in magic and myth* (2002 edition). Mineola, NY: Dover Publications.

Hurleya, K.D., Lamberta, M.C., Van Ryzinb, M., Sullivana, J., & Stevensc, A. (2013). Therapeutic alliance between youth and staff in residential group care: Psychometrics of the therapeutic alliance quality scale. *Children and Youth Services Review, 35*(1), 56–64.

Jackson, L. (November 17, 2014). *Olympic Girl Power: The Incredible Story of Lis Hartel.* Retrieved from: www.horsenation.com/2014/11/17/olympic-girl-power-the-incredible-story-of-lis-hartel/

Janura, M., Peham, C., Dvorakova, T., & Elfmark, M. (2009). An assessment of the pressure distribution exerted by a rider on the back of a horse during hippotherapy. *Human Movement Science, 28*(3), 387–393.

Johansen, S.G., Wang, C.E.A., Binder, P.E., & Malt, U.F. (2014). Equine-facilitated body and emotion-oriented psychotherapy designed for adolescents and adults not responding to mainstream treatment: A structured program. *Journal of Psychotherapy Integration, 24*(4), 323–335.

Kang, H., Jung, J., & Yu, J. (2012). Effects of hippotherapy on the sitting balance of children with cerebral palsy: A randomized control trial. *Journal of Physical Therapy Science, 24*(9), 833–836.

Kaplan, R., & Kaplan, S. (1989). *The experience of nature: A psychological perspective.* (Manuscript, University of Nevada, Reno). Cambridge, UK: Cambridge University Press.

Kaplan, S. (1995). The restorative benefits of nature: Toward an integrative framework. *Journal of Environmental Psychology, 15*, 169–182.

Kellert, S.R., & Wilson, E.O. (1993). *The biophilia hypothesis.* Washington, DC: Island Press.

Kendall, E., Maujean, A., Pepping, & Wright, J.J. (2014). Hypotheses about the psychological benefits of horses. *Explore: The Journal of Science and Healing, 10*(2), 81–87.

Kern-Godal, A., Arnevik, E.A., Walderhaug, E., & Ravndal, E. (2015). Substance use disorder treatment retention and completion: A prospective study of EAT for young adults. *Addiction Science and Clinical Practice, 10*(21), 3–12.

Kim, S., Yuk, G.C., & Gak, H. (2013). Effects of the horse riding simulator and ball exercises on balance of the elderly. *Journal of Physical Therapy Science, 25*(11), 1425–1428.

Kohanov, L. (2001). *The Tao of Equus: A woman's journey of healing and transformation through the way of the horse.* San Francisco, CA: New World Library.

Kohanov, L. (2007). *Riding between worlds: Exploring our potential through the way of the horse.* San Francisco, CA: New World Library.

Krejčí, E., Janura, M., & Svoboda, Z. (2015). The benefit of hippotherapy for improvement of attention and memory in children with cerebral palsy: A pilot study. *Acta Gymnica, 45*(1), 27–32.

Lac, V. (2016). Amy's story: An existential-integrative equine-facilitated psychotherapy approach to anorexia nervosa. *Journal of Humanistic Psychology*, 1–12. http://doi.org/10.1177/0022167815627900

Lanning, B., & Krenek, N. (2013). Guest editorial: Examining effects of equine-assisted activities to help combat veterans improve quality of life. *Journal of Rehabilitation Research and Development*, *50*(8), vii–xiii.

Larson, G., Karlsson, E.K., Perri, A., et al. (2012). Rethinking dog domestication by integrating genetics, archeology, and biogeography. *Proceedings of the National Academy of Sciences*, *109*(23), 8878–8883.

Leck, C., Evans, N., & Upton, D. (2014). Agriculture—Who cares? An investigation of "care farming" in the UK. *Journal of Rural Studies*, *34*, 313–325.

Lee, C.W., Kim, S.G., & Na, S.S. (2014). The effects of hippotherapy and a horse riding simulator on the balance of children with cerebral palsy. *Journal of Physical Therapy Science*, *26*(3), 423–425.

Levine, G.N., Allen, K., Braun, L.T., Christian, H.E., Friedmann, E., Taubert, K.A., Thomas, S.A., Wells, D.L., & Lange, R.A. (2013). Pet ownership and cardiovascular risk: A scientific statement from the American Heart Association. *Circulation*, *127*, 2353–2363.

Levinson, B.M. (1962). The dog as co-therapist. *Mental Hygiene*, *46*, 59–65.

Louv, R. (2008). *Last child in the woods: Saving our children from nature-deficit disorder*. Chapel Hill, NC: Algonquin Books.

Louv, R. (2012). *The nature principle: Reconnecting with life in a virtual age*. Chapel Hill, NC: Algonquin Books.

Maber-Aleksandrowicz, S., Avent, C., & Hassiotis, A. (2016). A systematic review of animal-assisted therapy on psychosocial outcomes in people with intellectual disability. *Research in Developmental Disabilities*, *49*(50), 322–338.

Macauley, B.L., & Gutierrez, K.M. (2004). The effectiveness of hippotherapy for children with language-learning disabilities. *Communication Disorders Quarterly*, *25*(4), 205–217.

Maujean, A., Pepping, C.A., & Kendall, E. (2015). A systematic review of randomized controlled trials of animal-assisted therapy on psychosocial outcomes. *Anthrozoos*, *28*(1), 23–36.

McCormick, A., & McCormick, M. (1997). *Horse sense and the human heart: What horses can teach us about trust, bonding, creativity and spirituality*. Deerfield Beach, FL: Health Communications, Inc.

McGreevy, P. (2012). *Equine behavior: A guide for veterinarians and equine scientists* (2nd edition). London: UK: Saunders, an imprint of Elsevier Ltd.

Meinersmann, K.M., Bradberry, J., & Roberts, F.B. (2008). Equine-facilitated psychotherapy with adult female survivors of abuse. *Journal of Psychosocial Nursing and Mental Health Services*, *46*(12), 36–42.

Meregillano, G. (2004). Hippotherapy. *Physical Medicine and Rehabilitation Clinics of North America*, *15*, 843–854.

Morrison, M. (2007). Health benefits of animal-assisted interventions. *Complementary Health Practice Review*, *12*(1), 51–62.

O'Haire, M.E., McKenzie, S.J., Beck, A.M., & Slaughter, V. (2013). Social behaviors increase in children with autism in the presence of animals compared to toys. PLoS One, 8(2): e57010. https://doi.org/10.1371/journal.pone.0057010

Ormerod, E.J., Edney, A.T.B., Foster, S.J., & Whyham, M.C. (2005). Therapeutic applications of the human-companion animal bond. *Veterinary Record*, *157*(22), 689–691.

Park, J.H., Shurtleff, T., Engsberg, J., Rafferty, S., You, J.Y., & You, I.Y. (2014). Comparison between the robo-horse and real horse movements for hippotherapy. *Bio-Medical Materials and Engineering, 24*(6), 2603–2610.

Pedersen, I., Nordaunet, T., Martinsen, E.W., Berget, B., & Braastad, B.O. (2011). Farm animal-assisted intervention: Relationship between work and contact with farm animals and change in depression, anxiety, and self-efficacy among persons with clinical depression. *Issues in Mental Health Nursing, 32*(8), 493–500.

Pet Partners. (2016). Retrieved from: https://petpartners.org/

Porter-Wenzlaff, L. (2007). Finding their voice: Developing emotional, cognitive, and behavioral congruence in female abuse survivors through equine-facilitated psychotherapy. *Explore: The Journal of Science and Healing, 3*(5), 529–534.

Professional Association of Therapeutic Horsemanship International (PATH Intl.). (2016a). *Find a Center*. Retrieved from: www.pathintl.org/path-intl-centers/find-center

Professional Association of Therapeutic Horsemanship International (PATH Intl.). (2016b). *History*. Retrieved from: www.pathintl.org/about-path-intl/about-path-intl/history

Rogers, C. (1951). *Client-centered therapy*. Cambridge, MA: The Riverside Press.

Rothe, E., Vega, B., Torres, R., Soler, S., & Pazos, R. (2005). From kids and horses: Equine facilitated psychotherapy for children. *International Journal of Clinical and Health Psychology, 5*(2), 373–383.

Salotto, P. (2001). *Pet assisted therapy: A loving intervention and an emerging profession: Leading to a friendlier, healthier, and more peaceful world*. Norton, MA: D. J. Publications.

Selby, A., & Smith-Osborne, A. (2013). A systematic review of effectiveness of complementary and adjunct therapies and interventions involving equines. *Health Psychology, 32*(4), 418–432.

Selhub, E.M., & Logan, A.C. (2012). *Your brain on nature*. Ontario, Canada: Wiley Publishing.

Sempik, J., Hine, R., & Wilcox, D. (2010). *Green care: A Conceptual Framework: A Report of the Working Group on Health Benefits of Green Care*. Retrieved from: www.umb.no/statisk/greencare/green_carea_conceptual_framework.pdf

Serpell, J.A. (2006). Animal-assisted interventions in historical perspective. In A.H. Fine (Ed.), *Handbook on animal-assisted therapy: Theoretical foundations and guidelines for practice* (2nd edition, chap. 1, pp. 3–19). New York, NY: Academic Press.

Snider, L., Korner-Bitensky, N., Kammann, C., Warner, S., & Saleh, M. (2007). Horseback riding as therapy for children with cerebral palsy: Is there evidence of its effectiveness? *Physical & Occupational Therapy in Pediatrics, 27*(2), 5–23.

Sobo, E.J., Eng, B., & Kassity-Krich, N. (2006). Canine visitation (pet) therapy: Pilot study data on decrease in child pain perception. *Journal of Holistic Nursing, 24*, 51–57.

Steiger, B., & Steigner, S.H. (2004). *Horse miracles: Inspirational true stories of remarkable horses*. Fort Collins, CO: Adams Media.

Steward, L. (April 5, 2017). *What Is Your Pet Telling You?* Retrieved from: www.youtube.com/watch?v=oTVlCnenYeE

Sung, Y.H., Kim, C.J., Yu, B.K., & Kim, K.M. (2013). A hippotherapy simulator is effective to shift weight bearing toward the affected side during gait in patients with stroke. *NeuroRehabilitation, 33*(3), 407–412.

Taylor, A.F., & Kuo, F.E. (2009). Children with attention deficits concentrate better after walk in the park. *Journal of Attention Disorders, 12*(5), 402–409.

Taylor, R.R., Kielhofner, G., Smith, C., et al. (2009). Volitional change in children with Autism: A single-case design study of the impact of hippotherapy on motivation. *Occupational Therapy in Mental Health, 25*, 192–200.

Temcharoensuk, P., Lekskulchai, R., Akamanon, C., et al. (2015). Effect of horseback riding versus a dynamic and static horse riding simulator on sitting ability of children with cerebral palsy: A randomized controlled trial. *Journal of Physical Therapy Science*, *27*(1), 273–277.

Thompson, C.W., Roe, J., Aspinall, P., Mitchell, R., Clow, A., & Miller, D. (2012). More green space is linked to less stress in deprived communities: Evidence from salivary cortisol patterns. *Landscape and Urban Planning*, *103*(3), 221–229.

Tissot, J.C. (1964). *Gymnastique Medicinale et Chirurgicale*. New Haven, CT: Elizabeth Licht.

Trotter, K.S., Chandler, C.K., & Goodwin-Bond, D.C. (2008). A comparative study of the efficacy of group equine assisted counseling with at-risk children and adolescents. *Journal of Creativity in Mental Health*, *3*, 254–284.

Uchiyama, H., Ohtani, N., & Ohta, M. (2011). Three-dimensional analysis of horse and human gaits in therapeutic riding. *Applied Animal Behaviour Science*, *135*(4), 271–276.

Ulrich, R.S. (1979). Visual landscapes and psychological well-being. *Landscape Research*, *4*, 17–23.

Ulrich, R.S., Simons, R.F., Losito, B.D., Fiorito, E., Miles, M.A., & Zelson, M. (1991). Stress recovery during exposure to natural and urban environments. *Journal of Environmental Psychology*, *11*, 201–230.

Ungermann, C. M., & Gras, L. Z. (2011). Therapeutic riding followed by rhythmic auditory stimulation to improve balance and gait in a aubject with orthopedic pathologies. *The Journal of Alternative and Complementary Medicine*, *17*(12), 1191–1195.

van den Berg, A.E., Maas, J., Verheij, R.A., & Groenewegen, P.P. (2010). Green space as a buffer between stressful life events and health. *Social Science Medicine*, *70*, 1203–1210.

Van Haaften, E.H., & Van De Vijver, F.J. (1996). Psychological consequences of environmental degradation. *Journal of Health Psychology*, *1*(4), 411–429.

Vidrine, M., Owen-Smith, P., & Faulkner, P. (2002). Equine-facilitated group psychotherapy: Applications for therapeutic vaulting. *Issues in Mental Health Nursing*, *23*(6), 587–603.

Wach, S.M. (2014). *Interactions with Horses Is Associated with Higher Mindfulness and Heart Rate Aariability and Lower Electrodermal Response in College Students*. Retrieved from: http://scholarcommons.sc.edu/aiken_psychology_theses

Waite, C., & Bourke, L. (2013). "It's different with a horse": Horses as a tool for engagement in a horse therapy program for marginalised young people. *Youth Studies Australia*, *32*(4), 13–21.

Wanneberg, P.L. (2014). Disability, riding, and identity: A qualitative study on the influence of riding on the identity construction of people with disabilities. *International Journal of Disability, Development and Education*, *61*(1), 67–79.

Willis, D. (1997). Animal therapy. *Rehabilitation Nursing*, *22*(2), 78–81.

Yalom, I. (2003). *The gift of therapy: An open letter to a new generation of therapists and their patients* (1st edition). Harper Perennial.

Yorke, J., Adams, C., & Coady, N. (2008). Therapeutic value of equine-human bonding in recovery from trauma. *Anthrozoös*, *21*(1), 17–30.

2 Understanding Equine-Assisted Therapy

☐ Defining Equine-Assisted Therapy

Equine-assisted therapy is considered part of the larger industry called "equine-assisted activities and therapies". Services are organized as either non-therapy "activities" such as adaptive riding or equine-assisted learning, or "therapies" in which the horse is included in physical therapy, occupational therapy, speech therapy, or mental health services provided by licensed professionals.

Although these therapies are provided by thousands of professionals from around the world, and treat conditions ranging from cerebral palsy to post-traumatic stress disorder, there remains a great need to concisely define, describe, and clarify the terminology and practical guidelines of equine-assisted therapy (Debuse, et al., 2005; Smith-Osborne & Selby, 2010; Thompson, et al., 2012; Brandt, 2013; Angsupaisal, et al., 2015; Lentini & Knox, 2015; Pham & Bitonte, 2016).

Therapy Services (Equine-Assisted Therapy)

Equine-assisted therapy broadly refers to any type of therapy or treatment that includes equine interactions, activities, or treatment strategies, and the equine milieu. Services are regulated by healthcare laws and provided by appropriately educated, trained, and credentialed (licensed or registered) healthcare professionals. These individuals act within their scope of practice, and focus on addressing the patient's clinical treatment goals. Patients (or their parents or legal guardians in specific cases) seek therapy as a treatment for physical or psychological illness or disability, and agree to the treatment by signing an informed consent form and actively engaging in the treatment planning process.

Specific to equine-assisted therapy, typically physical therapists, occupational therapists, speech therapists, mental health professionals, nurses, and on some occasions, medical doctors, are the licensed healthcare professionals who most commonly provide some form of equine-assisted therapy. Most professionals who offer equine-assisted therapy are required to obtain additional training, education, supervision, and certification (when available) prior to adding a new technique or area of practice specialization (Cook, 2011; ACA, 2016; APA, 2016; NASW, 2016; AOTA, 2016; APTA, 2016a).

Licensed healthcare professionals do not conceptualize equine-assisted therapy as a distinct or separate service or profession (Ekholm Fry, 2013; Pham & Bitonte, 2016, AHA, 2017). Rather, professionals continue to practice whatever form of conventional healthcare they are licensed to provide—such as physical, occupational, and speech therapy; or psychology, counseling, social work, or marriage and family therapy—while incorporating horses and the farm milieu into the patient's treatment plan. Regardless of where the service is conducted and whether or not a horse is present, these professionals remain bound by the same laws and ethics associated with the profession in which they are licensed.

Physical, occupational, and speech therapists commonly use activities conducted in the farm milieu or while mounted on a horse (usually called "hippotherapy") to improve functional outcomes. Licensed mental health professionals use various forms of equine-assisted mental health including equine-facilitated psychotherapy, equine-assisted counseling, or the Equine-Assisted Growth and Learning (EAGALA) model of equine-assisted psychotherapy to address treatment goals or aid in the treatment process.

Types of Equine-Assisted Therapy Services

Just like any form of conventional healthcare, when physical therapists, occupational therapists, speech therapists, and licensed mental health professionals provide equine-assisted therapy, they do so within the limits of their scope of practice, treating only patients whose conditions would typically be treated by their distinct healthcare practice. Adding a horse to therapy does not change a professional's scope of practice, or enable them to treat populations or conditions they would not otherwise treat (ACA, 2016; AOTA, 2016; APA, 2016; APTA, 2016a; ASHA, 2016b; NASW, 2016).

Although there may be overlap between the populations or conditions served by the various forms of equine-assisted therapy, each type of therapy addresses a different aspect of the problem. For example, a patient suffering from a traumatic brain injury might see a physical therapist to help with balance, mobility, and increased coordination, an occupational therapist to help reintegrate into the work place, a mental health professional to address co-occurring post-traumatic stress disorder or mood disorders, and a speech therapist to help with issues of cognitive-communication skills.

As a point of clarification, since "equine-assisted therapy," "hippotherapy," "equine-assisted psychotherapy," or any of the other approaches to including horses in human healthcare are not distinct or separate professions or services, patients should not be referred to any of these directly.

Rather, patients should be referred to the appropriate type of professional for their condition, like a licensed physical, occupational, speech, or mental health therapist. These professionals may choose to incorporate equine movement, equine activities, or the farm milieu in the patient's treatment plan, but their primary responsibility is to use clinical reasoning and their extensive training, education, and experience to treat the presenting condition using whatever treatment method is deemed most effective. The equine interaction is only one tool among many others in a skilled and knowledgeable professional's repertoire.

In an effort to help the public better understand that "hippotherapy" or "equine-assisted therapy" are not stand-alone services that could be provided by non-licensed individuals, the American Hippotherapy Association, Inc. (AHA) advises healthcare professionals to specify their distinct areas of licensure to ensure it is clear what regulated healthcare service the professional provides (AHA, 2016); for example, equine-assisted physical therapy.

Understanding that each type of healthcare professional includes horses in their clinical practices differently is a critical step towards developing referent and provider competence, and protecting the safety of patients seeking treatment.

Equine-Assisted Physical Therapy

When licensed physical therapists see patients at the farm and incorporate equine activities and the farm milieu in a patient's treatment plan, they are providing equine-assisted physical therapy. Although current statistics seem to indicate that physical therapists are the second most common professionals to include horses in human healthcare (Stroud & Hallberg, 2016), there is yet to be published research that investigates the professional practice of equine-assisted physical therapy.

According to the American Physical Therapy Association (APTA, 2016a), "Physical therapists are health care professionals who help individuals maintain, restore, and improve movement, activity, and functioning, thereby enabling optimal performance and enhancing health, well-being, and quality of life" (para. 1). Physical therapy focuses on treating impairments of body function and structure, and helping to minimize or eliminate physical restrictions that may impact human performance and engagement in activities (APTA, 2015). When physical therapists incorporate horses and the farm milieu in treatment, they address these and other goals.

Although not unique to equine-assisted physical therapy, the movement of the horse is the primary tool used by physical therapists to achieve functional outcomes associated with physical therapy goals (Benda, et al., 2003; Lechner, et al., 2007; McGibbon, et al., 2009; Chang, et al., 2012; Kang, et al., 2012; Angoules, et al., 2015). The warmth of the horse is also cited as a therapeutic benefit, helping to improve circulation, reduce abnormal muscle tone, and relax muscle spasticity (Kang, et al., 2012; Angoules, et al., 2015), and motivation and socialization are considered aspects of equine-assisted physical therapy (Benda, et al., 2003).

Although perhaps less common in equine-assisted physical therapy, use of the farm milieu is also considered a treatment component. Physical therapists may use activities around the barnyard to help achieve functional outcomes (Shurtleff, et al., 2009, AHA, 2017).

Sample populations or conditions commonly treated by equine-assisted physical therapy may include but are not limited to:

- Autism spectrum disorder
- Cerebral palsy
- Developmental delays
- Elderly populations and others dealing with balance disorders
- Learning disabilities
- Stroke
- Traumatic brain injury

Equine-Assisted Occupational Therapy

Equine-assisted occupational therapy refers to the inclusion of horses and the farm milieu in an occupational therapy session. The scope of practice of occupational therapists is very broad, which as Corcoran (2006) points out is both an "asset and a challenge."

Occupational therapists may concentrate on mental health issues; assist with rehabilitation, disability, and participation challenges; and guide patients through productive aging, or they might focus on overall patient health and wellness (AOTA, 2014). Although understanding exactly what occupational therapists do is too detailed for this book, at the core of occupational therapy seems to be an emphasis on whole person wellness and enhancing participation in the activities of living.

This broad scope of practice informs how occupational therapists could include horses in clinical practice, and a few scholars have published papers related to the role and practice of occupational therapists who use equine-assisted therapy (Millhouse-Flourie, 2004; Cerquozzi, et al., 2007; Latella & Langford, 2008; Baker, 2015).

Latella & Langford (2008) suggest that equine-assisted occupational therapy is based upon sensory integration theory, and could be used to "address motor, process, and interaction skills to enhance occupational performance" (p. 16). Occupational therapists may also use equine-assisted occupational therapy to increase patient motivation and engagement and to promote social and emotional bonding and play through the use of activities like grooming or caring for the horses (Cerquozzi, et al., 2007; Latella & Langford, 2008; Baker, 2015).

Unlike physical therapists, occupational therapists could use techniques akin to mental health professionals, or teach patients new skills and enhance socialization (Baker, 2015, Ajzenman, 2012). However, occupational therapists might also use the movement of the horse or activities like steering through an obstacle course to achieve functional outcomes related to mobility, strength, or endurance, or to practice skills like taking turns, planning, and sequencing (Latella & Langford, 2008; Ajzenman, 2013).

Ajzenman states:

> The movement of the horse [in equine-assisted occupational therapy] assists with developing necessary strength, postural control, as well as providing necessary sensory input to assist with development of the proprioceptive, vestibular systems and other sensory systems, and assists with overall regulation (depending on patients under or over responsivity). This has a multi-layered impact where proximal stability allows for increased body awareness and the ability to stabilize and freely access and use upper extremities for daily activity engagement.
>
> (personal communication, June 25, 2017)

She goes on to note that equine-assisted occupational therapy "affords children opportunities to work on functional communication, socially problem solve, and learn to play as a primary occupation" (personal communication, June 25, 2017).

According to the American Occupational Therapy Association (AOTA, 2014), occupational therapists are "experts at analyzing the client factors, performance skills, performance patterns, and contexts and environments necessary for people to engage in their everyday activities and occupations" (p. 1). In equine-assisted occupational therapy, occupational therapists consider all the factors that might be compromising the fulfillment of a patient's life goals and daily activities. This includes lifestyle patterns or habits; physical wellness issues like mobility, strength, and endurance; social and interpersonal engagement including leisure and play; activities of daily living like eating, sleeping, dressing, personal hygiene, or driving, education and learning; and occupational or vocational considerations (Millhouse-Flourie, 2004; AOTA, 2014). Occupational therapists design treatment goals to address these areas using equine activities and the farm milieu.

Occupational therapists treat a wide range of populations and conditions using equine-assisted occupational therapy which may include but are not limited to:

- Autism spectrum disorder
- Cerebral palsy
- Developmental delays
- Elderly populations and others dealing with balance disorders

- Intellectual disabilities
- Learning disabilities
- Mental illness
- Sensory processing disorder
- Traumatic brain injury
- Stroke

Equine-Assisted Speech Therapy

Speech and language therapy addresses disorders of speech, language, communication, and swallowing. Although only three studies published in peer-reviewed journals could be identified specific to speech and language therapy incorporating horses (Macauley & Gutierrez, 2004; Keino, et al., 2009; Valle, et al., 2014), equine-assisted speech therapy seems uniquely positioned to aid in the treatment of such disorders.

The dynamic movement of the horse requires the integration of all body systems (Macauley & Gutierrez, 2004) and promotes sensory-motor development, both of which are highly important to speech and language function. According to Tina Rocco, "The patient receives proprioceptive input, vestibular input, tactile input, auditory input, olfactory input, and visual flow all simultaneously as the horse is moving" (Rocco, 2012, para. 8).

Further benefits of equine-assisted speech therapy include the motivation of working with horses and coming to the farm, and the social/emotional aspects included in the therapy like interacting with the horse, staff, volunteers, or other patients (Macauley & Gutierrez, 2004, Keino, et al., 2009).

Keino, et al. (2009) state, "In general, PDD [pervasive developmental disorder] children may lack spontaneity in seeking to share enjoyment, interests, or achievements with other people, and may also lack social or emotional reciprocity" (p. 87). The researchers go on to note an important aspect of their study was the shift in perspective about treatment participants experienced when engaging in equine-assisted speech therapy. They report, "The recognition of their environment, which changed from being 'harmful' to 'pleasant,' is a very important factor in aiding them to courageously seek to spontaneously share enjoyment, interests, or achievements with parents and later with important others" (p. 87).

Similar to the lack of established theory base or methodology in equine-assisted physical therapy, Valle, et al. (2014) report:

> No article or publication referring to any kind of theoretical basis in the speech therapy area was found in the literature. The absence of well-defined methodological lines is possibly due to this being a new area, thus demanding researchers to indicate the effectiveness of the speech therapy aspects dealt with.
>
> (p. 518)

It seems clear more research on the topic of how licensed speech therapists incorporate horses and the farm milieu in therapy sessions could greatly benefit professionals and the industry as a whole.

Conditions aided or treated by equine-assisted speech therapy may include but are not limited to:

- Articulation delays and disorders
- Auditory processing disorders
- Autism spectrum disorder
- Cerebral palsy
- Developmental delays
- Down syndrome
- Dysarthria
- Expressive language delays and deficits
- Oral motor delays
- Oral/verbal apraxia of speech
- Stuttering/fluency disorders
- Swallowing/feeding difficulty
- Voice issues (breath support, volume, vocal abuse and misuse)

Equine-Assisted Mental Health

Equine-assisted mental health is a specialty area of practice in which licensed mental health professionals (psychologists, counselors, psychotherapists, and social workers) provide regulated mental health services in a farm environment working with horses. The term "equine-assisted mental health" is sometimes used synonymously with "equine-assisted psychotherapy" to broadly describe including horses in mental health services.

The clinical practice of including horses and the farm milieu in mental health services appears to be the most commonly used type of equine-assisted therapy (Stroud & Hallberg, 2016) and is certainly the most researched of all types of equine-assisted therapy (Bates, 2002; Roberts, et al., 2004; Rothe, et al., 2005; Karol & Tac, 2007; Klontz, et al., 2007; Kirby, 2010; Masini, 2010; Swindell, 2010; Bachi, 2013; Brandt, 2013; Carlsson, et al., 2014; Notgrass & Pettinelli, 2015; Johns, et al., 2016). However, as Carlsson (2016) points out, "Results highlight the complexity in practice, making it difficult to evaluate" (p. 20).

Like other forms of mental health treatment, professionals providing equine-assisted mental health apply a wide range of psychological and human development principles and methods to treat pathology, address abuse and trauma, and decrease the symptoms of depression, anxiety, and other mental health conditions (Signal, et al., 2013; Wilson, et al., 2015; Nurenberg, et al., 2015; Earles, et al., 2015; Lac, 2016). These services are used to address a wide range of issues from mental illness, addiction, and family or marriage concerns, to everyday life challenges.

Researchers have theorized about the many ways horses may help people who are dealing with mental health issues. From the size of the horse, to its instinctual nature, its responses and reactions, its communication style, and the feelings of self-esteem and self-confidence that develop through the horse-human relationship, the opportunities for addressing clinical mental health goals are plentiful (Vidrine, et al., 2002; Frewin & Gardiner, 2005; Rothe, et al., 2005; Porter-Wenzlaff, 2007; Trotter, et al., 2008; Ford, 2013; Johansen, et al., 2014; Kern-Godal, et al., 2015).

The farm milieu is also considered an important component of equine-assisted mental health (Rothe, et al., 2005; Karol & Tac, 2007; Berget & Braastad, 2011; Schroeder & Stroud, 2015).

Populations or conditions treated by equine-assisted mental health services may include but are not limited to:

- Addiction
- ADD/ADHD
- Anxiety
- "At-risk" behaviors in children and adolescents
- Autism spectrum disorder
- Conduct disorder and oppositional defiant disorder
- Eating disorders
- Mood disorders including depression and bi-polar
- Personality disorders including borderline personality disorder and narcissistic personality disorder
- Schizophrenia and schizoaffective disorder
- Obsessive-compulsive disorder
- Post-traumatic stress disorder
- Relationship issues including marriage, family, and parenting
- Stress and stress-related conditions

Non-Therapy Services (Equine-Assisted Activities)

Equine-assisted activities refers to the non-therapy services that include horses and focus on teaching skills and enhancing quality of life. Consumers and referring professionals should be aware these services are not regulated by healthcare laws, ethics, competency requirements, or standards of practice in the United States. In essence, non-therapy services are a part of the free-market industry, which is self-regulating.

Individuals who provide non-therapy services may include riding instructors; relational horsemanship instructors; life, leadership, or executive coaches; and experiential educators. Since none of these professions are regulated by healthcare laws, they are free to choose whatever type of education, training, or certificate program they deem useful.

Non-therapy services capitalize upon the recognized benefits of social interaction, physical exercise, and skill building (Rimmer & Rowland,

2006; Pendry & Roeter, 2013; Hauge, et al., 2014; Lee, et al., 2015). While some providers focus on adaptive recreation by providing horseback riding lessons, others might use equine interactions to teach life skills, social skills, communication skills, or leadership skills while facilitating personal growth and increased self-awareness (DePauw, 1986; Ward, et al., 2013; Dell, et al., 2011; Kendall, et al., 2015; Meola, 2016).

By law, in the United States non-licensed individuals may not infringe upon the scope of practice of licensed healthcare professionals (Hinkley, 2015). It is illegal for non-licensed providers to offer services or use terminology that are protected by the various licensed professions (APTA, 2015; APTA, 2016b; AOTA, 2016; ASHA, 2016, NASW, 2016; NBCC, 2016). For example, a non-licensed individual cannot legally provide (or state they provide) any form of therapy that falls under the protection of a licensed profession, nor can they offer "treatment" for medical or mental health conditions unless directly supervised by a licensed healthcare professional, a signed consent for treatment is in place, and the team utilizes a clinically formulated treatment plan.

Referring professionals and those interested in attending non-therapy services should be aware that adaptive or "therapeutic" riding and equine-assisted learning including life, leadership, or executive coaching are not considered forms of therapy in the United States, and thus individuals should not seek out or be referred to these services to treat medical or mental health conditions unless the provider meets the previously listed criteria.

What is Equine-Assisted Learning?

Equine-assisted learning (EAL) is a non-therapy skills-based service that focuses on teaching life skills, social skills, communication skills, or leadership skills while facilitating personal growth and increased self-awareness through both mounted and non-mounted interactions with horses. Services are provided by educators, riding instructors, or life/professional development coaches. EAL providers may teach horsemanship skills, and even use riding and other mounted activities as a means to foster skills. This method is not manualized, and providers practice using a variety of approaches or theoretical beliefs.

What is Adaptive or "Therapeutic" Riding?

Adaptive riding is a non-therapy skills-based service in which instructors teach horseback riding and horsemanship skills to students with disabilities or special needs.

The AHA defines adaptive riding as "a riding lesson for individuals with special needs taught by specifically trained instructors. The primary goal of adaptive riding is to teach the recreational activity or sport of horseback riding to individuals with special needs" (2017, p. 1). Most adaptive riding instructors are certified through the Professional Association of Therapeutic Horsemanship, International (PATH Intl.).

☐ Terminology

When attempting to speak about including horses in healthcare professions, the plethora of terms utilized astounds and confounds most everyone, from patients and referents, to funding sources and researchers, to the very professionals providing the service.

At present, 63 different terms can be readily identified in research and in practice that describe the concept of including horses in human healthcare. To complicate matters, these terms are used either interchangeably to describe the same service, or used to describe completely different services (Angsupaisal, et al., 2015).

In a 1992 article, Norma Lang states when talking about the nursing profession, "If we cannot name it, we cannot control it, practice it, teach it, finance it, or put it into public policy" (Clark & Lang, 1992, p. 109).

In healthcare settings, the use of standardized language is imperative to help ensure the wellbeing of the patient, to understand and communicate treatment outcomes, and to legitimize the profession (Maas & Delaney, 2004; Thoroddsen & Ehnfors, 2007; Rutherford, 2008). Dr. Judith Warren suggests that using standardized terminology is essential to supporting research activities, retrieving and coding data, auditing the quality of a service, making sound clinical decisions, and promoting a sense of shared understanding across cultures, languages, and systems (Warren, 2012).

Cross-cultural differences in language and treatment practices further complicate the terminology struggle. Laws and competency standards are different in each country, and this affects the use of terms. For instance, a term that is considered accurate in American may not be accurate in German. Questions arise about who should set the standardized terms, and if such a task force would truly be able to capture a cross-cultural and multilingual audience. The various membership associations provide terms and their associated definitions, but there is little agreement or cohesion between them, making it further difficult for researchers, authors, students, consumers, and referents.

History of Terminology

From the 1970s to the 1990s, the terms "hippotherapy," "therapeutic riding," "horseback riding for the disabled," "horseback riding for the handicapped," "equestrian therapy," "riding therapy," "rehabilitative horseback riding," "equine therapy," "horse therapy," and "equine-movement therapy" appeared in the research to describe including horses in human healthcare.

As evidenced by those terms, prior to the 1990s, verbs used to describe the role of the horse in human healthcare were non-existent in terminology. According to a personal correspondence with Michael Kaufmann (September 20, 2016), the term "assisted" (as in "equine-assisted therapy") was adopted in the 1990s to align with the Delta Society (now Pet Partners) and the larger industry of animal-assisted activities and therapies. Based on the literature review conducted for this book, the term "assisted" appears first in research when Benda, et al. (2003) use "equine-assisted therapy (hippotherapy)" (p. 817), and a year later when Macauley & Gutierrez (2004) reference "equine-assisted activities" and "equine-assisted therapy" (p. 205), citing the Delta Society.

In 1996, the Equine-Facilitated Mental Health Association (EFMHA) initiated the use of the verb "facilitated," based upon their philosophical belief that horses "co-facilitated" mental health services. Kaufmann (personal communication, September 20, 2016) states this term "implied too much action and intentionality on the part of the horse" and goes on to note that many in the industry believed that the term "assisted" more accurately described the role of the horse at that time. EFMHA's choice to use "facilitated" introduced one of the first significant splits in language the industry encountered.

Since that time, the discussion about whether or not horses "assist" or "facilitate" has grown to include a proliferation of possible verbs used to describe the role of the horse. Some suggest horses "guide" or "mediate" services, while others see the horse as their "partner." These differing beliefs have led to the creation of new terms such as "equine-mediated therapy," or "equine-guided education." This has caused confusion in research, as in some cases the use of a different verb (i.e. "assisted" vs. "facilitated") actually indicates a distinct theoretical approach. This compounds the challenges researchers face, as it can be unclear if they are comparing like services even though the term used to describe the service is different.

Finally, specific methods or approaches have arisen over the years that are taught by organizations or individuals. Examples include:

- The EAGALA model of equine-assisted psychotherapy and equine-assisted learning
- The Eponaquest model of equine-facilitated learning
- The Adventures in Awareness™ model of equine-facilitated experiential learning
- The Equine Psychotherapy Institute model of equine-assisted psychotherapy
- The Gestalt Equine Psychotherapy™ model of equine-assisted psychotherapy
- The Human-Equine Alliances for Learning (HEAL) approach to equine-facilitated psychotherapy and learning

- The Human-Equine Relational Development Institute (HERD) model of equine-facilitated psychotherapy and learning
- The Natural Lifemanship model of equine-assisted psychotherapy

It is important to note that throughout this book, the term "assisted" will be used as the common verb to describe the role of the horse in human healthcare. The use of this term does not imply a philosophical belief or a methodological approach, unless specifically indicated (e.g. the EAGALA model of equine-assisted psychotherapy).

Hippotherapy and "Therapeutic" Riding

The term "hippotherapy" is defined by the AHA as the manner in which "occupational, therapy, physical therapy, and speech-language pathology professionals use evidence-based practice and clinical reasoning in the purposeful manipulation of equine movement to engage sensory, neuromotor and cognitive systems to achieve functional outcomes" (AHA, 2017, p. 3).

Hippotherapy is a noteworthy term because it is the most clearly and consistently defined and understood in research throughout time and across culture as exampled by Lechner, et al. (2003), Debuse, et al. (2005), Buswell & Leriou (2007), Snider, et al. (2007), Honkavaara & Rintala (2010), Kwon, et al. (2011), Granados & Agís (2011), Chang, et al. (2012), Bunketorp Käll, et al. (2012), El-Meniawy & Thabet (2012), Shurtleff & Engsberg (2012), Ajzenman (2013), and Kwon, et al. (2015). All of these researchers clearly articulate that hippotherapy is used during the provision of a regulated physical, occupational, or speech therapy service by licensed therapists to achieve functional outcomes.

Unlike hippotherapy, the use of the term "therapeutic riding" is not consistently defined. There is significant confusion as to whether or not the service is therapy, who provides it, what the goals are, and how it is provided as evidenced in the research (Bertoti, 1988; Bizub, et al., 2003; Debuse, et al., 2005; Bass, et al., 2009; Beinotti, et al., 2010; Cuypers, et al., 2011; Munoz-Lasa, et al., 2011; Bunketorp Käll, et al., 2012; Ihara, et al., 2012).

The confusion in terms between hippotherapy and therapeutic riding is first evidenced by Bertoti's (1988) groundbreaking research article, in which she writes:

> In therapeutic riding, the horse is used as a treatment modality similar to the use of therapy balls and bolsters typically seen in a pediatric physical therapy clinic. To facilitate particular postural responses, the therapist may place the rider in various positions on the horse such as prone, side lying, side sitting, or sitting. In many cases, the

therapist and rider will ride together so that the therapist can facilitate the movement or desired response as needed.

(p. 1505)

Later, Bass, et al. (2009) state, "Therapeutic horse-back riding is defined as using horseback riding treatment to improve posture, balance, and mobility while developing a therapeutic bond between the patient and horse" (p. 1261).

Two years later, Munoz-Lasa, et al. (2011) write, "Equine-assisted therapies, such as therapeutic horseback riding (THR) and hippotherapy (HT), are physical therapy treatment strategies with known positive effects in some neurological diseases with motor disability" (p. 462).

As a solution to this problem, the AHA (AHA, 2015) recommends not using the term "therapeutic riding" at all, stating:

Therapeutic is a term that falls under one of several billable codes used by therapists (occupation therapists, physical therapists, or speech-language pathologists). Use of this term outside the realm of therapy can lead to confusion when a licensed therapist is not present.

(p. 3)

The AHA's point is supported by Merriam-Webster's medical definition of "therapy" as a "therapeutic treatment of, or relating to, the treatment of illness" (Merriam-Webster Online Dictionary, 2016). Instead, the AHA recommends using the term "adaptive riding," defining it as "A [non-therapy] riding lesson for individuals with special needs taught by specifically trained instructors. The primary goal of adaptive riding is to teach the recreational activity or sport of horseback riding to individuals with special needs" (AHA, 2017, p. 1).

The use of the term "adaptive riding" causes some disagreement within the industry. One aspect of the disagreement appears to be that "therapeutic riding" instructors don't necessarily agree that they "adapt" their services to meet the needs of people with special needs. This could be arguable since it seems nearly every aspect of a "therapeutic" riding lesson is adapted in some way—from the training of the horses, instructors, and staff; to the use of volunteers who support the riders; to the facility and equipment and the policies, procedures, standards and the specialty liability insurance required to provide riding lessons to people with special needs (Thompson, et al., 2012; AHA, 2017). Others argue that "therapeutic" riding is just what it says it is: therapeutic. They believe the service provides health benefits and should be advertised and marketed as such. This is a passionate issue as the term "therapeutic riding" has been used for many years, and holds great meaning to many people.

Although wishing to be respectful of those who feel the term "therapeutic riding" should remain the standard, the research clearly demonstrates that use of this term is causing significant confusion both nationally and internationally that is negatively affecting the industry as a whole. Therefore, for the sake of clarifying the difference between therapy and non-therapy services, the term "adaptive riding" will be used throughout this book.

Equine-Assisted Mental Health and Equine-Assisted Learning

Similarly to the confusions between hippotherapy and "therapeutic" riding, research shows a nearly total lack of industry-wide understanding or agreement about the difference between equine-assisted mental health and equine-assisted learning. Researchers confuse the two by suggesting the non-therapy method of equine-assisted learning is a mental health strategy used to provide treatment for mental health diagnoses (Ewing, et al., 2007; Burgon, 2011; Pendry & Roeter, 2013; Pendry, et al., 2014; Duncan, et al., 2014; Newton-Cromwell, et al., 2015; Lentini & Knox, 2015; Frederick, et al., 2015; Lee, et al., 2016).

For example, Duncan, et al. (2014) report, "The EAL [equine-assisted learning] industry is uniquely positioned to provide an appropriate form of experiential learning therapy for veterans and their spouses/partners suffering from the effects of OSI [occupational stress injury]" (p. 65).

Pendry & Roeter (2013) state:

> One type of approach that has caught the attention of researchers and mental health professionals is equine facilitated learning, which combines the experience of equine human interaction with counseling-based processing skills to increase participants' awareness and control of their emotions, cognitions, and behaviors.
>
> (p. 2)

Frederick, et al. (2015) suggest that equine-assisted learning can be used as a treatment intervention for decreasing levels of depression in at-risk youth.

Ewing, et al. (2007) confuse equine-facilitated psychotherapy and equine-facilitated learning as one service. They state, "Equine-facilitated psychotherapy or learning (EFP/L) is an experiential methodology that uses a 'hands-on' approach" (p. 60). Later they make reference to treatment, and call the participants clients, stating, "EFP/L is unique in that the clients go to the animal: They must experience the treatment in its natural environment" (p. 61). And finally, they state, "To continue the lead of current, promising research, the purpose of this study was to evaluate the effectiveness of equine-facilitated therapy with adolescents diagnosed with severe emotional disorders" (p. 61).

Lee, et al. (2016) highlight the confusion between equine-assisted learning and equine-assisted psychotherapy, stating, "We included these EAL [equine-assisted learning] studies because it is hard to clearly distinguish between EAP [equine-assisted psychotherapy] and EAL, as they are typically practised together, with an overlap between EAP and EAL" (p. 226).

Although the two types of services may look similar in their use of activities and in the populations they serve, they are distinctly different. Equine-assisted mental health is a clinical intervention regulated by healthcare laws and provided by licensed professionals. Unless supervised by a licensed professional, equine-assisted learning is not therapy, and does not provide "treatment" for mental or behavioral healthcare issues. For legal and ethical reasons, it is important this distinction is made clear in research, published literature, promotional materials, and in practice.

☐ The Importance of Differentiating Between Services

Some might argue that just being around horses is healing for people, regardless of what service occurs, who provides it, what it is called, or how it is described—and therefore, why all the fuss about clearly differentiating between services? However, there are serious issues to take into consideration that, if handled carelessly, could be detrimental to individuals and to the industry as a whole.

Consumer Safety

Professional healthcare licensure has competency standards for a specific reason. Human beings are complicated. Although on the surface a condition might seem obvious and its "treatment" intuitive, the more information, training and education one has, the more clearly articulated the complications and risks become. Licensed healthcare professionals go through a standardized and regulated education, training and credentialing process. This process guarantees a level of competence and mastery within the profession. Non-therapy providers are not required by law to demonstrate or adhere to any specific education, training, competency, or licensing requirements.

If an individual providing a non-therapy service uses language that misleads the consumer or referent into thinking the service will reduce serious medical or mental health symptoms, or provide a type of "treatment" for a complicated condition or diagnosis, the provider could unintentionally cause harm due to a lack of education, training, and experience. In some cases, the harm may go unnoticed or may not be understood by the provider. This is especially relevant for those offering services that address psychological conditions. The work with horses can be provocative, and may open people up to thoughts, feelings and memories they may not be ready to process, or have the support in place to process safely. Providers who are not trained in mental health may not recognize the signs of someone becoming emotionally triggered by an activity.

In the case of adaptive riding or equine-assisted learning, this could occur when a program or provider states their service can treat or help reduce the effects of PTSD in returning veterans.

Examples of this can be found on many websites offering adaptive riding or equine-assisted learning. For instance, Cadence Therapeutic Riding Center (www.cadenceriding.org) states the purpose of equine-assisted learning is "To treat Post Traumatic Stress Disorder (PTSD) and Traumatic Brain Injury (TBI)" and "To reduce stress, anxiety and the risk of suicide" (http://cadenceriding.org/equine-assisted-therapies-riding/).

Due to perceived stigma associated with "therapy," a veteran might attend a program like that offered through Cadence Therapeutic Riding center, thinking it will "treat" PTSD. If the veteran believes the program is equipped to address or handle his/her symptoms, he/she is likely to be more vulnerable, and less likely to seek the appropriate service. PTSD, especially in returning veterans, is extremely complex, as is its treatment. Veterans may be triggered by smells, noises, touch, movement, or topics discussed, and may have flashbacks that are re-traumatizing and destabilizing (U.S. Department of Veterans Affairs, 2016). If the program staff believes they are helping with these symptoms, they may not seek guidance or consultation, and they may not think to refer the participant to the appropriate service provider. This can be very dangerous for the participant, and can place the program at risk for legal action.

If the program advertises adaptive riding lessons or equine-assisted learning sessions for veterans, but clearly articulates the appropriate goals associated with adaptive riding or equine-assisted learning, a veteran may choose the service for non-medical reasons such as recreation, exercise, fun, improving quality of life, or enhancing experience of community. If the veteran happens to be triggered by something the program or instructor does, he or she can be appropriately referred to a licensed therapist to address the trigger or symptoms that arise.

BraveHearts (www.braveheartsriding.org), a program that serves veterans through equine-assisted services, provides an example of using appropriate goals for their non-therapy programming which include, "to learn horsemanship skills, to participate in unique, positive recreational activities with their entire family, to create opportunities for positive interaction and sharing of common interests, and to build a community of veteran families" (www.braveheartsriding.org/veterans). BraveHearts also offers a retreat for veterans, which is obviously psychotherapeutic, but they are clear that these events are led by counselors from the Veterans Administration.

Issues exist with physical health conditions as well. Parents may seek out adaptive riding to help their child achieve functional health-related treatment outcomes. They may do this because the program or provider states their service will help treat medical conditions, and it costs less and is more available than therapy. If the non-therapy provider misleads the parent or referent into believing they can assess and treat health-related conditions via a non-therapy service, they are putting both the participate and themselves at risk.

Finally, even licensed professionals must be careful to only accept specialty populations (such as returning veterans) or agree to treating an unfamiliar condition (such as PTSD) if they have received additional training, education, and supervision specific to the population or condition (ACA, 2016; APA, 2016; NASW, 2016; AOTA, 2016; APTA, 2016a). If a licensed professional is interested in accepting new patients that fall outside of their typical patient profile, they are advised to seek additional training and consultation to determine the best course of action. This could include receiving supervision from another licensed professional who is experienced working with the population, attending trainings, and reading current research and treatment protocols—or the licensed professional could determine it is most ethical to refer the patient to a more experienced provider.

Most participants do not know the difference between therapy and non-therapy services. They read the description and if it sounds like the service will help them or address a need they have, they may participate regardless of who is providing it and what that person's training, education, and licensure is. As such, it falls upon the provider to be ethical and responsible about how they market their services and how they use a system of appropriate referrals.

Scope of Practice

Licensed healthcare professionals operate under strict scope of practice laws unique to each profession. Scope of practice laws define the procedures, processes, and actions a healthcare provider may perform. Scope of practice also explains the limits or extent to which a healthcare provider is allowed to practice. In the United States, each state has specific stipulations related to scope of practice, and healthcare professionals are responsible for remaining firmly within their legal boundaries, regardless if they include horses or not. If they act outside of their scope, they face legal action and could lose their license.

Non-therapy providers do not have a scope of practice, as their services are not regulated. However, in the United States, it is illegal for non-licensed individuals to offer services provided by a licensed healthcare professional, to use protected titles to describe their services, or to offer duplicate services using a different non-protected title (Glosoff, et al., 1995; AOTA, 2007; APTA, 2016b; Human Services Guide, 2016). At present, the lines between non-therapy services like equine-assisted learning or adaptive riding and therapy services provided by licensed healthcare professionals are blurred in many cases. This does not help the industry in its attempts to gain credibility within the larger medical community, or provide the public with a clear understanding of equine-assisted therapy.

Non-therapy providers have important services to offer. The key lies in providing opportunities that are uniquely different from the protected scope of practice of licensed professionals. By doing this, non-licensed providers can remove themselves from direct competition with licensed professionals, and can create a niche market that can be used as an important part of the continuum of care spectrum through effective referral.

Research

Without standardized language and internationally accepted terminology, it is nearly impossible to code and measure concepts and treatment strategies effectively (Maas & Delaney, 2004; Rutherford, 2008; Lee, et al., 2016). If researchers and practitioners use different language and different definitions for terminology, it becomes challenging to accurately understand the causal factors linking a professional practice with clinical outcomes.

Much of the research done on equine-assisted therapy uses inconsistent terminology, so it is difficult to be certain researchers are investigating the same intervention. Thompson, et al. (2012) write, "Because terminology used to describe different types of equine programs is used inconsistently, uniformity among programs of the same name cannot be assumed" (p. 374).

Mixing therapy and non-therapy approaches further confounds the issue. A targeted clinical intervention provided by a licensed professional is significantly different than a non-clinical, adaptive recreation activity. Debuse, et al. (2005) state:

> What complicates the evidence base for hippotherapy is the fact that some authors seem to blur the boundaries between hippotherapy and the other areas within therapeutic riding as set out earlier, both in their intervention and in their measurements by using non-specific concepts such as "therapeutic riding programs."
>
> (p. 221)

Finally, Angsupaisal, et al. (2015) add, "The limited evidence on effectiveness [of equine-assisted activities and therapies] may be partially explained by the heterogeneity in the therapies applied. This heterogeneity is reflected in past and present terminology" (p. 1152).

It is clear, from a comprehensive review of existing research, that there is little standardization in terminology including the definitions of terms, and the application of clinical practices. This affects everyone involved:

- Participants cannot feel assured the service they are paying for and engaging in actually helps their condition.

- Medical professionals cannot write accurate prescriptions for services, nor can they be certain which service to refer to for what condition or what the optimum dosing amount is.
- Insurance companies are unwilling to reimburse for services they feel do not meet the criteria for "evidence-based" practices. The only way a service can become "evidence-based" is if there is conclusive, high-quality, empirical research backing up provider claims of efficacy.

☐ Conclusion

The safety and wellbeing of patients who engage in equine-assisted therapy should be the first priority for both licensed healthcare professionals providing therapy and individuals offering non-therapy services. Both parties have an ethical and legal responsibility to offer only the services they are trained, educated, and licensed to provide, and to adhere to scope of practice laws.

All professionals and industry associations can help in this effort by committing to using the same terminology, and by promoting a clearer understanding of the important differences between therapy and non-therapy services.

The industry as a whole is accountable for engaging in better self-regulation regarding how services are advertised and provided, and by whom. This internal regulation will only make the industry safer for consumers, and will help improve the quality of the services offered, and the research conducted. These efforts will benefit providers and consumers alike.

☐ References

Ajzenman, H.F. (2012). [Hippotherapy practice model: Promoting occupational performance and participation for children with physical and developmental disabilities]. Unpublished manuscript.

Ajzenman, H.F. (2013). Effect of hippotherapy on motor control, adaptive behaviors, and participation in children with autism spectrum disorder: A pilot study. *American Journal of Occupational Therapy, 67*(6), 653–663.

American Counseling Association (ACA). (2016). *ACA Code of Ethics*. Retrieved from: www.counseling.org/resources/aca-code-of-ethics.pdf

American Hippotherapy Association, Inc. (AHA). (2015). *AHA, Inc. Terminology*. Retrieved from: www.americanhippotherapyassociation.org/wp-content/uploads/2015/02/AHA-Inc-Terminology-Final_Ver_JT_2_16.pdf

American Hippotherapy Association, Inc. (AHA). (2016). Retrieved from: www.american hippotherapyassociation.org/

American Hippotherapy Association, Inc. (AHA). (2017). *AHA, Inc. Terminology*. Retrieved from: www.americanhippotherapyassociation.org/wp-content/uploads/2015/02/Final-AHA-Terminology-Paper-3-9-2017.pdf

American Occupational Therapy Association (AOTA). (2007). *Model Occupational Therapy Practice Act*. Retrieved from: www.aota.org/-/media/corporate/files/advocacy/state/resources/practiceact/model%20practice%20act%20final%202007.pdf

American Occupational Therapy Association (AOTA). (2014). Scope of practice. *American Journal of Occupational Therapy, 68*, S34–S40.

American Occupational Therapy Association (AOTA). (2016). *Occupational Therapy Code of Ethics, 2015*. Retrieved from: www.aota.org/-/media/corporate/files/practice/ethics/code-of-ethics.pdf

American Physical Therapy Association (APTA). (2015). *Code of Ethics for a Physical Therapist*. Retrieved from: www.apta.org/uploadedFiles/APTAorg/About_Us/Policies/Ethics/CodeofEthics.pdf

American Physical Therapy Association (APTA). (2016a). *The Physical Therapist Scope of Practice*. Retrieved from: www.apta.org/ScopeOfPractice/

American Physical Therapy Association (APTA). (2016b). *Term and Title Protection*. Retrieved from: www.apta.org/TermProtection/

American Psychological Association (APA). (2016). *Ethical Principles of Psychologists and Code of Conduct*. Retrieved from: www.apa.org/ethics/code/

American Speech-Language-Hearing Association (ASHA). (2016a). *Code of Ethics*. Retrieved from: www.asha.org/Code-of-Ethics/

American Speech-Language-Hearing Association (ASHA). (2016b). *Scope of Practice*. Retrieved from: www.asha.org/policy/SP2016-00343/

Angoules, A., Koukoulas, D., Balakatounis, K., Kapari, I., & Matsouki, E. (2015). A review of efficacy of hippotherapy for the treatment of musculoskeletal disorders. *British Journal of Medicine and Medical Research, 8*(4), 289–297.

Angsupaisal, M., Visser, B., Alkema, A., Meinsma-van der Tuin, M., Maathuis, C.G.B., Reinders-Messelink, H., & Hadders-Algra, M. (2015). Therapist-designed adaptive riding in children with cerebral palsy: Results of a feasibility study. *Physical Therapy, 95*(8), 1151–1162.

Bachi, K. (2013). Application of attachment theory to equine-facilitated psychotherapy. *Journal of Contemporary Psychotherapy, 43*(3), 187–196.

Baker, S. (2015). Emerging practice areas: Occupational therapy and hippotherapy. *Connections, 12*(5), 14–15.

Bass, M.M., Duchowny, C.A., & Llabre, M.M. (2009). The effect of therapeutic horseback riding on social functioning in children with autism. *Journal of Autism and Developmental Disorders, 39*, 1261–1267.

Bates, A. (2002). Of patients & horses: Equine-facilitated psychotherapy. *Journal of Psychosocial Nursing and Mental Health Services, 40*(5), 16–9.

Beinotti, F., Correia, N., Christofoletti, G., & Borges, G. (2010). Use of hippotherapy in gait training for hemiparetic post-stroke. *Arquivos de Neuro-Psiquiatria, 68*(6), 908–913.

Benda, W., McGibbon, N.H., & Grant, K.L. (2003). Improvements in muscle symmetry in children with cerebral palsy after equine-assisted therapy (hippotherapy). *Journal of Alternative and Complementary Medicine, 9*(6), 817–825.

Berget, B., & Braastad, B.O. (2011). Animal-assisted therapy with farm animals for persons with psychiatric disorders. *Ann Ist Super Sanità, 47*(4), 384–390.

Bertoti, D.B. (1988). Effect of therapeutic horseback riding on posture in children with cerebral palsy. *Physical Therapy, 68*(10), 1505–1512.

Bizub, A., Joy, A., & Davidson, L. (2003). "It's like being in another world": Demonstrating the benefits of therapeutic horseback riding for individuals with psychiatric disability. *Psychiatric Rehabilitation Journal, 26*(4), 377–384.

Brandt, C. (2013). Equine-facilitated psychotherapy as a complementary treatment intervention. *Practitioner Scholar: Journal of Counseling & Professional Psychology, 2*(1), 23–42.

Bunketorp Käll, L., Lundgren-Nilsson, Å., Blomstrand, C., Pekna, M., Pekny, M., & Nilsson, M. (2012). The effects of a rhythm and music-based therapy program and therapeutic riding in late recovery phase following stroke: A study protocol for a three-armed randomized controlled trial. *BMC Neurology, 12,* 141–153.

Burgon, H.L. (2011). "Queen of the world": Experiences of "at-risk" young people participating in equine-assisted learning/therapy. *Journal of Social Work Practice, 25*(2), 165–183.

Buswell, D., & Leriou, F. (2007). Perceived benefits of students' service-learning experiences with hippotherapy. *Palaestra, 23*(1), 20–25.

Carlsson, C. (February 14, 2016). A narrative review of qualitative and quantitative research in equine-assisted social work or therapy: Addressing gaps and contradictory results. *Animalia an Anthrozoology Journal.* doi 10.1007/s10615-016-0613-2

Carlsson, C., Ranta, D.N., & Traeen, B. (2014). Equine assisted social work as a mean for authentic relations between clients and staff. *Human-Animal Interaction Bulletin, 2*(1), 19–38.

Cerquozzi, C., Cerquozzi, E., Darragh, A., & Miller-Kuhaneck, H. (2007). An exploratory survey of occupational therapists' role in hippotherapy. *American Occupational Therapy Association's Developmental Disabilities Special Interest Section Quarterly, 30*(3), 1–4.

Chang, H.J., Kwon, J.Y., Lee, J.Y., & Kim, Y.H. (2012). The effects of hippotherapy on the motor function of children with spastic bilateral cerebral palsy. *Journal of Physical Therapy Science, 24*(12), 1277–1280.

Clark, J., & Lang, N. (1992). Nursing's next advance: An internal classification for nursing practice. *International Nursing Review, 39*(4), 109–111.

Cook, R. (2011). Incidents and injury within the hippotherapy milieu: Four years of safety study data on risk, risk management, and occurrences. *Scientific and Educational Journal of Therapeutic Riding,* 57–66.

Corcoran, M. (2006). The scope of occupational therapy: Our asset and our challenge. *The American Journal of Occupational Therapy, 60*(3), 247–248.

Cuypers, K., De Ridder, K., & Strandheim, A. (2011). The effect of therapeutic horseback riding on 5 children with attention deficit hyperactivity disorder: A pilot study. *Journal of Alternative and Complementary Medicine, 17*(10), 901–908.

Debuse, D., Chandler, C., & Gibb, C. (2005). An exploration of German and British physiotherapists' views on the effects of hippotherapy and their measurement. *Physiotherapy Theory and Practice, 21*(4), 219–242.

Dell, C.A., Chalmers, D., Bresette, N., Swain, S., Rankin, D., & Hopkins, C. (2011). A healing space: The experiences of First Nations and Inuit youth with equine-assisted learning (EAL). *Child and Youth Care Forum, 40*(4), 319–336.

DePauw, K. (1986). Horseback riding for individuals with disabilities: Programs, philosophy, and research. *Adapted Physical Activity Quarterly, 3*(3), 217–226.

Duncan, C.R., Critchley, S., & Marland, J. (2014). Can praxis: A model of equine assisted learning (EAL) for PTSD. *Canadian Military Journal, 14*(2), 64–69.

Earles, J., Vernon, L., & Yetz, J. (2015). Equine-assisted therapy for anxiety and posttraumatic stress symptoms. *Journal of Traumatic Stress, 28,* 149–152.

Ekholm Fry, N. (2013). Equine-assisted therapy: An overview. In M. Grassberger, R.A. Sherma, O.S. Gileva, C.M.H. Kim, & K.Y. Mumcuoglu (Eds.), *Biotherapy: History, principles, and practice* (pp. 255–258). Netherlands: Springer.

El-Meniawy, G.H., & Thabet, N.S. (2012). Modulation of back geometry in children with spastic diplegic cerebral palsy via hippotherapy training. *Egyptian Journal of Medical Human Genetics, 13*(1), 63–71.

Ewing, C.A., MacDonald, P.M., Taylor, M., & Bowers, M.J. (2007). Equine-facilitated learning for youths with severe emotional disorders: A quantitative and qualitative study. *Child Youth Care Forum, 36*, 59–72.

Ford, C. (2013). Dancing with horses: Combining dance/movement therapy and equine facilitated psychotherapy. *American Journal of Dance Therapy, 35*(2), 93–117.

Frederick, K.E., Hatz, J.I., & Lanning, B. (2015). Not just horsing around: The impact of equine-assisted learning on levels of hope and depression in at-risk adolescents. *Community Mental Health Journal, 51*(7), 809–817.

Frewin, K., & Gardiner, B. (2005). New age or old sage? A review of equine assisted psychotherapy. *The Australian Journal of Counselling Psychology, 6*, 13–17.

Glosoff, H.L., Benshoff, J.M., Hosie, T.W., & Maki, D.R. (1995). The 1994 ACA model legislation for licensed professional counselors. *Journal of Counseling & Development, 74*, 209–220.

Granados, A.C., & Agís, I. (2011). Why children with special needs feel better with hippotherapy sessions: A conceptual review. *Journal of Alternative and Complementary Medicine, 17*(3), 191–197.

Hauge, H., Kvalem, I.L., Berget, B., Enders-Slegers, M.J., & Braastad, B.O. (2014). Equine-assisted activities and the impact on perceived social support, self-esteem and self-efficacy among adolescents: An intervention study. *International Journal of Adolescence and Youth, 19*(1), 1–21.

Hinkley, K.N. (2015). *National Conference of State Legislatures: Scope of Practice Overview.* Retrieved from: www.ncsl.org/research/health/scope-of-practice-overview.aspx

Honkavaara, M., & Rintala, P. (2010). The influence of short term, intensive hippotherapy on gait in children with cerebral palsy. *European Journal of Adapted Physical Activity, 3*(2), 29–36.

Human Services Guide. (2016). *Counselor vs. Therapist vs. Psychologist.* Retrieved from: www.humanservicesedu.org/counselor-vs-psych-vs-therapist.html#context/api/listings/prefilter

Ihara, M., Ihara, M., & Doumura, M. (2012). Effect of therapeutic riding on functional scoliosis as observed by roentgenography. *Pediatrics International, 54*(1), 160–162.

Johansen, S.G., Arfwedson Wang, C.E., Binder, P.-E., & Malt, U.F. (2014). Equine-facilitated body and emotion-oriented psychotherapy designed for adolescents and adults not responding to mainstream treatment: A structured program. *Journal of Psychotherapy Integration, 24*(4), 323–335.

Johns, L., Bobat, S., & Holder, J. (2016). Therapist experiences of equine-assisted psychotherapy in South Africa: A qualitative study. *Journal of Psychology in Africa, 26*(2), 199–203.

Kang, H., Jung, J., & Yu, J. (2012). Effects of hippotherapy on the sitting balance of children with cerebral palsy: A randomized control trial. *Journal of Physical Therapy Science, 24*(9), 833–836.

Karol, J., & Tac, N. (2007). Applying a traditional individual psychotherapy model to equine-facilitated psychotherapy (EFP): Theory and method. *Clinical Child Psychology and Psychiatry, 12*(1), 77–90.

Keino, H., Funahashi, A., Keino, H., et al. (2009). Psycho-educational horseback riding to facilitate communication ability of children with pervasive developmental disorders. *Journal of Equine Science/Japanese Society of Equine Science, 20*(4), 79–88.

Kendall, E., Maujean, A., Pepping, C.A., Downes, M., Lakhani, A., Byrne, J., & Macfarlane, K. (2015). A systematic review of the efficacy of equine-assisted interventions on psychological outcomes. *European Journal of Psychotherapy & Counselling, 2537*(17), 57–79.

Kern-Godal, A., Arnevik, E.A., Walderhaug, E., & Ravndal, E. (2015). Substance use disorder treatment retention and completion: A prospective study of EAT for young adults. *Addiction Science and Clinical Practice, 10*(21), 3–12.

Kirby, M. (2010). Gestalt equine psychotherapy. *Gestalt Journal of Australia and New Zealand, 6*(2), 60–68.

Klontz, B.T., Bivens, A., & Leinart, D. (2007). The effectiveness of equine-assisted experiential therapy: Results of an open clinical trial. *Society & Animals, 15,* 257–267.

Kwon, J.-Y., Chang, H.J., Lee, J.Y., Ha, Y., Lee, P.K., & Kim, Y.-H. (2011). Effects of hippotherapy on gait parameters in children with bilateral spastic cerebral palsy. *Archives of Physical Medicine and Rehabilitation, 92*(5), 774–779.

Kwon, J.-Y., Chang, H.J., Yi, S.-H., Lee, J.Y., Shin, H.-Y., & Kim, Y.-H. (2015). Effect of hippotherapy on gross motor function in children with cerebral palsy: A randomized controlled trial. *The Journal of Alternative and Complementary Medicine, 21*(1), 15–21.

Lac, V. (2016). Amy's story: An existential-integrative equine-facilitated psychotherapy approach to anorexia nervosa. *Journal of Humanistic Psychology,* 1–12. http://doi.org/10.1177/0022167815627900

Latella, D., & Langford, S. (2008). Hippotherapy: An effective approach to occupational therapy intervention. *Occupational Therapy Practice, 13*(2), 16–20.

Lechner, H.E., Feldhaus, S., Gudmundsen, L., Hegemann, D., Michel, D., Zäch, G., & Knecht, H. (2003). The short-term effect of hippotherapy on spasticity in patients with spinal cord injury. *Spinal Cord: The Official Journal of the International Medical Society of Paraplegia, 41*(9), 502–505.

Lechner, H.E., Kakebeeke, T.H., Hegemann, D., & Baumberger, M. (2007). The effect of hippotherapy on spasticity and on mental well-being of persons with spinal cord injury. *Archives of Physical Medicine and Rehabilitation, 88*(10), 1241–1248.

Lee, C.W., Kim, S.G., & An, B.W. (2015). The effects of horseback riding on body mass index and gait in obese women. *Journal of Physical Therapy Science, 27*(4), 1169–1171.

Lee, P.T., Dakin, E., & Mclure, M. (2016). Narrative synthesis of equine-assisted psychotherapy literature: Current knowledge and future research directions. *Health and Social Care in the Community, 24*(3), 225–246.

Lentini, J.A., & Knox, M.S. (2015). Equine-facilitated psychotherapy with children and adolescents: An update and literature review. *Journal of Creativity in Mental Health, 10*(3), 278–305.

Maas, M.L., & Delaney, C. (2004). Nursing process outcome linkage research. *Medical Care, 42,* II-40–II-48.

Macauley, B.L., & Gutierrez, K.M. (2004). The effectiveness of hippotherapy for children with language-learning disabilities. *Communication Disorders Quarterly, 25*(4), 205–217.

Masini, A. (2010). Equine-assisted psychotherapy in clinical practice. *Journal of Psychosocial Nursing, 48*(10), 30–34.

McGibbon, N.H., Benda, W., Duncan, B.R., & Silkwood-Sherer, D. (2009). Immediate and long-term effects of hippotherapy on symmetry of adductor muscle activity and functional ability in children with spastic cerebral palsy. *Archives of Physical Medicine and Rehabilitation, 90*(6), 966–974.

Meola, C.C. (2016). Addressing the needs of the Millennial workforce through equine assisted learning. *Journal of Management Development, 35*(3), 294–303.

Merriam-Webster Online Dictionary. (2016). Retrieved from: www.merriam-webster.com/dictionary/therapeutic

Millhouse-Flourie, T. (2004). Physical, occupational, respiratory, speech, equine and pet therapies for mitochondrial disease. *Mitochondrion, 4*(5–6), 549–558.

Munoz-Lasa, S., Ferriero, G., Valero, R., Gomez-Muniz, F., Rabini, A., & Varela, E. (2011). Effect of therapeutic horseback riding on balance and gait of people with multiple sclerosis. *Giornale Italiano di Medicina del Lavoro Ed Ergonomia, 33*(4), 462–467.

National Association of Social Workers (NASW). (2016). *Code of Ethics of the National Association of Social Workers.* Retrieved from: www.socialworkers.org/pubs/Code/code.asp

National Board for Certified Counselors (NBCC). (2016). *Understanding National Certification and State Licensure.* Retrieved from: www.nbcc.org/Certification/Certificationor Licensure

Newton-Cromwell, S.A., McSpadden, B.D., & Johnson, R. (2015). Incorporating experiential learning for equine-assisted activities and therapies with an in-house equine therapy program for veterans. *Journal of Equine Veterinary Science, 35*(5), 458.

Notgrass, C.G., & Pettinelli, J.D. (2015). Equine assisted psychotherapy: The equine assisted growth and learning association's model overview of equine-based modalities. *Journal of Experiential Education, 38*(2), 162–174.

Nurenberg, J.R., Schleifer, S.J., Shaffer, T.M., et al. (2015). Animal-assisted therapy with chronic psychiatric inpatients: Equine-assisted psychotherapy and aggressive behavior. *Psychiatric Services, 66*(1), 80–86.

Pendry, P., Carr, A.M., Smith, A.N., & Roeter, S.M. (2014). Improving adolescent social competence and behavior: A randomized trial of an 11-week equine facilitated learning prevention program. *The Journal of Primary Prevention, 35,* 281–293.

Pendry, P., & Roeter, S. (2013). Experimental trial demonstrates positive effects of equine facilitated learning on child social competence. *Human-Animal Interaction Bulletin, 1*(1), 1–19.

Pet Partners. (2016). Retrieved from: https://petpartners.org/

Pham, C., & Bitonte, R. (2016). Hippotherapy: Remuneration issues impair the offering of this therapeutic strategy at Southern California rehabilitation centers. *NeuroRehabilitation, 38*(4), 411–417.

Porter-Wenzlaff, L. (2007). Finding their voice: Developing emotional, cognitive, and behavioral congruence in female abuse survivors through equine-facilitated psychotherapy. *Explore: The Journal of Science and Healing, 3*(5), 529–534.

Rimmer, J.A., & Rowland, J.L. (2006). Physical activity for youth with disabilities: A critical need in an underserved population. *Developmental Neurorehabilitation, 11,* 141–148.

Roberts, F., Bradberry, J., & Williams, C. (2004). Equine-facilitated psychotherapy benefits students and children. *Holistic Nursing Practice, 18*(1), 32–35.

Rocco, T. (January 23, 2012). *Hippotherapy as a Speech Therapy Treatment Strategy.* Retrieved from: http://speechinmotion.com/blog/2012/01/23/hippotherapy-as-a-speech-therapy-treatment-strategy/

Rothe, E., Vega, B., Torres, R., Soler, S., & Pazos, R. (2005). From kids and horses: Equine facilitated psychotherapy for children. *International Journal of Clinical and Health Psychology, 5*(2), 373–383.

Rutherford, M. (2008). Standardized nursing language: What does it mean for nursing practice? *Online Journal of Issues in Nursing, 13*(1), 1–7.

Schroeder, K., & Stroud, D. (2015). Equine-facilitated group work for women survivors of interpersonal violence. *The Journal for Specialists in Group Work, 3922,* 1–22.

Shurtleff, T.L., & Engsberg, J. (2012). Long-term effects of hippotherapy on one child with cerebral palsy: A research case study. *British Journal of Occupational Therapy, 75*(8), 359–366.

Shurtleff, T.L., Standeven, J.W., & Engsberg, J.R. (2009). Changes in dynamic trunk/head stability and functional reach after hippotherapy. *Archives of Physical Medicine and Rehabilitation, 90*(7), 1185–1195.

Signal, T., Taylor, N., Botros, H., Prentice, K., & Lazarus, K. (2013). Whispering to horses: Childhood sexual abuse, depression and the efficacy of equine facilitated therapy. *SAANZ Journal, 5*(1), 24–32.

Smith-Osborne, A., & Selby, A. (2010). Implications of the literature on equine-assisted activities for use as a complementary intervention in social work practice with children and adolescents. *Child and Adolescent Social Work Journal, 27*, 291–307.

Snider, L., Korner-Bitensky, N., Kammann, C., Warner, S., & Saleh, M. (2007). Horseback riding as therapy for children with cerebral palsy: Is there evidence of its effectiveness? *Physical & Occupational Therapy in Pediatrics, 27*(2), 5–23.

Stroud, D., & Hallberg, L. (2016). [Horses in healthcare: An international assessment of the professional practice of equine-assisted therapy]. Unpublished raw data.

Swindell, M. (2010). Equine therapy and social work: A winning combination. *Social Work*, 1–4.

Thompson, J.R., Iacobucci, V., & Varney, R. (2012). Giddyup! or whoa nelly! Making sense of benefit claims on websites of equine programs for children with disabilities. *Journal of Developmental and Physical Disabilities, 24*, 373–390.

Thoroddsen, A., & Ehnfors, M. (2007). Putting policy into practice: Pre-and posttests of implementing standardized languages for nursing documentation. *Journal of Clinical Nursing, 16*(10), 1826–1838.

Trotter, K.S., Chandler, C.K., & Goodwin-Bond, D.C. (2008). A comparative study of the efficacy of group equine assisted counseling with at-risk children and adolescents. *Journal of Creativity in Mental Health, 3*, 254–284.

U.S. Department of Veterans Affairs, National Center for PTSD. (2016). Retrieved from: www.ptsd.va.gov/index.asp

Valle, L.M.O., Nishimori, A.Y., & Neme, K. (2014). Speech therapy in hippotherapy. *Atualizacao Cientifica em Fonoaudiologia e Educacao, 16*(2), 511–523.

Vidrine, M., Owen-Smith, P., & Faulkner, P. (2002). Equine-facilitated group psychotherapy: Applications for therapeutic vaulting. *Issues in Mental Health Nursing, 23*(6), 587–603.

Ward, S., Whalon, K., Rusnak, K., Wendell, K., & Paschall, N. (2013). The association between therapeutic horseback riding and the social communication and sensory reactions of children with autism. *Journal of Autism and Developmental Disorders, 43*, 2190–2198.

Warren, J.J. (2012). *Importance of Standardized Terminology in Healthcare Information Systems*. Retrieved from: www.aacn.nche.edu/qsen-informatics/2012-workshop/presenta tions/warren/Importance-of-Standardized-Terminology-Warren.pdf

Wilson, K., Buultjens, M., Monfries, M., & Karimi, L. (2015). Equine-assisted psychotherapy for adolescents experiencing depression and/or anxiety: A therapist's perspective. *Clinical Child Psychology and Psychiatry*, 1–18. doi 10.1177/1359104515572379

3 Professional Competencies in Equine-Assisted Therapy

☐ Developing Professional Competencies in Equine-Assisted Therapy

When considering professional competencies in equine-assisted therapy, it is very important that individuals interested in adding equine-assisted therapy to their clinical practices are already competent, comfortable, and experienced providing whatever conventional healthcare service they are licensed to provide. Including animals in human healthcare is complex and dynamic, as it requires the professional to understand the function of their clinical practice and also integrate animal interactions and the natural setting. This chapter is written with the assumption that licensed professionals are already experienced in their areas of conventional practice, and the competencies included here will be added to those existing skills.

Physical, occupational, and speech therapists are likely to be credentialed through the American Hippotherapy Certification Board (AHCB). This entity outlines specific areas of competency that can help guide and direct these professionals towards appropriate training and education. Although less well known or widely supported, the Certification Board for Equine Interaction Professionals (CBEIP) also provides recommended competencies, which can help licensed mental health professionals make decisions about developing competency in equine-assisted therapy.

However, none of the state licensing boards require that a professional obtain any type of certificate in any form of equine-assisted therapy, and at present, only the American Counseling Association (ACA) mandates specific competency requirements related to including animals in a counseling session. This means that most professionals must use their best judgement to determine what they consider competence in this developing area of practice.

In 2016, the ACA took a historic step forward towards standardizing the areas in which a licensed mental health professional should demonstrate mastery when it released the 2016 ACA Animal-Assisted Therapy in Counseling Competencies (ACA, 2016b). Although required only for licensed counselors who are ACA members, this document outlines areas of competency that are applicable to any professional including animals in human healthcare. These competency requirements are more extensive and inclusive than those provided by either the AHCB or the CPEIP, and the content is extremely useful for all types of licensed healthcare providers as it is based on rigorous scholarly research, and not upon the personal opinions or beliefs of individuals.

This groundbreaking effort was developed out of Dr. Leslie Stewart's 2014 dissertation research, and speaks to a growing concern many professionals have about the widespread inclusion of animals in human healthcare without proper training, education, and supervision. Stewart is quoted saying:

> It seems like enthusiasm about the human-animal bond has been steadily growing, and that's wonderful. But at the same time there is a lack of awareness that this is a specialty area of practice within counseling that requires training and knowledge beyond [a counselor's graduate coursework].
>
> (in Bray, 2016, para. 4)

The recommended areas of competency included in this chapter are loosely based on exam content from the AHCB and the CBEIP, and include aspects of the ACA's Animal-Assisted Therapy in Counseling Competencies. Each of the credentialing boards provides a handbook its respective website that includes the areas of content included in the exam, and the full Animal-Assisted Therapy in Counseling competencies can be located on the ACA's website.

All professionals, regardless of licensure type, are encouraged to obtain training and education in these areas and demonstrate competency in their practical application of this information. Other areas of recommended competency including understanding clinical practices, business acumen, and program administration are addressed in the following chapters of this book, or are presented in greater detail in the accompanying workbook.

In-Depth Knowledge of Horses

It is the ethical responsibility of any licensed professional who employs animals to work in a healthcare setting to be able to protect the animal from harm, and to assess the wellbeing of the animal during a session (PATH Intl., 2014; AHA, 2016a; ACA, 2016b; Pet Partners, 2016). The professional is responsible for making changes to the animal's level of engagement or to the therapeutic activity based upon the responses and reactions of the animals (PATH Intl., 2014; ACA, 2016b; Pet Partners, 2016).

As with any species of animal, horses have unique characteristics, behaviors, physiology, and psychology. Although there are certain common characteristics among breeds, each individual horse has his/her own history, personality, and quirks. Ethically, and from a safety standpoint, it is important for licensed professionals to know how each horse demonstrates enjoyment, relaxation, stress, agitation, and burnout, and how they react to specific handling techniques or environmental stimuli. If a horse is in pain or experiencing burnout, he/she may not be appropriate to work with, and his/her reactions and responses will be different than usual, potentially increasing the risk of equine-assisted therapy (Cook, 2014; Merkies, et al., 2014). If licensed professionals aren't knowledgeable about equine physiology, psychology, and behavior they will not be able to appropriately assess the wellbeing of the horse(s), and thus could unknowingly support unsafe or unethical activity.

The therapeutic value of equine-assisted therapy is primarily based on interactions with horses. For some professionals, this involves understanding how the movement of the horse affects the human body (Benda, et al., 2003; Lechner, et al., 2007; McGibbon, et al., 2009; Debuse, et al., 2009; Chang, et al., 2012; Angoules, et al., 2015), while for others it is the ethology of the species that is believed to influence human change (Vidrine, et al., 2002; Frewin & Gardiner, 2005; Rothe, et al., 2005; Porter-Wenzlaff, 2007; Trotter, et al., 2008; Ford, 2013; Johansen, et al., 2014). To be considered competent when using a new or novel treatment or specialty area of practice, it is essential for professionals to be trained and educated about the mechanisms of change used during that treatment. In the case of equine-assisted therapy, this translates to understanding horses and the impact of the farm milieu.

Industry certification for physical, occupational, and speech therapists addresses the clinical importance of understanding equine physiology, psychology, and behavior, as well as demonstrating competency in horse handling techniques, horse care, riding skills, and safety practices. These professionals must also prove their knowledge related to the use of the horse's movement as a therapeutic strategy (AHCB, 2016). This in-depth knowledge of horses and proficiency testing related to equine competency is not the standard for mental health professionals providing equine-assisted therapy. In some cases, licensed mental health professionals have even abdicated their responsibility for understanding horses and for designing the equine-specific therapeutic activities to an "equine specialist" or "horse handler."

This is concerning since legally and ethically, it is the responsibility of the licensed healthcare professional to oversee the treatment process and make educated and informed clinical decisions about how to use any type of treatment. This includes determining the most appropriate treatment activity to use that will safely and effectively address the treatment goal(s). If the service is billed as therapy, it is the legal and ethical responsibility of the licensed professional to ensure the safety of the patient during treatment (ACA, 2016a; APA, 2016; NASW, 2016). If mental health professionals are unfamiliar with the species, and lack knowledge and training related to understanding equine communication, behavior, and psychology, it is difficult to conceive how they could manage the inherent risk associated with including horses in healthcare and be considered competent to use this treatment approach (Lee, et al., 2016).

Finally, there are times when including a second person or a team of people isn't therapeutically appropriate for the needs of the patient. Healthcare providers are responsible for upholding the dignity and confidentiality of their patients (ACA, 2016a; APA, 2016; NASW, 2016; APTA, 2016a, AOTA, 2016). At various times during treatment, a patient may feel vulnerable doing certain activities, talking about a medical or mental health condition, or discussing feelings they have related to their health in front of a non-therapist staff member or volunteer. The licensed professional needs to be competent enough to recognize when this is occurring, and be comfortable facilitating an appropriate (and safe) horse-human interaction, or farm-based intervention, that does not necessitate other people.

Risk Management

Statistically, working with or riding horses has been shown to be more dangerous in terms of accidents per hour than motorcycling, skiing, football, and automobile racing (Silver, 2002; Ball, et al., 2007; Carmichael, et al., 2014; Papachristos, et al., 2014). Although the risks involved with equine-assisted therapy differ from those of recreational, sport, or competitive riding, 47 states in the United States still consider any type of equine interaction to hold "inherent risk" due to the following dangers or conditions (Walson, 2003; Fershtman, 2016):

- The propensity of the animal to behave in ways that may result in injury, harm, or death to persons on or around them.
- The unpredictability of the animal's reaction to such things as sounds, sudden movement, and unfamiliar objects, persons, or other animals.
- Certain hazards such as surface and subsurface conditions.
- Collisions with other animals or objects.
- The potential of a participant to act in a negligent manner that may contribute to injury to the participant or others, such as failing to maintain control over the animal or not acting within the participant's ability.

This information is not presented to deter people from equine-assisted therapy. Rather, it is provided to bring awareness to the fact that being around horses can be dangerous, especially if people are not trained in equine behavior.

Merkies, et al. (2014) state:

Horse behavior, almost always associated with a fear response from the horse, is the most common factor related with injuries. The unpredictable nature of horses is often cited as the cause of injuries, when in reality it may simply be a lack of understanding of the equine ethogram and/or a failure to appropriately apply learning theory that leads to confusion and conflict behavior responses by the horse.

(p. 242)

As a highly communicative prey animal who lives naturally in a herd, there are instinctual traits unique to the species. Their reactions and responses are based both on their innate characteristics, and their individual personalities (Goodwin, 1999; McGreevy, 2012). In order to be effective in harnessing the potential therapeutic value of the horse-human relationship while being respectful and mindful of safety, licensed professionals who include horses in clinical practice have a responsibility to understand how horses communicate and behave, and to understand and mitigate the risks associated with the therapeutic intervention (Rothe, et al., 2005; Cook, 2011).

According to research, there are two effective risk mitigation strategies to address the inherent risk of working with horses. The first is to provide education and training in the areas of equine behavior, communication, and physiology, and ensure that staff, volunteers, and participants are prepared to safely interact with horses (Hausberger, et al., 2008; Cuenca, et al., 2009; Hawson, et al., 2010; Cook, 2011; Merkies, et al., 2014; Carmichael, et al., 2014). The second is wearing protective equipment, especially an appropriately rated helmet, when working on the ground with a horse or while mounted (Abu-Zidan & Rao, 2003; Ball, et al., 2007; Cuenca, et al., 2009; Cook, 2011; Carmichael, et al., 2014; Papachristos, et al., 2014).

Along with the basic inherent physical risk of including horses in human healthcare, there are risks specific to the various types of equine-assisted therapy. Physical, occupational, and speech therapists encounter different circumstances than do licensed mental health professionals. Dependent upon which type of therapy a professional provides, he/she is responsible for understanding the unique risks associated with that approach and attempting to mitigate those risks.

Different populations also require flexibility and sensitivity in regards to risk mitigation strategies. Skilled professionals understand when it is important to increase safety protocols, and when they should relax those protocols. The key in this decision-making process is knowledge, training, education, and experience.

Some equine-assisted therapy professionals voice concerns about the overuse of risk management, suggesting, "Creativity, spontaneity and experimentation suffocated in the quagmire of risk management" (McKelvy, 2002, p. 11), citing loss of therapy time, missed opportunities for problem solving because the therapist was overly controlling, and a lack of autonomy caused by standardized risk management practices.

Similarly, some professionals believe that communicating the risks associated with horses might negatively impact the patient's participation in the service. This is a slippery slope. Patients have a right to be fully informed and aware of whatever risks are associated with any treatment approach (ACA, 2016a; APA, 2016; NASW, 2016; APTA, 2016a, AOTA, 2016; ASHA, 2016). According to the American Psychological Association (APA), in therapeutic situations "for which generally recognized techniques and procedures have not been established, psychologists inform their clients/patients of the developing nature of the treatment, the potential risks involved, alternative treatment that may be available, and the voluntary nature of their participation" (APA, 2016, 10.01b). Of course licensed professionals do not want to frighten their patients, but ethically, they must share enough information for the patient to make an informed and educated choice about the intervention (Tseng, et al., 2012). Usually, providing the patient with information and education about how the risk will be mitigated will actually help to offset the fear.

Although the professional providing the service is probably not afraid of horses and may not be concerned by the risk, patients likely are. Even if they don't put words to their feelings, most people who haven't worked with horses or know anything about them have some level of concern (as they should). If professionals downplay the risks, or don't address them, this can leave patients feeling self-conscious and afraid to talk about their concerns. Typically, it is helpful to openly discuss the fears and concerns of working with horses prior to asking the patient to engage with the horses. Merkies, et al. (2014) states, "Horses demonstrate more relaxed behavior with humans having positive attitudes toward horses (Chamove, et al., 2002), whereas being stroked by a negatively thinking person causes an increase in horse HR [heart rate] (Hama, et al., 1996)" (p. 243). These researchers explain that nervousness in humans can cause adverse reactions in horses, and suggest, "A crowd of nervous and inexperienced people can create a potentially dangerous situation for both the participants and the horses" (p. 242).

Allowing the patient to watch the horses interact and teaching him/her about horse communication, body language, and general behaviors will help the patient feel safer and more comfortable (Hawson, et al., 2010). As Brandt (2013) states, "Care should be taken to ensure that the incorporation of equine activities is not rushed, particularly if clients present with fear or have little to no experience around horses" (p. 30). Also, it is of the utmost importance that patients feel empowered to voice concerns and to choose not to participate in specific activities without the fear of ridicule or shame (Brandt, 2013).

Risk mitigation doesn't only protect the patient—it also protects the horses. Horses are not prone to kick, bite, knock into or over, or otherwise cause injury to humans unless they are frightened, hurt, or not listened to, or if their spatial needs aren't being respected (Goodwin, 1999;

Christensen, et al., 2005). Simply teaching staff, volunteers, and patients how to read basic body language and respect the needs of the horses will decrease accidents significantly (Cuenca, et al., 2009; Hawson, et al., 2010). By doing this, the horse is likely to experience less stress related to equine-assisted therapy, and may feel safer and more comfortable when working with patients.

Specific Equine-Assisted Therapy Training

A knowledgeable provider recognizes that simply applying an existing treatment approach to the work with horses is not enough to ethically and intentionally offer this novel treatment. The equine environment is far more dynamic than a four-walls office, and requires additional training, education, and supervision.

As addressed earlier, the ethical codes of most licensed professionals who offer equine-assisted therapy state that licensed professionals will obtain additional training, education, supervision, and certification (if available) prior to adding any new treatment specialization to their clinical practice. In the absence of generally recognized standards, these professionals are expected to research the efficacy of the intervention, seek consultation, and strive to obtain the highest degree of competency possible to protect the safety of their patients (ACA, 2016a; APA, 2016; NASW, 2016; AOTA, 2016; APTA, 2016a).

To provide equine-assisted therapy ethically and safely, and to achieve the most from the intervention, the professional understands and utilizes the broad foundational theories of human-animal-nature bonding and the unique characteristics of the equines themselves, and employs applicable risk management strategies. Professionals must receive additional training in the use of clinical reasoning when choosing equine activities, and should demonstrate competency incorporating equines, equine activities, and the farm milieu in the treatment planning process.

Many different options exist for training in equine-assisted therapy, and some of these options will be explored in greater depth later in this chapter.

Clinical Intentionality

As the authors of the ACA's Animal-Assisted Therapy in Counseling Competencies point out, animal-assisted therapy is "more than owning/ loving animals" (ACA, 2016b). Even if a licensed healthcare provider loves horses, and enjoys being outside at the barn more than in the office, there must be an identified clinical rationale for providing equine-assisted therapy (AHA, 2016b). Without specialty training in equine-assisted therapy, professionals may not understand the clinical rationale, and rely only upon their love of horses or experiences with horses. Usually, this is not adequate to demonstrate competency and adhere to professional practices ethics and standards.

Through training, education, supervision, and experience, professionals learn to ask themselves, "Is this service clinically indicated for the patient?" and if so, "Can I articulate this need in the form of a treatment plan?" and "Whose needs am I addressing by offering equine-assisted therapy, mine or the patient's?"

Animal and Patient Advocacy

When considering including horses or the farm milieu in a therapy session, it is important to be aware of the ethical issues related to both the inclusion of an animal in human healthcare, and the use of a novel intervention.

Animal Advocacy

When we include animals in therapy, we are in essence appropriating them for human benefit. Amy Johnson, a co-contributor to the ACA's animal-assisted therapy competencies states, "These animals [animal-assisted therapy animals] are living, sentient beings, not just a tool," and suggests that animals have "needs and sensitivities" counselors must be trained to take into consideration (in Bray, 2016, para. 5).

Little research has been done to understand the effects of equine-assisted therapy on the horses themselves (O'Rourke, 2004; Kaiser, et al., 2006; Minero, et al., 2006; Fazio, et al., 2013). The few studies that have been conducted show that horses do react differently to equine-assisted therapy than they do to other forms of interaction (Minero, et al., 2006; Kaiser, et al., 2006; Fazio, et al., 2013). Little meaning has been made related to these findings, other than it appears that different populations may bring about physiological changes in the horses studied. As an example, Kaiser, et al. (2006) report the horses demonstrated signs of stress when working with at-risk youth, whereas they did not show stress when working with "physically or psychologically handicapped individuals" (p. 43) or those with learning disabilities. Their observations included a reflection about the attitudes of the at-risk patients and how their view of the horse as a "tool" might have impacted their behaviors towards the horses. The researchers suggest that these findings should not dissuade professionals from working with at-risk populations, but rather professionals should consider educating their patients about the horse as a sentient partner in equine-assisted therapy, and hold them accountable for treating the horse appropriately for the species, and with respect (Kaiser, et al., 2006).

Equine-assisted therapy providers have an ethical responsibility to assess the horses they work with for signs of stress, burnout, pain, and agitation, and to step in and help resolve these issues should they arise. This can be challenging, as people who are overexposed to the same horses may not be able to observe abnormal behaviors, and instead assume the behaviors are standard or normal (Anderson, et al., 1999; Lesimple, et al., 2014). To quote Lesimple, et al. (2014), "Over-exposure appeared also here as a major factor and the findings support the idea that the abnormal behaviors observed may somehow become the standard" (p. 4). In another statement taken from Lesimple, et al. (2014), researchers report that horse caretakers may underestimate the indicators of poor welfare, and they suggest this lack of concern could lead to decreased motivation to "decode" (p. 3) or understand these behaviors.

Reports related to personality or even general characteristics of horses provided by instructors, caretakers, or owners of the horses have shown similarly questionable validity (Anderson, et al., 1999; Lesimple, et al., 2014). Anderson, et al. (1999) report, "The therapeutic [adaptive] riding instructors did not often agree on the temperament of horses. Instructors only agreed on an average of 33% of their center's horses, and most of that agreement was only between two instructors, not all three" (p. 22). These researchers go on to state, "The instructors' lack of agreement is a very interesting finding because most instructors are very confident in their ability to judge a horse's temperament" (p. 22). Although Anderson, et al. (1999) did not investigate how accurate these instructors were at gauging equine health or wellness, their findings certainly support the idea that equine assessment could be greatly improved by the use of non-biased outsider evaluation. In some cases, this could even be provided (in part) by licensed professionals who do not own the horses they work with, and see these horses only on a semi-regular basis.

Beyond assessing horses for job dissatisfaction, burnout or pain, providers of equine-assisted therapy must ensure the horses they work with have all of their physical and emotional health needs met. This includes (but is not limited to) veterinary care, hoof care, diet and nutrition, exercise and training, time off, and herd socialization. These topics are addressed in greater length in Chapter Seven of this book.

Patient Advocacy

Use of a novel treatment approach requires careful consideration and sound clinical decision making in order to protect patient welfare. Novel treatments are interventions or strategies that have yet to be substantiated by conclusive research results (Anestis, et al., 2014). Although physical, occupational, speech, and mental health therapy are all forms of conventional healthcare supported by insurance companies and backed by the conclusive findings of many years of research, including equine activities or the equine milieu in any of these conventional therapies is still considered novel due to the lack of consistent, high-quality research (Tseng, et al., 2012; Bachi, 2012; Selby & Smith-Osborne, 2013; Anestis, et al., 2014, Angsupaisal, et al., 2015).

In some cases, vulnerable populations may seek out novel treatments as a "last-ditch effort" after trying many other options, and may put great stock in the potential outcomes. Borgi, et al. (2016) state, "Parents of children with ASD [autism spectrum disorder] may choose to use complementary and alternative treatments with their children in addition to, or in place of, conventional treatments, entering these programs with high expectations" (p. 2).

Probably one of the more dangerous decisions a licensed professional could make is to offer a novel treatment intervention to a vulnerable population he/she has little past experience working with simply because of the hype surrounding it (Anestis, et al., 2014). The steps a professional can take to avoid such a situation include:

- Demonstrating competence in working with the vulnerable population outside the farm milieu prior to inviting that population out to the farm.
- Reading existing research with an objective eye to understand the benefits/concerns related to treating this population with equine-assisted therapy.
- If the decision is made to use equine-assisted therapy, the professional will inform the patient of all possible risks involved, and carefully monitor the patient to ensure the intervention is not causing harm.

When considering the use of a novel treatment, patients have the right to be informed and educated about the risks and potential benefits of the service (Tseng, et al., 2012; APA, 2016). Not all patients are comfortable with horses or the farm milieu, and in some cases, their conditions may be precautionary or even contraindicated for intervention. Therapists who provide equine-assisted therapy are probably very comfortable in the equine environment, and may even seek it out above the office setting. This may cause therapists to be more likely to recommend equine-assisted therapy over other forms of therapy conducted in a conventional setting. Therefore, it is of great ethical importance that therapists assess their patients using sound clinical reasoning, and be as non-biased and respectful as possible in determining if the patient is a good fit for the service, wants to participate, and feels safe and comfortable to do so (Brandt, 2013).

In some cases, patients with a fear of horses, specific conditions, or life histories may become so distracted by the animals or the farm environment that they cannot engage in the therapeutic process effectively (Globisch, et al., 1999; Kirby, 2010). Cultural differences are also important to consider in the decision-making process. Not all cultures or religions view animals similarly, and may have different beliefs about the human-animal bond that could negatively alter treatment outcomes. Of course, if the patient is interested in challenging his/her own views or beliefs, and is open to working with animals, that is a different situation.

☐ Personal Competencies in Equine-Assisted Therapy

Competency has historically been measured by academic success resulting in passing exams and attaining licensure in one's profession. More recently, employers and educators have begun to see the value in assessing for personal attributes that lead to increased interpersonal and work-related competence (Van Dusseldorp, et al., 2011; Walker, et al., 2013; Zeidner & Hadar, 2014; Rasheed, 2015; Vlachou, et al., 2016). Although these personal competencies are important in any healthcare setting, the necessity for professionals to be skilled in these areas increases significantly with the inclusion of horses.

Self-Awareness and Authenticity

Rasheed (2015) defines self-awareness as "getting to know about one self as a person and the important things in life which influences us in different ways" (p. 212). Self-awareness also includes the ability to objectively examine one's motivations, beliefs, and behaviors for the purpose of better understanding his/her impact on others (Jack & Miller, 2008; Rasheed, 2015).

Although self-awareness is considered a critical skill for anyone in the healthcare professions (Jack & Miller, 2008; Walker, et al., 2013), when working with horses the need to be aware of one's own feelings, emotions, behaviors, and beliefs is intensified. Due to the instinctual nature of horses, they are prone to respond and react to changes in human physiology, especially when related to anxiety, nervousness, or fear (Keeling, et al., 2009; Merkies, et al., 2014). Since horses do not differentiate between the patient and the professional, the horse may respond and react to the feelings and emotions of the professional, the staff, or the volunteers just as it does to the patient. This can be confusing, and even result in less-than-positive outcomes for the horse or the patient (Lee, et al., 2016).

The use of authenticity is commonly paired with self-awareness. Authenticity is a powerful tool that must be carefully administered (Yalom, 2003; Gullo, et al., 2012), and licensed professionals who include horses in their healthcare practices have the opportunity to practice this skill even more than they might in a conventional treatment setting (Selby & Smith-Osborne, 2013; Carlsson, et al., 2014). Using appropriate authentic sharing not only refocuses an interaction, but simultaneously teaches an important life skill through role modeling. Taking responsibility for one's own feelings and emotions is key to building respect and trust. If the licensed professional recognizes he/she has been acting anxious, distracted, or snappy, putting words to this and apologizing in front of patients, volunteers, and staff demonstrates self-awareness and maturity.

For example, if a physical therapist is incorporating equine movement into a therapy session, and the horse responds by acting unusually difficult, the therapist can use self-awareness techniques to check in and see if anything is going on personally. If the therapist discovers he/she is distracted and anxious about something occurring at home, it would be a good time to stop the session briefly, and suggest the team take a moment to breathe and relax. If appropriate, the therapist may even disclose something like, "I don't know about any of you, but I notice I am feeling a little tense this morning." This allows everyone a moment of self-soothing and emotional regulation, and gives the horse a break from whatever tension he/she is experiencing.

In another example, the mental health professional providing equine-assisted psychotherapy might assume the horse is "mirroring" the patient, demonstrating anxiety or agitation, when in fact the horse is responding to the feelings and emotions of the therapist him/herself.

In both of these examples, it is likely the horse isn't the only one who notices something isn't quite right. The patient, the staff, or the volunteers may personalize the therapist's behavior or attitude, assuming it was something they did to cause the feelings of tension or anxiety they feel. If the licensed professional puts words to his/her own feelings and suggests the horse might actually be responding to those feelings, tensions may be alleviated, and a greater sense of equality and compassion will be established between the professional and the team.

If the professional is practicing self-awareness, the first question to be asked if the horse is acting in an unusual manner is, "How am I doing today?" or "How are my staff/volunteers doing today?" and "Am I (or are they) influencing the horse?" These questions may sound more familiar to mental health professionals, but physical therapists, occupational therapists, and speech therapists all can benefit from increased recognition of their impact on the horses, and thus on the patients and the session as a whole.

The practice of self-awareness and the use of authenticity offers opportunities for increased learning and growth for everyone involved. Activities like centering and grounding before a session or even during one, and evaluating one's own mental and physical state—both prior to and during engagement with horses—can help increase the effectiveness of the equine-assisted therapy intervention.

Social Intelligence

Social intelligence includes the ability to communicate effectively, work as a team, handle interpersonal conflicts, and seek support (Walker, et al., 2013). In essence, social intelligence enables people to live and work well together. Social intelligence skills are innate in most, but can be enhanced through self-growth, continuing education, and training.

The industry of equine-assisted therapy has been fraught with interpersonal and professional struggles that suggest there may be a need for a reinvigorated focus on specific skills of social intelligence. There is a joke, "What is the one thing two horse people can agree upon?" The answer is, "That they can't agree on anything at all." This concept is supported by the findings of Kidd, et al. (1984), who suggest horse owners may be less cooperative than other animal owners, stating, "Horse owners were found to have high levels of assertiveness and self-concern, but low levels of cooperativeness, novelty-seeking and nurturance" (in Robinson, 1999, p. 44).

Healthcare literature speaks to both the interpersonal benefits of a collaborative approach, and to the broader ramifications of collaboration within the healthcare industry (Walker, et al., 2013; Wu, et al., 2014). Key aspects of a collaborative relationship include understanding and abiding by scope of practice laws, using a shared decision-making process, and demonstrating mutual respect and trust (Schadewaldt, et al., 2014).

It would seem that focusing on collaboration rather than vying to be the "best" or the "only" way to provide equine-assisted therapy would be advisable. No one person or organization can be everything to everybody. Recognizing strengths and weaknesses, and learning to reach out and rely upon the talents and resources of others, is a powerful growth opportunity. This approach naturally leads to greater diversity, and the creation of a robust and healthy industry.

☐ Credentialing and Certificate Programs for Licensed Professionals

The credentialing process and certificate programs serve distinctly different purposes. Understanding the key differences between the two, and knowing how to utilize each can help advance the professional practice of equine-assisted therapy.

Credentialing

Credentialing is a process by which a third party validates the qualifications and competencies of a professional. To sit for a credentialing exam, the professional must demonstrate a specific level of education and experience within his/her field or discipline (ICE, 2016; NEHA, 2016).

Credentialing requires a separation between the education source (i.e. a college degree program or a trade-specific certificate program) and the credentialing body in order to promote non-biased, ethical evaluation. Credentialing bodies do not provide training or education, and support the broad acquisition of knowledge from diverse sources. Credentialing bodies are non-biased in that they do not align with any specific models of practice, nor do they assess for methodological knowledge.

Although credentialing bodies may require specific types and amounts of education and experience, the credentialing body cannot dictate where the applicate obtains the education or experience (ICE, 2016; NEHA, 2016).

In the equine-assisted therapy industry, both the AHCB and the CBEIP were designed to meet the Institute for Credentialing Excellence (ICE) standards by supporting the separation of education, training, and credentialing.

The American Hippotherapy Certification Board (AHCB)

The AHCB was founded in 1998 to develop and maintain an objective testing tool to evaluate and validate the skills and knowledge of physical, occupational and speech therapists interested in providing equine-assisted therapy. Professionals sitting for the exam must demonstrate prior education, training, and experience in equine-assisted therapy as well as existing licensure in their respective fields.

Although AHCB has a close relationship with American Hippotherapy Association, Inc. (AHA), it is an independent board made up of professionals in the industry who work collaboratively to ensure the exams remain up-to-date, accurate, and relevant. AHCB also works closely with the Professional Testing Corporation® which administers the test biannually to maintain the fairness and validity of the exams. The AHCB holds a strong reputation within the physical, occupational, and speech therapy communities and is considered the gold standard for those wishing to incorporate equines and the farm milieu into their clinical practices.

AHCB provides two levels of certification. The AHCB Certification Exam is the entry level option for licensed physical, occupational, or speech therapists, and physical or occupational therapy assistants with at least one year of experience in their area of clinical practice. The Hippotherapy Clinical Specialist Exam is an advanced level certification limited to licensed physical, occupational, or speech therapists who have three or more years of clinical experience (AHCB, 2016).

The Certification Board for Equine Interaction Professionals (CBEIP)

The CBEIP was founded with the goal of establishing a universal body of knowledge that could be used to guide and assess the professional practices of equine-assisted mental health and equine-assisted learning.

Like the AHCB, the CBEIP provides independent testing through the Professional Testing Corporation®. To sit for the exam, professionals must prove existing competency through documentation of education, training, and experience. Professionals can obtain the required training and experience in any manner they deem appropriate.

Those who pass the exam are awarded a certification that demonstrates a level of competency in their area of practice. Mental health professionals receive the Certified Equine-Interaction Professional-MH (CEIP-MH) and education professionals receive the Certified Equine-Interaction Professional-ED (CEIP-ED) (CBEIP, 2016).

CBEIP was initially critiqued as being biased in favor of the philosophical beliefs of the Equine-Facilitated Mental Health Association (EFMHA), which provided the seed money to develop the exam. The critique included observations about how the initial body of knowledge and exam content was crafted and by whom. This led to concerns that the process was not truly independent, and thus CBEIP did not receive the support it had sought from the Equine Assisted Growth and Learning (EAGALA) and other associations (Equine Assisted Assets, 2016).

CBEIP's challenges may be due in part to timing. The founding board of CBEIP was visionary in its understanding of the direction the industry would need to go to gain professional credibility. But, at the time of CBEIP's inception, the industry was simply not developed enough to manifest the vision. The lack of empirical research and scholarly writing in the industry forced CBEIP to use anecdotal resources that were opinion-based to craft both the body of knowledge and the corresponding exam content. This led to long-standing concerns about the validity of the exam and its usefulness in assessing competency.

The industry has grown and matured greatly over the years, building a body of knowledge through empirical research and scholarly writing. This will help the CBEIP greatly as it can now align exam content with current knowledge, research, and professional practices. Assuming the CBEIP takes the necessary steps to update the exam content so as to be grounded in empirical research rather than based upon opinion materials, and is given the support to do so, the CBEIP can be a valuable asset to this industry.

Training and Certificate Programs

A training and certificate program is an educational opportunity that results in a certificate of completion rather than a degree or a credential. A certificate of completion is not designed to assess for, or validate, broad competency. Instead, participants are taught specific information and skills, and are assessed based only on their knowledge related to the training program's content (ICE, 2016; NEHA, 2016). Obtaining a certificate of completion does not demonstrate overall competency, nor does it suggest that a professional is broadly qualified.

In many cases, certificate programs offer a model or a manualized approach that is proprietary, and participants receive a certificate of completion that demonstrates competency and knowledge only related to the specific training organization and its approach. In these cases, the training organization may stipulate standards and ethics of practice related to their model, but should support adherence to overarching standards and ethics of practice established by national membership associations. In other cases, certificate programs are administrated through college or university programs, and teach broadly-based theoretical and practical applications, but still should not be confused with a credentialing process.

It is unlikely that any one model or approach will address the needs of all patients. The beauty of continuing education and training is that there is room for many diverse approaches, and professionals can choose to attend various trainings in order to expand the possible techniques they could use in clinical practice, thereby enhancing their ability to serve their patients.

For mental health professionals, a plethora of training and certificate programs exist around the world for those interested in learning more about the various models and approaches to providing equine-assisted therapy. Although larger training and certificate organizations like the EAGALA may be better known, smaller training and certificate programs and college and university certificate programs should not be overlooked. In many cases, these organizations offer more comprehensive training and provide best practice guidelines, safety standards, ethics, and a replicable model of practice.

Physical, occupational, and speech therapists have less available training, but the training they commonly receive seems quite standardized and less methodologically based. Given the current educational opportunities, it seems physical, occupational, and speech therapists could begin developing additional training options for others in their professions who may be interested in including farm-based or other non-mounted activities in their practices.

The American Hippotherapy Association, Inc. (AHA)

Although the AHA is categorized primarily as a professional membership association in this book, this organization provides the bulk of the training and education for physical, occupational, and speech therapists who wish to include horses in their clinical practices.

Courses are held both in person and online, and are taught by AHA-approved faculty. At present, the AHA offers 10 different courses that range from introductory-level equine skills courses to more advanced courses educating therapists about specific populations and treatment techniques.

Therapists who obtain their training and education through AHA generally continue on to sit for one of the two exams offered by the AHCB.

The Equine Assisted Growth and Learning Association (EAGALA)

The Equine Assisted Growth and Learning Association (EAGALA) was founded in 1999 to support "professionals incorporating horses to address mental health and personal development needs" (EAGALA, 2016a). EAGALA is best known for its training and certificate program, but also maintains a membership branch that supports those interested in the EAGALA model of equine-assisted psychotherapy and learning. EAGALA hosts national and international conferences, provides networking opportunities, and offers its members a variety of other EAGALA-specific resources.

Given the organization's heavy emphasis on training and its singular focus on the EAGALA model of equine-assisted therapy and learning, the association is categorized in this book as a training and certificate program, rather than a professional membership association.

EAGALA is by far the largest training and certificate organization in the industry to date, reporting 4,500 members and 700 centers in 50 countries (EAGALA, 2016a). It is unclear how many of these individuals are also certified in the EAGALA model of equine-assisted psychotherapy and learning.

EAGALA certifies people in its manualized model of non-mounted and non-horsemanship equine-assisted psychotherapy and learning, which is provided by a team composed of a mental health professional and an "equine specialist."

EAGALA's training includes:

- Pre-training online webinar.
- Five-day fundamentals of the EAGALA model training
- Post-training online assessment.
- Professional development portfolio that includes questions about why an individual might want to provide the EAGALA model of equine-assisted psychotherapy and learning, agreeing to EAGALA's ethics and standards of practice, and submitting a resume.

EAGALA requires the following prerequisites for mental health professionals:

- Educational training and a degree in a mental health field, such as social work, psychology, marriage and family therapy, or others that include mental health as their scope of practice.
- Adherence to all applicable laws and regulations governing the professional's scope of practice.
- Licensure and/or registration to practice under a governing board/body or as a member of a professional association that requires strict accountability (or under professional supervision by a supervisor that is held accountable by a governing board/association), i.e. a board that can revoke registration, certification, accreditation, or licensure for ethical or scope of practice violations relating to mental health practice.

There is no distinction in EAGALA's training or certification between psychotherapy and learning. Everyone interested in the EAGALA model goes through the same training. Once an individual has been certified in the EAGALA model, he or she must adhere to the EAGALA standards of practice and code of ethics. EAGALA closely monitors its membership to ensure adherence.

A common critique of EAGALA's approach is its use of ground-based loose-horse activities that involve patients chasing horses, moving horses, or attempting to place equipment onto horses without horsemanship and safety training. Another critique is that through EAGALA's marketing and public relations efforts, it may be perceived as the only way to provide mental health services that include horses. In fact, EAGALA's website states it is the "global standard in therapy and personal development" (EAGALA, 2016a; EAGALA, 2016b) and suggests it "stands alone in the world of equine-assisted therapy due to a strict commitment to standards, code of ethics, continuing education, and a replicable framework" (EAGALA, 2016b, p. 3). To suggest that EAGALA is the only training and certificate program that adheres to standards, offers a code of ethics, or is replicable is simply untrue, and does consumers and the industry as a whole a great disservice.

It is also important to re-state that EAGALA is not a credentialing body, and therefore a certificate from EAGALA does not suggest broad competency in equine-assisted mental health.

Eponaquest

Founded in 1997 by author and horse trainer Linda Kohanov, Eponaquest offers trainings, workshops, and an apprenticeship program in the Eponaquest Approach™. This holistic approach encourages participants to explore "assertiveness, stress reduction and emotional fitness skills, strengthening self-esteem and personal empowerment in the process" (Eponaquest, 2016a).

Although Eponaquest provides a certificate program for equine-facilitated experiential learning (EFEL), the organization notes that licensed mental health professionals may choose to use the Eponaquest Approach™ when providing equine-facilitated psychotherapy.

Eponaquest Approved Instructors complete three nine-day mandatory seminars over a six-month period (Eponaquest, 2016b), and prior to being accepted into the program must demonstrate they possess the following prerequisites:

- Own or have routine access to a horse for the duration of the certificate program
- Have 5 years or 2,000 hours of prior horse experience
- Have experience participating in groups, and are comfortable with group process and group dynamics
- Must be mentally and emotionally stable and exhibit a level of personal maturity
- Must be physically fit and in good health

Eponaquest instructors adhere to the Eponaquest Best Practice Guidelines, and maintain ethical standards of practice. Over 300 Approved Instructors can be found worldwide.

Adventures in Awareness™

Adventures in Awareness™ was founded by Barbara Rector in the early 1990s. Ms. Rector is considered a pioneer in the equine-assisted mental health industry, and is credited with developing an equine-facilitated experiential learning model which has been translated to psychotherapy practices worldwide. The goal of the Adventures in Awareness™ model is to "Develop awareness and expand consciousness while enhancing an individual's self-confidence through work with horses" (AIA, 2016a).

Adventures in Awareness™ offers workshops, trainings, and an internship program for professionals interested in incorporating the model into their own practices.

The internship program includes a 14-day core curriculum which covers theory, principles, facilitation skills, equestrian skills, and a focus on the equine perspective. Participants also attend three three-day courses offered by Adventures in Awareness™ of which one horsemanship skills course is mandatory but participants can choose the other two courses based upon their own interests or schedules. Along with the core curriculum and the in-person workshops the following is required:

- Reading assignments
- Journaling assignments
- 300 logged hours of volunteer or paid practical experience using the Adventures in Awareness™ model
- Co-facilitation of an Adventures in Awareness™ short course workshop
- A portfolio
- Mentoring sessions

Those who successfully complete the internship program receive a certificate of completion, and those who graduate with "merit" are given permission to use the Adventures in Awareness™ name and materials (AIA, 2016b).

All Adventures in Awareness™ certificate holders have a commitment to adhere to AIA standards of safety and ethical humane practices.

The Equine Psychotherapy Institute

The Equine Psychotherapy Institute offers one of the more comprehensive training models for licensed mental health professionals interested in adding equine-assisted psychotherapy to their practices. This innovative and experiential approach to counseling, psychotherapy, and mental health "supports clients of all ages in addressing therapeutic goals, with horses as assistants, co-facilitators and teachers in this process" (EPI, 2016).

The Equine Psychotherapy Institute model of equine-assisted psychotherapy was founded on a set of practice standards and ethics that include:

- Understanding the theoretical and experiential foundations of equine-assisted psychotherapy.
- Understanding horses and learning how to engage with horses safely.
- Understanding the unique dynamics and processes of equine-assisted psychotherapy, including how to facilitate the therapeutic process of change when including horses.

The Equine Psychotherapy Institute training takes place over a 12-month period and requires the following for certification:

- Successful completion of three intensive trainings (a total of 15 days)
- Four hours of Skype/phone supervision sessions
- Three integration papers (500–1,000 words) submitted at the end of each intensive
- A final assessment which is an open book exam including theoretical, practical, personal questions, and case study
- A horsemanship video including horse handling and I-thou horsemanship skills

The Equine Psychotherapy Institute also offers an annual conference and additional training in advanced practice specializations.

The Gestalt Equine Institute of the Rockies

The Gestalt Equine Institute of the Rockies offers comprehensive training in a specialization of equine-assisted psychotherapy called Gestalt Equine Psychotherapy (GEP)™. The institute offers a two-year training that combines aspects of Gestalt psychotherapy with equine interactions (GEIR, 2016). The program focuses on professional and personal development, as well as emphasizes the importance of horsemanship skills.

Successful completion of the program includes:

- Attending eight four-day intensives
- Writing a 1–2-page integration paper
- Passing the equine assessment that includes horsemanship knowledge and riding skills
- Participating in three in-person meetings to assess equine skills throughout the duration of the training program
- Completing 16 hours of supervision
- Completing a Gestalt Theory Assessment
- Completing a final project

The Human-Equine Alliances for Learning (HEAL)

The Human-Equine Alliances for Learning offers a five-month training in the HEAL Model™ of equine-facilitated psychotherapy and learning. The training "prepares participants to facilitate horse activities for experiential psychotherapy or learning, helping clients increase relational ability, emotional well-being, self-awareness and empowerment" (HEAL, 2016).

The HEAL Model™ is "trauma-sensitive," focusing on the limbic/emotional communications between horse and human. The model provides a "respectful and safe" way for humans to engage therapeutically with horses.

The training includes 2 weeks of on-site instruction and a summer distance learning component that includes mentored practice in equine-facilitated psychotherapy. The following prerequisites are required:

- A Master's level or equivalent education in clinical counseling, or related field such as psychology or psychotherapy, social work, teaching or coaching
- Two years of experience in their field of human services
- A minimum of 3 years recent and regular horse experience is highly recommended
- Attend HEAL Keys to Connection workshop or 8-hour private intensive with a HEAL Trainer

Natural Lifemanship

The Natural Lifemanship program was founded in 2010 by Tim Jobe and Bettina Shultz and offers training and a certificate of completion in a model they call "trauma-focused equine-assisted psychotherapy".

The website claims "Natural Lifemanship is the new standard in equine assisted psychotherapy" (NL, 2017a), and states their model is "based on the neuroscience of human and horse brain development, the impact of trauma, and the role of relationships in recovery and healing" (NL, 2017a). The Natural Lifemanship model of trauma-focused equine-assisted psychotherapy "utilizes horses, sound principles of equine psychology, and an awareness of human brain development to repair and enhance all of life's relationships" (NL, 2017d).

Professionals interested in obtaining a certificate of completion in the Natural Lifemanship model attend a "Fundamentals of Natural Lifemanship" training and then continue on to take the "Natural Lifemanship Intensive" training. Other requirements include:

- Between 18 and 21 sessions of individual and group consultation
- Sixty practice hours
- Ongoing Natural Lifemanship membership
- Other non-specified assignments

Although the Natural Lifemanship website suggests its model is "the new standard," there is no evidence of supportive research, and no best practice guidelines, safety standards, or ethics specific to the model are included in its materials.

The Human-Equine Relational Development (HERD) Institute

The HERD Institute offers training and certificates in both equine-facilitated psychotherapy and equine-facilitated learning. Its mission is to "create a global community, of students and practitioners for Equine-Facilitated Psychotherapy and Learning, committed to furthering the work of the pioneers of our field" (HERD Institute, 2017).

The HERD Institute's training program for licensed mental health professionals is "Founded on experiential learning principles and academic excellence" (HERD Institute, 2017), offers continuing education units (CEUs) through the National Association of Social Workers (NASW) and the National Board for Certified Counselors (NBCC), and is pending CEU approval by the American Psychological Association (APA).

The course of study is structured over 12 months and participants must complete the following to graduate:

- Complete five four-day workshops (140 hours)
- Complete four online learning modules
- Participate in 22 hours of supervision with a faculty member
- Submit four 2,000-word theoretical papers
- Submit a personal process paper after every training workshop
- Demonstration of personal therapy requirements
- Completion of horsemanship skills development requirements, which includes 20 hours of continuing education for horsemanship skills
- Completion of Horsemanship Skills Test
- Completion of 10 mentored hours of live practice in EFP

The HERD Institute also offers workshops and retreats as well as weekly and monthly groups.

☐ Membership Associations

Professionals providing equine-assisted therapy find support, mentorship, and continuing education opportunities through joining membership associations. Professional membership associations also support the unique needs of specific licensed professionals by hosting national and regional conferences and networking opportunities, providing or connecting members to continuing education opportunities, and collecting and sharing data related to professional practice patterns.

Typically, professional associations maintain oversight of a professional practice or a clinical specialty through setting broad standards and ethics, defining terms, regulating compliance, and helping to educate and safeguard the public. Professional associations (similar to credentialing bodies) are not model- or method-specific. Rather, they support the needs of all licensed professionals within a specific trade or professional discipline regardless of what treatment approaches or strategies the professional chooses to use. This is why it is common to see only one professional membership association per discipline, while multiple training and certificate programs exist comfortably. If there are duplicate professional membership associations, that simultaneously attempt to establish standards, ethics, and terminology, conflict and confusion are bound to arise.

In most cases, professional associations adhere to the standards set forth by organizations like the ICE, which require a separation between credentialing and education. Generally, this means these associations do not offer certification, although they may offer training and continuing education opportunities.

The Professional Association of Therapeutic Horsemanship International (PATH Intl.)

Established in 1969 as the North American Riding for the Handicapped Association (NARHA), the association changed its name in 2011 to the Professional Association of Therapeutic Horsemanship International (PATH Intl.). It primarily serves non-licensed instructors and educators who teach adaptive horsemanship, riding, and driving lessons, and those offering equine-facilitated learning. It does provide some support for licensed physical, occupational, speech, and mental health professionals. As of 2015, PATH Intl. had 8,037 individual members and 877 center members spanning 41 countries (PATH Intl, 2015). PATH Intl. members can attend the association's national conference, or participate in educational content at a regional level.

PATH Intl. is known for establishing and maintaining industry standards for equine-assisted activities and therapies. These standards are created and reviewed by a committee of members whose task it is to keep the standards up to date and applicable to the membership. Precautions and contraindications are included to help providers understand what populations and conditions are appropriate for the service. PATH Intl. also offers accreditation for centers providing equine-assisted activities or therapies. These centers are required to adhere to the PATH Intl. standards. The benefit of this process is that these accredited centers may be safer for participants and for horses.

Given PATH Intl.'s history and membership composition, its expertise lies more prominently in the area of adaptive riding rather than therapy services provided by licensed professionals. This can lead to a focus on the needs of non-licensed adaptive riding instructors rather than a concentration on current practice trends and important issues for licensed professionals.

Finally, PATH Intl. does not adhere to the credentialing standards recommended by the ICE at this time, and is known as the leader in providing both training and certification for adaptive riding instructors. These individuals can be certified as "Registered," "Advanced," or "Master" based upon their level of experience, time, and additional training. Specialty certificates are also offered for driving and vaulting instructors, and non-therapist "equine specialists" who assist during equine-facilitated psychotherapy sessions.

The Equine Facilitated Mental Health Association (EFMHA)

The EFMHA was founded in 1996 and operated as a subgroup of NARHA until it was absorbed into PATH Intl. during the name change process in 2011. EFMHA no longer exists, although the acronym of EFMH (equine-facilitated mental health) is still used occasionally.

EFMHA is important to include here because it is credited with bringing a mental health focus to the work with horses. EFMHA developed key philosophical beliefs about including horses in mental healthcare. Namely, EFMHA believed the horse to be a sentient being who co-facilitates psychotherapy sessions. This led to the development of the terms "equine-facilitated psychotherapy" and "equine-facilitated learning."

The American Hippotherapy Association, Inc. (AHA)

The AHA began as a section of NARHA in 1992 and existed under the umbrella of NARHA until 2003 when it began its own non-profit association. AHA provides training, education, and support for physical therapists, occupational therapists, and speech therapists who provide equine-assisted therapy services. In 2016, AHA had 1,100 members in 18 countries (AHA, 2016a). AHA offers a variety of online and hands-on continuing education courses, and organizes a bi-annual conference.

Unlike PATH Intl., AHA adheres to the professional practice of separating education and credentialing. Therapists who wish to be certified to provide hippotherapy may obtain their training through AHA or in any other manner they so choose. Once they feel prepared, they can sit for an exam offered by the AHCB.

Federation of Horses in Education and Therapy International (HETI)

Officially, HETI was founded as the Federation of Riding for the Disabled International (FRDI) in 1991, although conversations about its creation began as early as 1985 (August 9, 2016, personal correspondence with

HETI Executive Director Gisela Rhodes). In 2009, the organization began a name change process from the Federation of Riding for the Disabled International to the Federation of Horses in Education and Therapy International. The name change was formally implemented in 2012.

HETI offers "Federation," "Institute," "Business," and "Associate" level membership. It serves a wide audience from large associations like PATH Intl. and institutes of higher learning to programs providing services and individuals in private practice. In 2016, HETI had 54 Federation members across 30 different countries, four Institutional members, 11 Business members, and 164 Associate members. Its membership spans 47 countries (HETI, 2016).

HETI hosts an International Congress every 3 years in different locations around the world. A Congress is a professional gathering where research is presented, much like a conference in the United States. HETI also publishes a yearly international peer-reviewed journal called the Scientific and Educational Journal of Therapeutic Riding. It offers a directory of education and training services with the goal of connecting professionals to continuing education and training opportunities.

☐ College and University Equine-Assisted Therapy Programs

For those seeking a Master's degree specialization or advanced training in some form of equine-assisted therapy from a recognized educational institution, the options are still limited at this time. To date, the industry of equine-assisted therapy does not have an agreed-upon body of knowledge that guides the development of academic curriculum.

Hart & Baehr (2013) write, "When the body of knowledge (BOK) defines a field, it serves to mark that particular field as a profession. The boundaries of that knowledge are often interdisciplinary and include theories, practices, standards, research, and general information both tacit and codified" (p. 260). A body of knowledge also includes agreed-upon terminology, standards of practice, and concepts related to the profession.

Without an established body of knowledge, each individual college or university creates its own curriculum. This poses challenges for those interested in hiring graduates, as there is no standardization in knowledge.

Out of the 28 academic programs reviewed for this book, all but two target only undergraduate students. Seven of these undergraduate programs offer a major related to equine-assisted activities or therapies, five offer a minor, and the rest offer courses, certificates, or provide services to the community with the help of students.

The University of Denver in Denver, Colorado and Prescott College in Prescott, Arizona are the only two programs to offer options for a Master's degree specialization, or post-Master's training.

University of Denver

The University of Denver offers a nine-month certificate program in equine-assisted mental health that combines a broad understanding of the theories and practices of equine-assisted mental health with hands-on learning experiences. An emphasis is placed on competent equine care and welfare, and students received one-on-one supervision. The online platform coupled with residential workshops makes the certificate possible for those living in other areas. Completion of the certificate program results in 52 continuing education credits (University of Denver, 2016). This program encourages graduates to sit for the Certification Board for Equine Interaction Professionals (CBEIP) national exam.

Prescott College

Prescott College offers a certificate program that adds 15 credits of specialized courses to the Master of Science in Counseling degree. Students attend four courses that meld e-learning with a four-day intensive residential workshop. The fifth class students take is a supervised clinical practicum.

Prescott College also offers a year-long post-Master's certification program in equine-assisted mental health that combines coursework with hands-on learning in the form of both residential workshops and additional practical experience. Students are expected to gain 100 hours of supervised practical experience, along with taking the four specialized courses in equine-assisted mental health. At the completion of the program, students receive 15 graduate credits, and are encouraged to sit for the CBEIP exam (Prescott College, 2016).

☐ Conclusion

Licensed healthcare professionals have a great responsibility to demonstrate personal and professional competency in any treatment or specialty area of practice they use, especially when the treatment is considered novel and research findings have yet to conclusively support its use.

Although the industry of equine-assisted therapy is young, and has yet to come together to lay the groundwork for a collaborative and mutually agreed-upon body of knowledge or framework of competency, progress is being made. Credentialing bodies have already been established, and there is a diverse range of training and certificate programs and membership associations to support professionals interested in providing equine-assisted therapy. College and university programs are also developing, and over time may play an important role in defining the industry and supporting its growth through empirical research and scholarly collaboration.

Within this dynamic industry, there is room for many different approaches, and it is exciting to think that individuals can find their own unique and eclectic way of practicing that adheres to important safety standards while meeting the needs of their equally colorful patients.

☐ References

Abu-Zidan, F.M., & Rao, S. (2003). Factors affecting the severity of horse-related injuries. *Injury: International Journal of the Care of the Injured, 34*(12), 897–900.

Adventures in Awareness™ (AIA). (2016a). *Learn about AIA*. Retrieved from: www.adven turesinawareness.net/about.htm

Adventures in Awareness™ (AIA). (2016b). *Internship Program*. Retrieved from: www. adventuresinawareness.net/internship/internship.htm

American Counseling Association (ACA). (2016a). *ACA Code of Ethics*. Retrieved from: www.counseling.org/resources/aca-code-of-ethics.pdf

American Counseling Association (ACA). (2016b). *Animal-Assisted Therapy in Counseling Competencies*. Retrieved from: www.counseling.org/docs/default-source/competencies/ animal-assisted-therapy-competencies-june-2016.pdf?sfvrsn=14

American Hippotherapy Association, Inc. (AHA). (2016a). Retrieved from: www.ameri canhippotherapyassociation.org/

American Hippotherapy Association, Inc. (AHA). (2016b). *Best Practice Statements for the Use of Hippotherapy by Occupational Therapy, Physical Therapy, and Speech-Language Pathology Professionals*. Retrieved from: www.americanhippotherapyassociation.org/wp-content/uploads/2015/02/FINAL_ver_Best-Practice_12_30_15.pdf

American Hippotherapy Certification Board (AHCB). (2016). Retrieved from: http://hip potherapycertification.org/

American Occupational Therapy Association (AOTA). (2016). *Occupational Therapy Code of Ethics, 2015*. Retrieved from: www.aota.org/-/media/corporate/files/practice/ethics/ code-of-ethics.pdf

American Physical Therapy Association (APTA). (2016a). *Code of Ethics for a Physical Therapist*. Retrieved from: www.apta.org/uploadedFiles/APTAorg/About_Us/Policies/ Ethics/CodeofEthics.pdf

American Physical Therapy Association (APTA). (2016b). *Term and Title Protection*. Retrieved from: www.apta.org/TermProtection/

American Psychological Association (APA). (2016). *Ethical Principles of Psychologists and Code of Conduct*. Retrieved from: www.apa.org/ethics/code/

American Speech-Language-Hearing Association (ASHA). (2016). *Code of Ethics*. Retrieved from: www.asha.org/Code-of-Ethics/

Anderson, M.K., Friend, T.H., Evans, J.W., & Bushong, D.M. (1999). Behavioral assessment of horses in therapeutic riding programs. *Applied Animal Behaviour Science, 63*, 11–24.

Anestis, M.D., Anestis, J.C., Zawilinski, L.L., Hopkins, T.A., & Lilienfeld, S.O. (2014). Equine-related treatments for mental disorders lack empirical support: A systematic review of empirical investigations. *Journal of Clinical Psychology*, 1–18.

Angoules, A., Koukoulas, D., Balakatounis, K., Kapari, I., & Matsouki, E. (2015). A review of efficacy of hippotherapy for the treatment of musculoskeletal disorders. *British Journal of Medicine and Medical Research, 8*(4), 289–297.

Angsupaisal, M., Visser, B., Alkema, A., Meinsma-van der Tuin, M., Maathuis, C.G.B., Reinders-Messelink, H., & Hadders-Algra, M. (2015). Therapist-designed adaptive riding in children with cerebral palsy: Results of a feasibility study. *Physical Therapy, 95*(8), 1151–1162.

Bachi, K. (2012). Equine-facilitated psychotherapy: The gap between practice and knowledge. *Society & Animals, 20,* 364–380.

Ball, C.G., Ball, J.E., Kirkpatrick, A.W., & Mulloy, R.H. (2007). Equestrian injuries: Incidence, injury patterns, and risk factors for 10 years of major traumatic injuries. *American Journal of Surgery, 193*(5), 636–640.

Benda, W., McGibbon, N.H., & Grant, K.L. (2003). Improvements in muscle symmetry in children with cerebral palsy after equine-assisted therapy (hippotherapy). *Journal of Alternative and Complementary Medicine, 9*(6), 817–825.

Borgi, M., Loliva, D., Cerino, S., et al. (2016). Effectiveness of a standardized equine-assisted therapy program for children with autism spectrum disorder. *Journal of Autism and Developmental Disorders, 46*(1), 1–9.

Brandt, C. (2013). Equine-facilitated psychotherapy as a complementary treatment intervention. *Practitioner Scholar: Journal of Counseling & Professional Psychology, 2*(1), 23–42.

Bray, B. (August 15, 2016). *ACA Endorses Animal-Assisted Therapy Competencies.* Retrieved from: http://ct.counseling.org/2016/08/aca-endorses-animal-assisted-therapy-competencies/

Carlsson, C., Ranta, D.N., & Traeen, B. (2014). Equine assisted social work as a mean for authentic relations between clients and staff. *Human-Animal Interaction Bulletin, 2*(1), 19–38.

Carmichael, S.P., Davenport, D.L., Kearney, P.A., & Bernard, A.C. (2014). On and off the horse: Mechanisms and patterns of injury in mounted and unmounted equestrians. *Injury: International Journal of the Care of the Injured, 45*(9), 1479–1483.

Certification Board for Equine Interaction Professionals (CBEIP). (2016). Retrieved from: www.cbeip.org/

Chang, H.J., Kwon, J.Y., Lee, J.Y., & Kim, Y.H. (2012). The effects of hippotherapy on the motor function of children with spastic bilateral cerebral palsy. *Journal of Physical Therapy Science, 24*(12), 1277–1280.

Christensen, J.W., Keeling, L.J., & Nielsen, B.L. (2005). Responses of horses to novel visual, olfactory and auditory stimuli. *Applied Animal Behaviour Science, 93,* 53–65.

Cook, R. (2011). Incidents and injury within the hippotherapy milieu: Four years of safety study data on risk, risk management, and occurrences. *Scientific and Educational Journal of Therapeutic Riding,* 57–66.

Cook, R. (2014). *Risk management and safety in hippotherapy.* Publisher: Rebecca Cook.

Cuenca, A.G., Wiggins, A., Chen, M.K., Kays, D.W., Islam, S., & Beierle, E.A. (2009). Equestrian injuries in children. *Journal of Pediatric Surgery, 44*(1), 148–150.

Debuse, D., Gibb, C., & Chandler, C. (2009). Effects of hippotherapy on people with cerebral palsy from the users' perspective: A qualitative study. *Physiotherapy Theory and Practice, 25*(3), 174–192.

Eponaquest. (2016a). *Overview.* Retrieved from: http://eponaquest.com/overview/

Eponaquest. (2016b). *Prerequisites and Applicable Process.* Retrieved from: http://eponaquest.com/prerequisites-application-process/

Equine Assisted Activities & Therapies Training Institute (EAATTI). (2017). *About.* Retrieved from: www.eaatti.com/about

Equine Assisted Assets. (2016). *Frequently Asked Questions.* Retrieved from: www.equineassistedassets.com/FAQs.htm

Equine Assisted Growth and Learning Association (EAGALA). (2016a). Retrieved from: www.eagala.org/

Equine Assisted Growth and Learning Association (EAGALA). (2016b). *EAGALA Certification Brochure*. Retrieved from: www.eagala.org/sites/default/files/attachments/EAGALA%20Certification%20Brochure%20WEB.pdf

Equine Psychotherapy Institute (EPI). (2016). *Certification, Ethics and Membership*. Retrieved from: www.equinepsychotherapy.net.au/certification/

Fazio, E., Medica, P., Cravana, C., & Ferlazzo, A. (2013). Hypothalamic-pituitary-adrenal axis responses of horses to therapeutic riding program: Effects of different riders. *Physiology and Behavior, 118*, 138–143.

Federation of Horses in Therapy and Education International (HETI). (2016). Retrieved from: www.frdi.net/

Fershtman, J.L. (September 21, 2016). *Can You Release Equine Activity Liability Act Liabilities? The Answer May Surprise You*. Retrieved from: www.equinelawblog.com/release-equine-activity-liabilities

Ford, C. (2013). Dancing with horses: Combining dance/movement therapy and equine facilitated psychotherapy. *American Journal of Dance Therapy, 35*(2), 93–117.

Frewin, K., & Gardiner, B. (2005). New age or old sage? A review of equine assisted psychotherapy. *The Australian Journal of Counselling Psychology, 6*, 13–17.

Gestalt Equine Institute of the Rockies (GEIR). (2016). *Gestalt Equine Psychotherapy (GEP) Training Program*. Retrieved from: www.gestaltequineinstitute.com/trainings.html

Globisch, J., Hamm, A.O., Esteves, F., & Öhman, A. (1999). Fear appears fast: Temporal course of startle reflex potentiation in animal fearful subjects. *Psychophysiology, 36*, 66–75.

Goodwin, D. (1999). The importance of ethology in understanding the behaviour of the horse. *Equine Veterinary Journal, 28*, 15–19.

Gullo, S., Lo Coco, G., & Gelso, C. (2012). Early and later predictors of outcome in brief therapy: The role of real relationship. *Journal of Clinical Psychology, 68*(6), 614–619.

Hart, H., & Baehr, C. (2013). Sustainable practices for developing a body of knowledge. *Technical Communication, 60*(4), 259–266.

Hausberger, M., Gautier, E., Biquand, V., Lunel, C., & Jégo, P. (2009). Could work be a source of behavioural disorders? A study in horses. *PLoS One, 4*(10), 2–9.

Hausberger, M., Roche, H., Henry, S., & Visser, K.E. (2008). A review of the human-horse relationship. *Applied Animal Behaviour Science, 109*(1), 1–24.

Hawson, L.A., McLean, A.N., & McGreevy, P.D. (2010). The roles of equine ethology and applied learning theory in horse-related human injuries. *Journal of Veterinary Behavior: Clinical Applications and Research, 5*(6), 324–338.

Human-Equine Alliances for Learning (HEAL). (2016). *Workshops/Trainings*. Retrieved from: http://humanequinealliance.com/efl-workshops-training/2018-heal-facilitator-training-redmond-wa-usa-near-seattle/

Human-Equine Relational Development Institute (HERD Institute). (2017). *EFPL Training and Certificate Overview*. Retrieved from: http://herdinstitute.com/efpl-training-certification/

Institute for Credentialing Excellence (ICE). (2016). *What Is Credentialing?* Retrieved from: www.credentialingexcellence.org/p/cm/ld/fid=32

Jack, K., & Miller, E. (2008). Exploring self-awareness in mental health practice. *Mental Health Practice, 12*(3), 31–35.

Johansen, S.G., Wang, C.E.A., Binder, P.E., & Malt, U.F. (2014). Equine-facilitated body and emotion-oriented psychotherapy designed for adolescents and adults not responding to mainstream treatment: A structured program. *Journal of Psychotherapy Integration, 24*(4), 323–335.

Kaiser, L., Heleski, C.R., Siegford, J., & Smith, K.A. (2006). Stress-related behaviors among horses used in a therapeutic riding program. *Journal of the American Veterinary Medical Association, 228*(1), 39–45.

Keeling, L.J., Jonare, L., & Lanneborn, L. (2009). Investigating horse-human interactions: The effect of a nervous human. *Veterinary Journal, 181*, 70–71.

Kidd, A.H., Kelley, H.T. and Kidd, R.M. (1984). Personality characteristics of horse, turtle, snake, and bird owners. In R.K. Anderson, B.L. Hart and L.A. Hart (Eds.), *The Pet Connection: Its Influence on Our Health and Quality of Life* (pp 200–206). Minneapolis, MN: Center to Study Human-Animal Relationships and Environments, University of Minnesota.

Kirby, M. (2010). Gestalt equine psychotherapy. *Gestalt Journal of Australia and New Zealand, 6*(2), 60–68.

Lechner, H.E., Kakebeeke, T.H., Hegemann, D., & Baumberger, M. (2007). The effect of hippotherapy on spasticity and on mental well-being of persons with spinal cord injury. *Archives of Physical Medicine and Rehabilitation, 88*(10), 1241–1248.

Lee, P.T., Dakin, E., & Mclure, M. (2016). Narrative synthesis of equine-assisted psychotherapy literature: Current knowledge and future research directions. *Health and Social Care in the Community, 24*(3), 225–246.

Lesimple, C., Hausberger, M., Hommel, B., & Staios, M. (2014). How accurate are we at assessing others' well-being? The example of welfare assessment in horses. *Frontiers in Psychology, 5*(21), 1–6.

McGibbon, N.H., Benda, W., Duncan, B.R., & Silkwood-Sherer, D. (2009). Immediate and long-term effects of hippotherapy on symmetry of adductor muscle activity and functional ability in children with spastic cerebral palsy. *Archives of Physical Medicine and Rehabilitation, 90*(6), 966–974.

McGreevy, P.D. (2012). *Equine behavior: A guide for veterinarians and equine scientists* (2nd edition). London: UK: Saunders, an imprint of Elsevier Ltd.

McKelvy, K.D. (March/April, 2002). Some risks of risk management. *EAGALA News*, 11–12.

Merkies, K., Sievers, A., Zakrajsek, E., Macgregor, H., Bergeron, R., & König Von Borstel, U. (2014). Preliminary results suggest an influence of psychological and physiological stress in humans on horse heart rate and behavior. *Journal of Veterinary Behavior: Clinical Applications and Research, 9*, 242–247.

Minero, M., Zucca, D., & Canali, E. (2006). A note on reaction to novel stimulus and restraint by therapeutic riding horses. *Applied Animal Behaviour Science, 97*, 335–342.

National Association of Social Workers (NASW). (2016). *Code of Ethics of the National Association of Social Workers.* Retrieved from: www.socialworkers.org/pubs/Code/code.asp

National Environmental Health Association (NEHA). (2016). *Difference between Credentials and Certifications.* Retrieved from: www.neha.org/professional-development/education-and-training/differences-between-credentials-certifications

Natural Lifemanship (NL). (2017a). *About Us.* Retrieved from: https://naturallifemanship.com/

Natural Lifemanship (NL). (2017b). *Become Certified.* Retrieved from: https://naturallifemanship.com/become-certified/

Natural Lifemanship (NL). (2017c). *NL Intensive Training.* Retrieved from: http://naturallifemanship.com/training-certification/intensive/

Natural Lifemanship (NL). (2017d). *NL Training and Certification.* Retrieved from: https://naturallifemanship.com/training-certification/

O'Rourke, K. (2004). Horse-assisted therapy: Good for humans, but how about horses? *Journal of the American Veterinary Medical Association, 225*(6), 817–817.

Papachristos, A., Edwards, E., Dowrick, A., & Gosling, C. (2014). A description of the severity of equestrian-related injuries (ERIs) using clinical parameters and patient-reported outcomes. *Injury: International Journal of the Care of the Injured, 45*(9), 1484–1487.

Pet Partners. (2016). *Learn the Pet Partners Difference*. Retrieved from: https://petpartners. org/learn/pet-partners-difference/

Porter-Wenzlaff, L. (2007). Finding their voice: Developing emotional, cognitive, and behavioral congruence in female abuse survivors through equine-facilitated psychotherapy. *Explore: The Journal of Science and Healing, 3*(5), 529–534.

Prescott College. (2016). *Equine-Assisted Mental Health*. Retrieved from: www.prescott. edu/academics/concentrations/equine-assisted-mental-health

Professional Association of Therapeutic Riding International (PATH Intl.). (2014). *Standards for Certification & Accreditation Manual*. Retrieved from: www.pathintl.org/images/ pdf/standards-manual/2014/2014-COMPLETE-PATH-Intl-Standards-Manual.pdf

Professional Association of Therapeutic Riding International (PATH Intl.). (2015). *2015 PATH Intl. Statistics*. Retrieved from: www.pathintl.org/images/pdf/about-narha/ documents/2015-fact-sheet-web.pdf

Rasheed, S.P. (2015). Self-awareness as a therapeutic tool for nurse/client relationship. *International Journal of Caring Sciences, 8*(1), 211–216.

Robinson, I.H.. (1999). The human-horse relationship: How much do we know? *Equine Veterinary Journal Supplement, 28*, 42–45.

Rothe, E., Vega, B., Torres, R., Soler, S., & Pazos, R. (2005). From kids and horses: Equine facilitated psychotherapy for children. *International Journal of Clinical and Health Psychology, 5*(2), 373–383.

Schadewaldt, V., McInnes, E., Hiller, J.E., & Gardner, A. (2014). Investigating characteristics of collaboration between nurse practitioners and medical practitioners in primary healthcare: A mixed methods multiple case study protocol. *Journal of Advanced Nursing, 70*(5), 1184–1193.

Selby, A., & Smith-Osborne, A. (2013). A systematic review of effectiveness of complementary and adjunct therapies and interventions involving equines. *Health Psychology, 32*(4), 418–432.

Silver, J.R. (2002). Spinal injuries resulting from horse riding accidents. *Spinal Cord: The Official Journal of the International Medical Society of Paraplegia, 40*, 264–271.

Trotter, K.S., Chandler, C.K., & Goodwin-Bond, D. (2008). A comparative study of the efficacy of group equine assisted counseling with at-risk children and adolescents. *Journal of Creativity in Mental Health, 3*, 254–284.

Tseng, S.-H., Chen, H.-C., & Tam, K.-W. (2012). Systematic review and meta-analysis of the effect of equine assisted activities and therapies on gross motor outcome in children with cerebral palsy. *Disability and Rehabilitation, 35*, 1–11.

University of Denver. (2016). *Equine-Assisted Mental Health Practitioner Certificate*. Retrieved from: http://portfolio.du.edu/equineassistedmentalhealth/page/57559

Van Dusseldorp, L.R.L.C., Van Meijel, B.K.G., & Derksen, J.J.L. (2011). Emotional intelligence of mental health nurses. *Journal of Clinical Nursing, 20*(3), 555–562.

Vidrine, M., Owen-Smith, P., & Faulkner, P. (2002). Equine-facilitated group psychotherapy: Applications for therapeutic vaulting. *Issues in Mental Health Nursing, 23*(6), 587–603.

Vlachou, E.M., Damigos, D., Lyrakos, G., & Chanopoulos, K. (2016). The relationship between burnout syndrome and emotional intelligence in healthcare professionals. *Health Science Journal, 10*(5), 1–9.

Walker, A., Yong, M., Pang, L., Fullarton, C., Costa, B., & Dunning, T.A.M. (2013). Work readiness of graduate health professionals. *Nurse Education Today*, *33*(2), 116–122.

Walson, H. (2003). *Detailed Discussion of the Equine Activity Liability Act*. Retrieved from: www.animallaw.info/article/detailed-discussion-equine-activity-liability-act

Wu, R.R., Kinsinger, L.S., Provenzale, D., King, H.A., Akerly, P., Barnes, L.K., Datta, S.K., Grubber, J.M., Katich, N., McNeil, R.B., Monte, R., Sperber, N.R., Atkins, D., and Jackson, G.L. (2014). Implementation of new clinical programs in the VHA healthcare system: The importance of early collaboration between clinical leadership and research. *Journal of General Internal Medicine*, *29*(4), 825–830.

Yalom, I. (2003). *The gift of therapy: An open letter to a new generation of therapists and their patients* (1st edition). New York: HarperPerennial.

Zeidner, M., & Hadar, D. (2014). Some individual difference predictors of professional well-being and satisfaction of health professionals. *Personality and Individual Differences*, *65*, 91–95.

4 Populations Served by Equine-Assisted Therapy

☐ Popular Beliefs

When reading the websites of national associations supporting equine-assisted therapy and the promotional materials of those providing services, one can understand the widespread popularity of the treatment approach. The information readily available to the public suggests that equine-assisted therapy is a highly effective treatment for many physical and mental health conditions.

In 2012, Thompson, et al. published the results of a study examining the benefits claims reported on websites of those providing equine-assisted activities or therapies. All 112 websites they reviewed during the course of their study suggest that interacting with horses could help with the following conditions:

- ADHD
- Autism
- Behavior disorders
- Cancer or terminally ill
- Deaf and hard of hearing
- Intellectual disability
- Learning disability
- Low vision and blindness
- Mental illness
- Physical disability
- Traumatic brain injury

Thompson and his fellow researchers point out that the benefits claims reported by these websites are not based on empirical study, stating, "The websites we reviewed led visitors to believe that equine programs provided participants with positive experiences and outcomes. However, the benefit claims summarized in Table 2 were never based on systematic empiricism" (Thompson, et al., 2012, p. 384).

Similarly, the Professional Association of Therapeutic Horsemanship, International (PATH Intl.) states that therapeutic activities with horses can have a "major" physical or emotional impact on a "wide variety" of issues and disabilities. The website suggests the following conditions benefit from both therapies provided with horses and non-therapy equine-assisted activities (PATH Intl., 2016):

- Amputations
- Attention-deficit disorder
- Autism spectrum disorder
- Brain injuries
- Cerebral palsy
- Cerebrovascular accident/stroke
- Deafness
- Developmental delay/cognitive delay
- Down syndrome
- Emotional disabilities
- Learning disabilities
- Multiple sclerosis
- Muscular dystrophy
- Spina bifida
- Spinal cord injuries
- Visual impairment

Although PATH Intl. cites a few research studies supporting some of the benefits claims made on its website, most of the claims have little if any conclusive research outcomes to substantiate them.

Likewise, the Equine Assisted Growth and Learning Association (EAGALA) states that equine-assisted psychotherapy helps patients "change and grow more effectively and quickly than traditional clinical and psycho-educational approaches" (EAGALA, 2016, para. 2). EAGALA's claims that equine-assisted psychotherapy is "more effective" than traditional talk therapy, or that it works more quickly than traditional approaches, lack empirical evidence, and the few studies cited are plagued with methodological issues that compromise their validity (Selby & Smith-Osborne, 2013; Anestis, et al., 2014; Kendall, et al., 2015).

It is to be assumed that those promoting efficacy claims unsupported by research are not doing so in an attempt to deceive the public or cause harm to patients. Rather, the claims are likely supported by personal beliefs, passions, and a true desire to help. However, as Thompson, et al. (2012) reminds us, treatments that are popularized without sound scientific research stand a fair chance of being discarded. Furthermore, due to the added expense, the difficultly associated with obtaining equine-assisted therapy services, and the lack of research conducted to determine if treatment is harmful, already vulnerable populations could be put in further jeopardy without sufficient evidence to suggest the risk is worth the gain.

Of course, without providing services and continuing to professionalize the industry through more rigorous research, practice standards, and competency requirements, there is no way to transition to a widely accepted and validated evidence-based practice. Therefore, it is hoped that professionals will continue to practice equine-assisted therapy with as much information and knowledge as possible, taking appropriately calculated risks, and guiding the industry towards sustainable and ethical growth.

To this end, it is important for professionals to know what evidence (or lack thereof) supports the use of equine-assisted therapy for various populations, and to make their own educated choices about who to serve and how to serve them.

☐ What Does Research Tell Us?

A comprehensive literature review was conducted for this book, and 227 articles were identified that met all inclusion criteria and directly addressed the use of equine-assisted therapy, equine-assisted learning, or adaptive riding to treat various health conditions.

Since current research commonly references therapy and non-therapy approaches used interchangeably to treat a variety of physical and mental health-related conditions, articles were coded and sorted into categories by population or condition rather than by therapy type. As discussed in earlier chapters of this book, the practice of using non-therapy approaches to "treat" any physical or mental health condition is not advised, and in some cases may be considered unethical or even illegal.

Due to the lack of specificity in therapy types, and the practice of combining therapy and non-therapy services in current research, for this section of the book the term "equine-assisted interactions" will be used to describe the wide range of therapy and non-therapy services studied.

Literature or Systematic Reviews

Systematic and literature reviews are very important when establishing a sound basis for evaluating a clinical practice. As Schlosser (2006) points out:

> The efficacy or effectiveness of a rehabilitation intervention is rarely established in a convincing manner with only one study. In fact, multiple studies are needed that are then synthesized to offer sound evidence in support of or to reject an intervention.
>
> (p. 2)

Systematic reviews analyze and synthesize the quality and outcomes of many different research projects. This process minimizes biases, and provides the most scientifically rigorous foundation from which to make benefits claims.

Out of 227 articles, 23 literature or systematic reviews were identified. In a developing area of study such as this, the large number of literature or systematic reviews is notable. Ten of these reviews focused on equine-assisted interactions for mental health use (Frewin & Gardiner, 2005; Lentini & Knox, 2009; Smith-Osborne & Selby, 2010; Cantin & Marshall-Lucette, 2011; Bachi, 2012; Anestis, et al., 2014; Lentini & Knox, 2015; Kendall, et al., 2015; Lee, et al., 2016; Carlsson, 2016b). Seven reviewed the use of equine-assisted interactions for cerebral palsy (Bond, 2007; Snider, et al., 2007; Sterba, 2007; Zadnikar & Kastrin, 2011; Tseng, et al., 2012; Whalen & Case-Smith, 2012; Wang, et al., 2015), and the remaining reviews addressed musculoskeletal disorders (Angoules, et al., 2015), multiple sclerosis (Bronson, et al., 2010), prison populations (Bachi, 2013), and the general benefits of therapeutic interactions with horses (MacKinnon, et al., 1995; Thompson, et al., 2012, Selby & Smith-Osborne, 2013).

The majority of the reviews state the tentatively hopeful, but inconclusive nature of the research, mostly due to methodological issues (MacKinnon, 1995; Whalen & Case-Smith, 2012; Tseng, et al., 2012; Bachi, 2012; Anestis, et al., 2014; Kendall, et al., 2015; Angoules, et al., 2015; Lentini & Knox, 2015; Wang, et al., 2015; Lee, et al., 2016; Carlsson, 2016b). The results of these reviews suggest the raising popularity of this novel treatment is not due to the overwhelmingly positive results of empirical investigation.

Carlsson (2016b) writes, "Not all studies indicate positive effects and the results are rarely significant" (p. 3). Kendell, et al. (2015) report, "The current state of the literature does not allow us to definitively conclude that equine-assisted interactions are efficacious" (p. 57), and Angoules, et al. (2015) state, "In conclusion, more well-designed studies are required to reach to safe conclusions about the position of hippotherapy in the treatment of the abovementioned health problems" (p. 296).

Challenges With Research

After reading over 200 published, peer-reviewed journal articles about every type of equine-assisted interaction, it is clear that issues with research methodology impact the quality and validity of the data. This finding is supported by nearly every systematic or literature review conducted to date (MacKinnon, et al., 1995; Bond, 2007; Lentini & Knox, 2009; Smith-Osborne & Selby, 2010; Cantin & Marshall-Lucette, 2011; Bachi, 2012; Whalen & Case-Smith, 2012; Tseng, et al., 2012; Selby & Smith-Osborne, 2013; Anestis, et al., 2014; Kendall, et al., 2015; Angoules, et al., 2015; Lentini & Knox, 2015; Wang, et al., 2015; Lee, et al., 2016; Carlsson, 2016b).

Interestingly, although reviewers have pointed out methodological shortcomings from the earliest reports (MacKinnon, et al., 1995; Pauw, 2000), the same issues seem to be repeated even in much of the recent research. Given the fact that methodological challenges can significantly compromise the validity of research, it is of great importance that both researchers and providers become more keenly aware of these issues, and work to remedy them whenever possible. Included here is a brief overview of the most common methodological issues addressed in current systematic or literature reviews.

Defining and Combining Treatment Types

In order to effectively study equine-assisted therapy, whatever type of therapy or treatment strategy or model used must be clearly defined and have a consistent (and replicable) treatment protocol in place (Wilson & Barker, 2003; Debuse et al., 2005; Bachi, 2012; Whalen & Case-Smith, 2012; Anestis, et al., 2014; Kendall, et al., 2015).

In many cases, the type of treatment utilized, the qualifications and licensure of the professional providing the service, the presenting concerns of research participants, and the design of the interaction aren't clearly defined or operationalized (Whalen & Case-Smith, 2012; Lee, et al., 2016).

Whalen & Case-Smith (2012) state, "Limitations of these studies include lack of specificity and detail in descriptions of the intervention" (p. 239), and they go on to note, "This review found that hippotherapy and THR [adaptive riding] trials lack consistency in intervention protocols. Not a single study used the same treatment duration and frequency" (p. 240).

Reviews also speak to the confusion caused by combining non-therapy and therapy services used to treat physical or mental health conditions (Snider, et al., 2007; Bachi, 2012; Kendell, et al., 2015; Wang, et al., 2015; Lee, et al., 2016). For example, many studies compare the effectiveness of using hippotherapy which is provided by a licensed healthcare professional, to a non-therapy service like adaptive riding provided by a non-licensed adaptive riding instructor for the treatment of various physical health conditions (Bond, 2007; Sterba, 2007; Bass et al., 2009; Munoz-Lasa, et al., 2011). In other cases, non-therapy services like equine-assisted learning are confused with therapy services, and are used to treat serious mental health conditions (Ewing, et al., 2007; Duncan, et al., 2014; Frederick, et al., 2015).

At present, a significant number of research projects investigate non-therapy approaches used to treat physical and mental health conditions. This is concerning, as non-therapy services are completely different from therapy services in design and implementation. Therefore, licensed healthcare professionals cannot, in good faith, use the results of these studies to validate or support their own services.

Sample Sizes and Generalizability of Results

Researchers comment that existing equine-assisted therapy studies are routinely limited by small sample sizes (Pauw, 2000; Wilson & Barker, 2003; Park, et al., 2013; Burgon, 2014; Kendall, et al., 2015; Lentini & Knox, 2015; Earles, et al., 2015; Lee, et al., 2016).

In theory, sample sizes must allow the statistics to be safely extrapolated to an entire population. If a sample selection is not representative of the larger population, the validity or generalizability of the research may be compromised (Kukull & Ganguli, 2012).

Burgon (2014) states, "It is acknowledged that the small sample size of this study makes drawing generalizations across populations limited" (p. 14). In another example, Kern-Godal, et al. (2016a) report, "Our findings are derived from a naturalistic study that used translated data from a small number of participants to explore their specific experience within a specific context. Transferability to other settings cannot be assumed" (p. 105). In both of these cases, the quality of the research isn't in question. Rather, these examples bring to light the idea that sample sizes can impact generalizability.

One of the ways to increase sample size is to use a multi-center approach. However, due to the significant differences in the applications of the treatment approach, and a lack of standardization in the tools used to measure outcomes, this has yet to be an effective option.

Control Groups

Another common critique of existing equine-assisted therapy research is the lack of control groups (Bachi, 2012; Whalen & Case-Smith, 2012; Anestis, et al., 2014; Kendall, et al., 2015; Park, et al., 2013). In some cases, the design of the research leads to the use of participants as their own control, while in others, control groups are necessary.

If control groups are used, in many cases the experimental group and the control group lack needed similarity (e.g. experimental group takes place at a farm doing equine-assisted psychotherapy and control group takes place at the school doing in-office group counseling). This challenge could be rectified by providing one farm-based physical, occupational, speech, or mental health therapy that does not include horses and one that does. This would help separate out and identify the role of the horse as a potential agent of change (Anestis, et al., 2014).

As researcher Ann Kern-Godal points out:

> Many studies seem to imply a causal relationship between the intervention and the positive outcomes reported. In most cases this is inaccurate and misleading, not least because few studies involve random allocation of participants to the intervention or to an alternative

comparable therapy. There are, however, exceptions such as Nurenberg, et al. (2015) which, in addition to having valuable results, provides useful "how to" lessons in research design.

(personal correspondence, May 4, 2017)

Novel Effects and Issues With Controlling Variabilities

Equine-assisted therapy is novel to most research participants. For most, it is an exciting and stimulating experience like nothing they have engaged in before. Many may be new to horses, and may not be used to the farm milieu. This creates complications for researchers.

The variabilities that could exist in the treatment environment are many, difficult to control, and impossible to replicate in another non-farm-based treatment environment. Although it is highly unlikely researchers will ever be able to control for all the possible variabilities, they can at least compare similar services as previously mentioned (Wilson & Barker, 2003; Anestis, et al., 2014; Borgi, et al., 2016). As Anestis, et al. (2014) suggests, other large, familiar farm animals could be used in the same setting as the equine-assisted therapy service, or the same type of therapy could be provided with one group including horses while the other does not.

Other variabilities include whether or not the participant engages in other forms of therapy during the provision of the equine-assisted therapy service (Pauw, 2000). It is unclear from many of these studies if equine-assisted therapy was used as an adjunctive service or a stand-alone therapy. Without this information, it is nearly impossible to ascertain if, in fact, equine-assisted therapy was the reason for the improvement, or if the improvement was caused by the combination of services.

Measuring Outcomes

For research studies to be considered valid or sound, measurements must be precise, accurate, and reproducible (Wilson & Barker, 2003). These tools must also be sensitive and responsive to the variables the researcher desires to measure (Debuse, et al., 2005).

Rosenbaum (2009) reports on the lack of statistically significant finding in a randomized clinical trial (RCT) conducted by Elise Davis and colleagues. He notes:

> It is also possible that the models we use to explain what our therapies are expected to do may be wrong. In the case of hippotherapy there may be benefits that were not thought about and therefore not measured in this study.

(p. 88)

In essence, he is speaking to the challenges inherent in choosing not only the right variables to measure, but also the right instrument to measure them with.

As Pauw (2000) points, out "Though the same variables were measured in different studies, different types of apparatus were used. This impedes the pooling of data from different studies and makes it more difficult to compare them" (p. 525). Pauw is referring to multiplicity of instruments used for data collection in equine-assisted therapy research. She is concerned with this especially because there is little standardization between the various tools used, and thus it is nearly impossible to consider a multi-center research project approach as a means to increase sample sizes (Pauw, 2000).

Wilson & Barker (2003) suggest strategies for increasing both precision and accuracy including to:

> operationally define and standardize all methods in the study, use standardized instruments that have been shown to both measure consistently across time (reliability) and accurately measure the construct of interest (validity), train and certify observers, assess agreement between any raters (interrater reliability), refine and automate instruments, and use the mean of repeated measurements [this is not included in the process of establishing accuracy].
>
> (p. 24)

Practitioner-Researcher Bias in Equine-Assisted Therapy

In equine-assisted therapy research, it is common to see practitioners both provide the service and conduct the research. Supporters of the practitioner-researcher approach argue that complete objectivity is impossible, and the benefits of this type of research such as the researcher's familiarity with the topic and with the population can outweigh the challenges. Those who object suggest these practitioner-researchers may misinterpret data because of personal bias, or make assumptions based upon a subconscious or conscious desire to support their own work, or prove their services are effective (Rooney, 2005).

Carlsson (2016b) comments on practitioner-researchers bias, stating, "Most who research human-horse relations are themselves biased and many practitioners are very enthusiastic about the field. It is possible that some are driven and influenced by their own relationships with horses" (p. 20). Quite simply put, it is plausible that the researcher's love of horses or passion about equine-assisted therapy may influence the design of the research, the interpretation of data, or even the outcomes of the research.

This may be evidenced by a practice common to equine-assisted interaction research in which therapists who provide the service also collect the treatment outcome ratings from patients (Anestis, et al., 2014). By doing this, the therapist may unintentionally convey their expectations or hopes related to treatment outcomes. Given the power differential between patients and healthcare providers, the participants may be influenced by the therapist, providing him/her with more positive responses than the participant actually experienced. As the researchers point out, the simple remedy to this problem is to employ non-biased raters who are not stakeholders in the research (Anestis, et al., 2014).

Another way in which the practitioner-researcher bias may influence research includes the topics chosen for research projects. As clearly evidenced by existing research, the focus is on "proving" that equine-assisted therapy is effective for a variety of conditions. To date, no research could be located that investigates if the horse is actually the primary factor causing change in humans, or if other factors are at play that significantly influence the research outcomes. Furthermore, no current research investigates if there are populations for whom equine-assisted therapy is *not* advantageous. Although the results of these types of studies may be uncomfortable, this information is essential in advancing the level of scientific knowledge.

An important area of personal bias to consider is if the researcher stands to gain or lose financially or professionally from the outcomes of the research. For example, if the researcher also runs an equine-assisted therapy business, and the outcome of the research shows that equine-assisted therapy isn't advantageous to a specific population he/she currently serves, how might that discovery impact business or his/her professional reputation?

As Mehra (2002) and Rooney (2005) suggest, one of the most important ways for researchers to address potential biases is through honest and open personal reflection, and discussions or supervision with peers and other professionals. Another way to address the issue of personal bias is through the use of self-disclosure, documenting what personal biases the researcher may hold so that readers can view the results through the particular researchers' personal lens.

Research Specific to Conditions or Populations

Although much of the existing research may be compromised due to the previously mentioned methodological issues, it is still important to understand the scope of research conducted to date related to various conditions and populations treated by equine-assisted interactions.

In this section, the reader will be introduced to current research by population or condition. Only those conditions or populations that have been investigated by five or more studies published in a peer-reviewed journal are included in this review. This organizational strategy clearly demonstrates which areas are currently being studied, and encourages readers to identify the gaps in existing research.

Cerebral Palsy

Beyond a doubt, cerebral palsy is the most researched of all possible conditions purportedly treated by an equine-assisted interaction. Forty-two research studies with outcomes written in English and published in peer-reviewed scientific journals were identified during the literature review conducted for this book. A number of systematic (or literature) reviews have also been conducted evaluating the quality and quantity of evidence supporting the benefits claims associated with equine-assisted interactions and cerebral palsy (Bond, 2007; Snider, et al., 2007; Sterba, 2007; Zadnikar & Kastrin, 2011; Whalen & Case-Smith, 2012; Tseng, et al., 2012; Wang, et al., 2015).

All of these reviews suggest that individuals with cerebral palsy may receive some benefits from equine-assisted interactions, although researchers do not appear to agree upon exactly what these benefits are, or who might be best served by the intervention. Beyond this disagreement, all of the reviews certainly do agree that challenges with research design impair outcomes.

Wang, et al. (2015) report:

> HT/THR/AS seems to improve the total score of the gross motor function via improvement of the walking, running, and jumping dimension. However, it is not likely to benefit the symmetry of postural muscle activity. Studies included in this review lack a sufficient number of subjects, and the number of high-quality RCTs is limited, which warrants further evaluation of these modalities using large-scale well-designed RCTs.
>
> (p. 221)

Tseng, et al. (2012) state, "Our meta-analysis corroborated the reported efficacy of HPOT [hippotherapy] on normalizing hip adductor muscle activity" (p. 98). But, they also state, "Our study could not confirm that any significant change occurred regarding gross motor activity status after long-term HPOT and TR (total riding time, 8–22 h) in children with spastic CP" (p. 98). With regard to study design, they state, "The methodological shortcomings identified in each study may also have had the potential to influence our findings" (p. 98).

Whalen & Case-Smith (2012) suggest:

> Although the current level of evidence remains limited, our synthesis identified that children with spastic CP, aged 4 years and above, are likely to have significant improvements with moderate to large treatment effects on gross motor function and mobility as a result of hippotherapy and THR [therapeutic riding].
>
> (p. 239)

However, they go on to state, "This review found that hippotherapy and THR [therapeutic riding] trials lack consistency in intervention protocols. Not a single study used the same treatment duration and frequency. A manualized approach for hippotherapy and THR is needed" (p. 240). Due to the challenges with research design, they conclude, "It is not clear who benefits from hippotherapy and THR or how outcomes may vary for children with different types or severity levels of CP" (p. 240).

Finally, both Tseng, et al. (2012) and Snider et al. (2007) found that hippotherapy may improve postural control and muscle tone in children with CP, but adaptive riding does not.

In 25 of the 42 papers, hippotherapy provided by a licensed healthcare professional was used as the treatment intervention (McGibbon, et al., 1998; Kulkarni-Lambore, et al., 2001; Benda, et al., 2003; Casady & Nichols-Larsen, 2004; Hamill, et al., 2007; McGibbon, et al., 2009; Debuse, et al., 2009; McGee & Reese, 2009; Shurtleff, et al., 2009; Shurtleff, et al., 2010; Honkavaara & Rintala, 2010; Zadnikar & Kastrin, 2011; Kwon, et al., 2011; Frank, et al., 2011; Shurtleff, 2012; Chang, et al., 2012; Kang, et al., 2012; El-Meniawy & Thabet, 2012; Yokoyama, et al., 2013; Manikowska, et al., 2013; Park, et al., 2014; Baik, et al., 2014; Krejčí, et al., 2015; Angsupaisal, et al., 2015; Kwon, et al., 2015). In most of these cases, the articles do not implicitly state what type of therapy was used (i.e. physical, occupational, or speech therapy), or identify the specific qualifications of the individuals who provided it. The remaining 17 articles investigated the use of adaptive riding or simulated hippotherapy provided on a mechanical horse.

Autism Spectrum Disorder

With an identified 24 published research papers, autism appears to be the second most researched condition to be treated by an equine-assisted interaction. No systematic reviews have been conducted limited to research on autism. However, Anestis, et al. (2014), Lentini & Knox (2015), and Kendall, et al. (2015) provide some synthesis in their broader reviews.

Generally, these reviews seem to show that equine-assisted interactions may be beneficial in reducing some symptoms of autism like inattention, distractibility, and avoidant behaviors, and may increase self-regulation, social interaction, social skills, and positive parent-child relationships (Lentini & Knox, 2015; Kendall, et al., 2015).

Only three of the twenty-four articles used a form of regulated therapy provided by a licensed healthcare professional (Taylor, et al., 2009; Memishevikj & Hodzhikj, 2010; Ajzenman, 2013), and in all three cases, services were provided by licensed occupational therapists or certified occupational therapy assistants. The remaining studies report that adaptive (therapeutic) riding or equine-assisted learning was used as the treatment method, and the services were conducted by an adaptive riding instructor or an equine-assisted learning instructor rather than a trained therapist.

Ajzenman's (2013) pilot study included 12 weeks of hippotherapy for six youth diagnosed with autism (aged 5–12). Ajzenman reports, "The results suggest that postural control, adaptive behaviors, and participation in everyday activities improved for children with ASD after involvement in a 12-wk HPOT [hippotherapy] intervention" (p. 659).

Memishevikj & Hodzhikj (2010) used an occupational therapy approach and noted that the improvements their study participants demonstrated in the areas of speech, socialization, and sensory/ cognitive awareness were not carried over in children with severe autism.

Gabriels, et al. (2015) conducted the first, large-scale randomized control trial involving 116 participants (aged 6–16) using a 10-week course of adaptive riding and a control group conducted at the farm using non-horse activities. They report, "Results show significant postintervention improvements in the THR [therapeutic riding] group compared to the BA control on the Irritability and Hyperactivity subscales of the ABC-C36 beginning by the fifth week of intervention" (p. 547).

Jenkins & DiGennaro Reed (2013) also used adaptive (therapeutic) riding and state:

> The results suggest that THR [therapeutic riding] did not produce clinically significant effects on participant affect, off-task behavior, problem behavior, compliance, or language (i.e., spontaneous initiations and responses to initiations) from baseline to treatment during center-based activities and home observations. The findings from the time-series analysis suggest that THR is not an effective intervention to improve performance on these dependent variables.
>
> (p. 738)

These researchers also suggest that parents consider therapeutic (adaptive) riding to be a leisure activity rather than a treatment for autism. These researchers used a multiple baseline across participants' design and a wait-list control group for comparison purposes. The outcome of this research was significantly different than other studies.

Similar to studies done on cerebral palsy, issues with research methodology likely impede results. There is little if any standardization between the design of the clinical activities and the sample sizes tend to be small and many lack control groups (Jenkins & DiGennaro Reed, 2013; Anestis, et al., 2014, Lanning, et al., 2014).

At-Risk Youth

Sixteen studies specific to "at-risk" youth were identified in the literature review. No specific systematic reviews have been conducted related to this population, but seven of the 23 reviews include commentary or a section dedicated to at-risk youth and equine-assisted interactions (Cantin & Marshall-Lucette, 2011; Bachi, 2012; Selby & Smith-Osborne, 2013; Anestis, et al., 2014; Kendall, et al., 2015; Lentini & Knox, 2015; Lee, et al., 2016).

Decreases in behavioral problems, criminal activities, and drug use have been noted (Bachi, 2012; Lentini & Knox, 2015), and increases in self-esteem, self-confidence, empathy, trust, and positive social interactions are also reported (Bachi, 2012; Kendall, et al., 2015; Lentini & Knox, 2015). Lentini & Knox (2015) state that studies resulted in "mild to moderate improvements in self-esteem, social development, self-control, transferrable skills, reduced adjudications, and reduced maladaptive behavior" (p. 292).

Both Bachi (2012) and Kendall, et al. (2015) report that although no statistical differences could be ascertained between the control group and the equine-assisted interaction group, a trend was observed towards increased self-control, trust, and life satisfaction in several studies.

Eight of the 16 studies utilized an equine-assisted mental health approach (Bowers & MacDonald, 2001; Trotter, et al., 2008; Bachi, et al., 2011; Drinkhouse, et al., 2012; Maujean, et al., 2013; Boshoff, et al., 2015; Kendall & Maujean, 2015; Wilkie, et al., 2016), two clearly identified using equine-assisted learning (Frederick, et al., 2015; Saggers & Strachan, 2016), and the remaining studies were unclear if a therapy or non-therapy approach was applied, or did not indicate that a licensed mental health professional provided the service (Kaiser, et al., 2006; Burgon, 2011; Holmes, et al., 2012; Waite & Bourke, 2013; Burgon, 2014; Gibbons, et al., 2016).

Lee, et al. (2016) report when non-therapy equine-assisted learning was used in an attempt to treat depressive symptoms (as in Frederick, et al., 2015), "the treatment group did not significantly increase from the pretest to posttest on the Generalised Self-Efficacy Scale and did not significantly decrease from pretest to posttest on the Major Depression Inventory" (p. 242–243). They note the study design only included "five EAL sessions to deal with adolescents' deep emotional problems, such as depression and low self-efficacy" (p. 242), and suggest that a mental health method like equine-assisted psychotherapy probably should have been used when attempting to address a serious mental health issue like depression.

Clearly, some individuals who are considered "at-risk" may benefit from a non-therapy program that teaches life skills, addresses learning differences, or helps to enhance self-esteem by hands-on learning activities (Burgon, 2014). However, there is a significant difference between this focus, and the use of a non-therapy service to treat serious mental health conditions.

The term "at-risk" is extremely vague, and without a clear, measureable definition is it difficult to know if the equine-assisted interaction was effective for a specific condition. This—coupled with the challenges caused by the use of a non-therapy equine-assisted interaction to treat serious mental health conditions—makes understanding or interpreting the current data difficult.

Non-Combat PTSD, Trauma, and Abuse

Fourteen studies were identified that investigated equine-assisted interactions as a treatment for non-combat PTSD, trauma, and abuse. No systematic reviews could be found specific to these conditions. In light of this, Bachi (2012), Selby & Smith-Osborne (2013), and Lentini & Knox (2015) provide some insight in the context of their broader reviews.

Bachi (2012) reports that equine-assisted activities and therapies (EAAT) may be used to serve diverse populations including adult female survivors of abuse and people recovering from trauma. She states, "However, most of these studies are inconclusive, as they fail to use a control group" (p. 370).

Selby & Smith-Osborne (2013) suggest that although limited, the research related to non-combat PTSD, trauma, or abuse could be promising, showing clinically significant, but not statically significant, outcomes. However, these researchers also report issues with research methodology, including a lack of control groups and small sample sizes.

Lentini & Knox (2015) include a section titled "other populations" and include sexual abuse and PTSD. They note, "Outcomes of these studies indicated improvements in 'warm emotion,' quality of life, empowerment, reduced anxiety, reduced depression, increased enthusiasm, and increases in happiness" (p. 293).

Earles, et al. (2015) examined the effects of interacting with horses on insight and mindfulness, theorizing that an increase in these two areas may decrease symptoms of anxiety and PTSD. The researchers report "Participants' PTSD symptoms, emotional distress, anxiety symptoms, depression symptoms, and alcohol use decreased significantly following program participation. Participants' mindfulness increased following treatment" (p. 150). But, they also note, "There were no significant changes in physical health, proactive coping, general perceived self-efficacy, social support, life satisfaction, or optimism" (p. 150).

Thirteen of the 14 studies identified in the literature review were conducted as a form of psychotherapy or mental health treatment (Schultz, et al., 2007; Porter-Wenzlaff, 2007; Meinersmann, et al., 2008; Yorke, et al., 2008; Froeschle, 2009; Signal, et al., 2013; Yorke, et al., 2013; Whittlesey-Jerome, 2014; Kemp, et al., 2014; Earles, et al., 2015; Schroeder & Stroud, 2015; McCullough, et al., 2015; Johansen, et al., 2016). The articles were not always clear as to the qualifications of the providers.

There is one example of non-mental health providers offering hippotherapy services to participants with a history of sexual and emotional abuse (Guerino, et al., 2015); this approach is highly cautionary as PTSD, trauma, and abuse are complicated mental health conditions that must be treated carefully to avoid causing additional harm.

The Elderly

Ten studies were located that investigated the effects of equine-assisted interactions for elderly populations. Two of these studies used a horseback riding simulator (Kim, et al., 2013; Kim & Lee, 2015) and the rest were conducted with living horses in either a hippotherapy or adaptive riding setting (de Araújo, et al., 2011; de Araújo, et al., 2013; Homnick, et al., 2013; Wehofer, et al., 2013; Dabelko-Schoeny, et al., 2014; Kim & Lee, 2014; Homnick, et al., 2015; Cho, et al., 2015).

Angoules, et al. (2015) reviewed the results of four of the live horse studies identified in this literature review. They state, "Conclusively there is promising evidence that hippotherapy promotes balance in the elderly contributing in fall prevention" (p. 293).

This statement is further validated by the results of additional research which shows improvements in balance (de Araújo, et al., 2013; Homnick, et al., 2013; Wehofer, et al., 2013; Kim & Lee, 2014), increased muscle strength (Wehofer, et al., 2013; de Araújo, et al., 2013), increased perception of general health (Homnick, et al., 2013), and the ability to recover after a fall (Wehofer, et al., 2013).

The only study that did not show positive results was conducted by de Araújo, et al. (2011). The researchers report they were unable to determine any significant differences at that time due to the short length of treatment. However, de Araújo conducted a follow up study in 2013 that did show positive results (de Araújo, et al., 2013).

Another area of study related to the elderly includes depression and dementia. Cho, et al. (2015) discovered that riding horses as a form of exercise increased serotonin and cortisol levels in elderly populations, and Dabelko-Schoeny, et al. (2014) learned that an equine-assisted interaction decreased behavioral problems.

Dabelko-Schoeny, et al. (2014) state:

> Pre-intervention measures showed that participants exhibited lower levels of disruptive behaviors compared with the control group on the days they were scheduled to work with the horses. Interestingly, cortisol levels, used as a physiological measure of coping with stress, were elevated after the intervention in participants with higher Mini Mental State Examination scores.
>
> (p. 141)

4 of 10 studies related to elderly populations used hippotherapy (de Araújo, et al., 2011; de Araújo, et al., 2013; Wehofer, et al., 2013; Kim & Lee, 2014), but it was not clear what type of licensed professional provided

the treatment. The remaining six studies used adaptive riding, "horseback riding exercise," or a mechanical horse to simulate horseback riding.

Given the growing number of elderly people in the United States, and the significant mental, behavioral, and physical healthcare needs this population presents, it seems there is an opportunity for licensed professionals (especially mental health professionals) who provide equine-assisted therapy to consider ways to include these individuals in their clinical services. Of course, safety is of the utmost importance with this population, and activities should be designed with the possible fragility of the patients in mind. Patient health screening prior to admittance is also highly recommended, and horses should be chosen who are well seasoned and calm.

Psychiatric Conditions or Mental Illness

Ten studies were identified that investigate equine-assisted interactions as a potential treatment for psychiatric conditions, severe behavioral conditions, or mental illness. Although some systemic reviews make mention of studies related to these conditions (Cantin & Marshall-Lucette, 2011; Selby & Smith-Osborne, 2013; Anestis, et al., 2014; Kendall, et al., 2015), none shed much light on the effectiveness of the treatment approach.

Of the 10 studies identified in this literature review, four included a variety of patients with unspecified "psychiatric disorders" (Bizub, et. al., 2003; Johansen & Malt, 2010; Nurenberg, et al., 2013; Nurenberg, et al., 2015), three were specific to the effects of equine-assisted interactions on patients diagnosed with schizophrenia or schizoaffective disorder (Cerino, et al., 2011; Corring, et al., 2013; Seredova, et al., 2016), and three studies addressed the use of equine-assisted interactions for children with severe mental illness (Ewing, et al., 2007; Chardonnens, 2009; Ansorge & Sudres, 2011).

Four of these studies used a form of psychotherapy as the equine-assisted interaction (Chardonnens, 2009; Johansen & Malt, 2010; Nurenberg, et al., 2013; Nurenberg, et al., 2015). Three used adaptive riding (Bizub & Davidson, 2003; Cerino, et al., 2011; Corring, et al., 2013), one used hippotherapy (Seredova, et al., 2016), and one used equine-assisted learning (Ewing, et al., 2007). In the final study, it was not clear what method was used (Ansorge & Sudres, 2011). In the studies that used adaptive riding, it appears trained clinical staff with mental health experience were included.

Ewing, et al. (2007) was the only study to report a lack of any significant positive change in the areas of self-esteem, empathy, depression, internal locus of control, or loneliness after equine-assisted learning. Although these researchers provide a number of possible reasons for the lack of positive results, one key area that seems most likely is the choice to use the non-therapy approach of equine-assisted learning to address a population suffering from severe emotional disorders.

According to researchers, their study participants included a young girl diagnosed with PTSD caused by sexual assault, physical violence, and emotional abuse; another girl with a history of sexual abuse and severe behavioral issues; a young man diagnosed with severe ADHD and a tendency towards pryomania, panic, and running away; and another boy with "situational depression" caused by his father's aggression and physical violence towards the boy's mother. The severity of these diagnoses, and symptomology presented by these four participants suggest that mental health services provided by licensed professionals would probably have been indicated rather than a non-therapy service.

With exception of Ewing, et al. (2007), generally the results of the studies show positive improvements in reducing symptomology. However, many of the studies are compromised because of methodological issues like no control groups, small sample sizes, and the overall design of the research (Anestis, et al., 2014). That being said, the existing research provides a starting point from which to further investigate the possible effects of equine-assisted interactions for patients diagnosed with psychiatric conditions.

Stroke

Eight published studies examine the effects of equine-assisted interactions on patients recovering from a stroke. Of those eight papers, five were conducted using a horseback riding simulator (Park, et al., 2013; Sung, et al., 2013; Baek & Kim, 2014; Kim, et al., 2014; Kim & D.-K. Lee, 2015). Two used adaptive riding (Bunketorp Käll, et al., 2012; Beinotti, et al., 2013) and only one studied the effects of hippotherapy conducted with living horses (Beinotti, et al., 2010). In this study, it was not clear what type of licensed therapist provided the treatment. No systemic reviews were identified that included the use of equine-assisted interactions for stroke patients.

Five of the seven studies investigated balance and gait in recovering stroke patients (Beinotti, et al., 2010; Park, et al., 2013; Sung, et al., 2013; Baek & Kim, 2014; Kim, et al., 2014; Kim & Lee, 2015). One of the studies examined quality of life (Beinotti, et al., 2013), and another considered the effects of combining rhythm and music with adaptive riding to improve overall health status and functioning of patients recovering from a stroke (Bunketorp Käll, et al., 2012).

Both Beinotti, et al. (2010) and Baek & Kim (2014) found that the outcomes of the experimental group were significantly different from those of the control group. Beinotti, et al. (2010) report:

> In conclusion, the hippotherapy associated with conventional physical therapy has proved to be a good resource in the treatment of gait training for hemiparetic patients after stroke. The improvements in

motor impairment of lower limbs, the independence of ambulation, of cadence and speed confirm this finding. Thus the patients in the experimental group showed a greater approximation of the normal gait standard than the control group.

(p. 913)

Baek & Kim (2014) agree, stating, "The differences between the two groups were not significant before the experiment, but were statistically significant ($p < 0.05$) after the intervention" (p. 1294), leading them to conclude, "To improve stroke patients' balance ability, diverse uses of horse riding simulation training should be considered" (p. 1295).

Finally, Beinotti, et al. (2013) felt that their results indicated improvement in quality of life for stroke patients when an equine-assisted interaction was used with a conventional physiotherapy treatment approach. Due to methodological limitations, it is not clear if these benefits could be generalized to an equine-assisted interaction if used alone.

Even through the quality of the existing research is high, the recommendations included in the studies still suggest some methodological issues like small sample sizes and challenges controlling for the many variables possible. Obviously, given the small number of research projects conducted to date, additional research is needed to establish a conclusive report.

Veterans and Active Military Personnel

Seven studies were identified that investigate the role of equine-assisted interactions in the treatment of returning veterans or active military personnel, all of which appear to suffer from significant methodological issues. Four are pilot studies (Lanning & Krenek, 2013; Duncan, et al., 2014; Burton & Burge, 2015; Ferruolo, 2015) with small sample sizes, and one took place as part of an experiential learning course at a university where students were allowed to assist in helping veterans learn to work with horses and outcomes seemed more related to benefits sustained by the students than the veterans (Newton-Cromwell, et al., 2015). The remaining two are single-participant case studies (Asselin, et al., 2012; Nevins, et al., 2013).

Three of the studies focused on mental health issues and appeared to use a form of equine-assisted mental health to address post-traumatic stress disorder (Burton & Burge, 2015), depression, anxiety and reintegration issues (Ferruolo, 2015), and general psychological functioning (Nevins, et al., 2013). Two studies investigated the use of adaptive riding for veterans to address spinal cord injury (Asselin, et al., 2012) and overall quality of life (Lanning & Krenek, 2013), and one used equine-assisted learning to treat symptoms of PTSD (Duncan, et al., 2014). It is important to note that no studies could be identified at this time that investigate the use of hippotherapy provided by licensed physical, occupational, or speech therapists for veterans or active military personnel.

According to the published studies, a total of fewer than 80 veterans or active military personnel have participated in equine-assisted interaction research specific to this population to date. Given that veterans returning home after deployment and active military personnel are considered a highly vulnerable population for whom trauma, suicide, domestic issues, substance abuse, crime, and homelessness are complicating factors (SAMHSA, 2016), there is a great need for additional high-quality research related to the efficacy of providing equine-assisted therapy for this population.

Anestis, et al. (2014) go as far as to say in their systematic review of existing research:

> We further urge major organizations, such as the United States Armed Forces and United States Department of Veterans Affairs, to hold off on the implementation of ERT [equine-related treatment] programs on a wide-scale basis unless and until a strong research foundation for this treatment emerges.
>
> (p. 15)

Although this author does not support the recommendation to cease all equine-assisted interactions with military populations, it is of the utmost importance that those offering equine-assisted interactions to returning veterans or active military personnel do so with great care, respect, and caution. It would be considered unethical for individuals to provide services outside of their scope of practice, or without prior experience, education, and training specific to this population to offer services due to the highly vulnerable nature of the clientele.

Non-mental health providers working with this population are urged to consider a team approach that includes a licensed mental health professional additionally trained and experienced in this area, and should not advertise that they offer "treatment" for mental or physical health diagnoses.

Due to the complex and co-existing nature of the conditions many veterans and active military personnel experience, professionals are cautioned about the transferability of research results. Choosing the right equine-assisted interaction based upon presenting conditions is very important with this population. It should not be assumed that just any equine-assisted interaction, or provider, is right for veterans or active military personnel.

Multiple Sclerosis

Six studies were located that address the use of equine-assisted interactions for the treatment of multiple sclerosis. One systematic review was conducted related to multiple sclerosis, but this review only included three studies, none of which were specific to multiple sclerosis (Bronson, et al., 2010).

Five of the six studies were conducted using hippotherapy (Hammer, et al., 2005; Silkwood-Sherer & Warmbier, 2007; Menezes, et al., 2013; Gencheva, et al., 2015; Lindroth, et al., 2015) and only one (Munoz-Lasa, et al., 2011) used a form of adaptive riding but state the instructors "worked closely with health professionals" (p. 463). It is unclear from the research which type of licensed professionals provided the hippotherapy services in all cases.

Although existing research seems to suggest that equine-assisted interactions might be helpful in treating this condition, limited research, small sample sizes, and complications caused by the diversity and multiplicity of symptoms make it difficult to provide definitive conclusions (Hammer, et al., 2005; Silkwood-Sherer & Warmbier, 2007; Munoz-Lasa, et al., 2011; Menezes, et al., 2013; Gencheva, et al., 2015; Lindroth, et al., 2015).

Addictions and Chemical Dependency

Six published research studies could be identified during this literature review that investigated the use of equine-assisted interactions for the treatment of addictions or chemical dependency. These conditions were also only briefly mentioned in current reviews (Cantin & Marshall-Lucette, 2011; Selby & Smith-Osborne, 2013; Anestis, et al., 2014), but no conclusive outcomes could be extracted.

Of the six research studies, three were conducted in Canada using a culturally-based equine-assisted learning program in the treatment of First Nations youth struggling with solvent abuse (Dell, et al., 2008; Dell, et al., 2011; Adams, et al., 2015), and three were conducted in Norway using a form of equine-assisted mental health to treat participants ranging in age from 16–30 who were involved in various stages of substance use treatment (Kern-Godal, et al., 2015; Kern-Godal, et al., 2016a; Kern-Godal, et al., 2016b).

The Norwegian studies examined if patients who participated in an equine-assisted interactionwere more likely to remain and complete their treatment for substance use disorders. In their first study, the researchers found a highly significant association between attending the equine-assisted interaction and retention and completion of treatment (Kern-Godal, et al., 2015). Two subsequent studies explored the contributing factors to these findings, discovering that both the horse and the stable psychosocial context were important components in the positive outcomes (Kern-Godal, et al., 2016a; Kern-Godal, et al., 2016b).

An emerging theme in four of the studies show research participants believed the farm was a safe space or context in which they could communicate, connect, and feel accepted and empowered (Dell, et al., 2011; Adams, et al., 2015; Kern-Godal, et al., 2016a; Kern-Godal, et al., 2016b).

Attention-Deficit/Hyperactivity Disorder

Five studies were identified specific to attention-deficit/hyperactivity disorder (ADHD) and equine-assisted interactions. ADHD is briefly mentioned in two systemic reviews (Anestis, et al., 2014; Kendall, et al., 2015). Both these systematic reviews include only one study conducted on ADHD (Cuypers, et al., 2011). The remaining four included here probably were not published at the time of either of these reviews.

The current research includes one pilot study on behavior, quality of life, and motor performance (Cuypers, et al., 2011), another pilot study on resting-state brain function (Yoo, et al., 2016), one controlled study on changes in gate balance and brain connectivity (Hyun, et al., 2016), and one prospective, open-label trial on the possible improvement of core ADHD symptoms (Jang, et al., 2015). The fifth study (Oh, et al., 2015) wasn't available in full text.

It is not clear from the research exactly what form of equine-assisted interaction was used during these studies, nor were the qualifications of the professionals providing the treatment discussed, but two of the studies did seem to suggest the approach was a combination of hippotherapy and adaptive riding (Cuypers, et al., 2011; Yoo, et al., 2016).

Since children with ADHD often experience motor problems (Fliers, et al., 2009), it seems logical that much of the research has been focused on hippotherapy or adaptive riding. However, it is notable that equine-assisted mental health approaches were unrepresented in the research, since many mental health professionals treat ADHD. It would seem there is an opportunity for a great deal more research in the area of ADHD and equine-assisted interactions, especially as it relates to mental health interventions.

Other Research

Four studies per topic have been conducted to date related to eating disorders (Christian, 2005; Lac, et al., 2013, Sharpe, 2014; Lac, 2016) and other neurological conditions (Encheff, et al., 2012; Nervick & Parent-Nichols, 2012; Sunwoo, et al., 2012; Cabiddu, et al., 2016).

Three studies per topic have been conducted related to prison populations (Cushing & Williams, 1995; Deaton, 2005; Hemingway, et al., 2015), anxiety (Scheidhacker, et al., 2002; Alfonso, et al., 2015; Wilson, et al., 2015), Down syndrome (Champagne & Dugas, 2010; Bevilacqua, et al., 2015; Ribeiro, et al., 2015), intellectual disabilities (Borioni, et al., 2012; Giagazoglou, et al., 2012; Giagazoglou, et al., 2013), and back pain (Håkanson, et al., 2009; Oh, et al., 2014; Yoo, et al., 2014).

Two studies per topic have been conducted related to cancer (Haylock & Cantril, 2006; Cerulli, et al., 2014), spinal cord injury (Lechner, et al., 2003; Lechner, et al., 2007), self-harm (Carlsson, et al., 2015; Carlsson, 2016a), and grief (Glazer, et al., 2004; Symington, 2012).

An additional 25 papers related to equine-assisted interactions used to treat a clinical condition were classified as "miscellaneous" as they could not be combined into any similar category, and 13 papers were identified that studied non-clinical populations.

☐ Conclusion

Although a good deal of research has been conducted to date, our understanding of equine-assisted therapy and its uses is still in its infancy. There is much we do not know, and much we have to learn. But, as anyone who has spent time in the presence of horses knows, simply being outside, connecting with another creature, and engaging the whole body in an activity that invigorates the senses and touches our souls *feels good*.

Over time, the quality and scope of research will begin to catch up with the enthusiasm of those providing the service. Until this happens, professionals are urged to speak about equine-assisted therapy as a novel treatment, one that necessitates a good deal of additional research before making claims about the benefits associated. Indicating the tentative, but hopeful nature of existing research, and sharing patient stories or the personal experiences of providers may be a more ethical way to communicate the excitement and passion for the industry until more can be gleaned from empirical study.

Equine-assisted therapy has inherent risks not found in office-based physical, occupational, speech, or mental health therapy (Fershtman, 2016; Walson, 2003; Cook, 2011), and if used incorrectly, could cause harm. Given this, it is of great importance that providers are careful not to mislead the public by suggesting it is a "proven" or even "evidence-based" practice. Patients have a right to understand the novel and investigational nature of equine-assisted therapy, and make personal choices given the risks associated.

Every provider can contribute to the growing body of knowledge about equine-assisted therapy by being curious and practicing the art of "never assuming." In truth, we don't know what factors cause change when a patient engages with a horse. Attempting to "prove" a treatment works without studying the mechanisms of change could unwittingly sacrifice important knowledge, while curiosity and exploration will guide us towards deeper and more complex understanding.

☐ References

Adams, C., Arratoon, C., Boucher, J., et al. (2015). The helping horse: How equine assisted learning contributes to the wellbeing of First Nations youth in treatment for volatile substance misuse. *Human-Animal Interaction Bulletin, 1*(1), 52–75.

Ajzenman, H. (2013). Effect of hippotherapy on motor control, adaptive behaviors, and participation in children with autism spectrum disorder: A pilot study. *American Journal of Occupational Therapy*, *67*(6), 653–663.

Alfonso, S.V., Alfonso, L.A., Llabre, M.M., & Isabel Fernandez, M. (2015). Project stride: An equine-assisted interactionto reduce symptoms of social anxiety in young women. *Explore: The Journal of Science and Healing*, *11*(6), 461–467.

Anestis, M.D., Anestis, J.C., Zawilinski, L.L., Hopkins, T.A., & Lilienfeld, S.O. (2014). Equine-related treatments for mental disorders lack empirical support: A systematic review of empirical investigations. *Journal of Clinical Psychology*, 1–18.

Angoules, A., Koukoulas, D., Balakatounis, K., Kapari, I., & Matsouki, E. (2015). A review of efficacy of hippotherapy for the treatment of musculoskeletal disorders. *British Journal of Medicine and Medical Research*, *8*(4), 289–297.

Angsupaisal, M., Visser, B., Alkema, A., Meinsma-van der Tuin, M., Maathuis, C.G.B., Reinders-Messelink, H., & Hadders-Algra, M. (2015). Therapist-Designed Adaptive Riding in Children With Cerebral Palsy: Results of a Feasibility Study. Physical Therapy, 95(8), 1151–1162. http://doi.org/10.2522/ptj.20140146

Ansorge, J., & Sudres, J.-L. (2011). Equine-assisted therapy in child psychiatry. *Soins Psychiatrie*, *277*, 40–44.

Asselin, G., Ward, C., Penning, J.H., Ramanujam, S., & Neri, R. (2012). Therapeutic horse back riding of a spinal cord injured veteran: A case study. *Rehabilitation Nursing*, *37*(6), 270–276.

Bachi, K. (2012). Equine-facilitated psychotherapy: The gap between practice and knowledge. *Society & Animals*, *20*, 364–380.

Bachi, K. (2013). Equine-facilitated prison-based programs within the context of prison-based animal programs: State of the science review. *Journal of Offender Rehabilitation*, *52*(1), 46–74.

Bachi, K., Terkel, J., & Teichman, M. (2011). Equine-facilitated psychotherapy for at-risk adolescents: The influence on self-image, self-control and trust. *Clinical Child Psychology and Psychiatry*, *17*(2), 298–312.

Baek, I.-H., & Kim, B.J. (2014). The effects of horse riding simulation training on stroke patients' balance ability and abdominal muscle thickness changes. *Journal of Physical Therapy Science*, *26*(8), 1293–1296.

Baik, K., Byeun, J.-K., & Baek, J.-K. (2014). The effects of horseback riding participation on the muscle tone and range of motion for children with spastic cerebral palsy. *Journal of Exercise Rehabilitation*, *10*(5), 265–270. http://doi.org/10.12965/jer.140124

Bass, M.M., Duchowny, C.A., & Llabre, M.M. (2009). The effect of therapeutic horseback riding on social functioning in children with autism. *Journal of Autism and Developmental Disorders*, *39*, 1261–1267.

Beinotti, F., Christofoletti, G., Correia, N., & Borges, G. (2013). Effects of horseback riding therapy on quality of life in patients post stroke. *Topics in Stroke Rehabilitation Journal*, *20*(3), 226–232.

Beinotti, F., Correia, N., Christofoletti, G., & Borges, G. (2010). Use of hippotherapy in gait training for hemiparetic post-stroke. *Arquivos de Neuro-Psiquiatria*, *68*(6), 908–913.

Benda, W., McGibbon, N. H., & Grant, K. L. (2003). Improvements in muscle symmetry in children with cerebral palsy after equine-assisted therapy (hippotherapy). *J Altern Complement Med*, *9*(6), 817–825.

Bevilacqua Junior, D.E., Ribeiro, M.F., Accioly, M.F., Ferreira, A.A., Antunes Teixeira, V.D.P., & Espindula, A.P. (2015). Heart rate variability in practitioners of hippotherapy with Down syndrome. *Physiotherapy*, *101*, e364.

Bizub, A., Joy, A., & Davidson, L. (2003). "It's like being in another world": Demonstrating the benefits of therapeutic horseback riding for individuals with psychiatric disability. *Psychiatric Rehabilitation Journal, 26*(4), 377–384.

Bond, M. (2007). Horseback riding as therapy for children with cerebral palsy: Is there evidence of its effectiveness? *Physical & Occupational Therapy in Pediatrics, 27*(2), 5–23.

Borgi, M., Loliva, D., Cerino, S., et al. (2016). Effectiveness of a standardized equine-assisted therapy program for children with autism spectrum disorder. *Journal of Autism and Developmental Disorders, 46*(1), 1–9.

Borioni, N., Marinaro, P., Celestini, S., Del Sole, F., Magro, R., Zoppi, D., et al. (2012). Effect of equestrian therapy and onotherapy in physical and psycho-social performances of adults with intellectual disability: A preliminary study of evaluation tools based on the ICF classification. *Disability and Rehabilitation, 34*(4), 279–287.

Boshoff, C., Grobler, H., & Nienaber, A. (2015). The evaluation of an equine-assisted therapy programme with a group of boys in a youth care facility. *Journal of Psychology in Africa, 25*(1), 86–90.

Bowers, M.J., & MacDonald, P.M. (2001). The effectiveness of equine-facilitated psychotherapy with at-risk adolescents: A pilot study. *Journal of Psychology and Behavioral Science, 15*, 62–76.

Bronson, C., Brewerton, K., Ong, J., Palanca, C., & Sullivan, S.J. (2010). Does hippotherapy improve balance in persons with multiple sclerosis: A systematic review. *European Journal of Physical and Rehabilitation Medicine, 46*(3), 347–353.

Bunketorp Käll, L., Lundgren-Nilsson, Å., Blomstrand, C., Pekna, M., Pekny, M., & Nilsson, M. (2012). The effects of a rhythm and music-based therapy program and therapeutic riding in late recovery phase following stroke: A study protocol for a three-armed randomized controlled trial. *BMC Neurology, 12*, 141–153.

Burgon, H.L. (2011). "Queen of the world": Experiences of "at-risk" young people participating in equine-assisted learning/therapy. *Journal of Social Work Practice, 25*(2), 165–183.

Burgon, H.L. (2014). Horses, mindfulness and the natural environment: Observations from a qualitative study with at-risk young people participating in therapeutic horsemanship. *International Journal of Psychosocial Rehabilitation, 17*(2), 51–67.

Burton, L.E., & Burge, M.R. (2015). Equine assisted therapy reduces symptoms in veterans with post-traumatic stress disorder. *Journal of Investigative Medicine, 63*(1), 165.

Cabiddu, R., Borghi-Silva, A., Trimer, R., Trimer, V., Ricci, P.A., Italiano Monteiro, C., et al. (2016). Hippotherapy acute impact on heart rate variability non-linear dynamics in neurological disorders. *Physiology and Behavior, 159*, 88–94.

Cantin, A., & Marshall-Lucette, S. (2011). Examining the literature on the efficacy of equine assisted therapy for people with mental health and behavioural disorders. *Mental Health and Learning Disabilities Research and Practice, 8*(1), 51–61.

Carlsson, C. (2016a). Triads in equine-assisted social work enhance therapeutic relationships with self-harming adolescents. *Clinical Social Work Journal.*

Carlsson, C. (February 14, 2016b). A narrative review of qualitative and quantitative research in equine-assisted social work or therapy: Addressing gaps and contradictory results. *Animalia an Anthrozoology Journal.*

Carlsson, C., Nilsson Ranta, D., & Traeen, B. (2015). Mentalizing and emotional labor facilitate equine-assisted social work with self-harming adolescents. *Child and Adolescent Social Work Journal, 32*(4), 329–339.

Casady, R.L., & Nichols-Larsen, D.S. (2004). The effect of hippotherapy on ten children with cerebral palsy. *Pediatric Physical Therapy, 16*(3), 165–172. http://doi.org/10.1097/01. PEP.0000136003.15233.0C

Cerino, S., Cirulli, F., Chiarotti, F., & Seripa, S. (2011). Non conventional psychiatric rehabilitation in schizophrenia using therapeutic riding: The FISE multicentre Pindar project. *Annali dell'Istituto Superiore Di Sanità, 47*(4), 409–414.

Cerulli, C., Minganti, C., De Santis, C., Tranchita, E., Quaranta, F., & Parisi, A. (2014). Therapeutic horseback riding in breast cancer survivors: A pilot study. *Journal of Alternative and Complementary Medicine, 20*(8), 623–629.

Champagne, D., & Dugas, C. (2010). Improving gross motor function and postural control with hippotherapy in children with Down syndrome: Case reports. *Physiotherapy Theory and Practice, 26*(8), 564–571.

Chang, H.J., Kwon, J.-Y., Lee, J.-Y., & Kim, Y.-H. (2012). The effects of hippotherapy on the motor function of children with spastic bilateral cerebral palsy. *Journal of Physical Therapy Science, 24*(12), 1277–1280. http://doi.org/10.1589/jpts.24.1277

Chardonnens, E. (2009). The use of animals as co-therapists on a farm: The child-horse bond in person-centred equine-assisted psychotherapy. *Person-Centered & Experiential Psychotherapies, 8*(4), 319–332.

Cho, S.-H., Kim, J.-W., Kim, S.-R., & Cho, B.-J. (2015). Effects of horseback riding exercise therapy on hormone levels in elderly persons. *Journal of Physical Therapy Science, 27*(7), 2271–2273.

Christian, E. (2005). All creatures great and small: Utilizing equine-assisted therapy to treat eating disorders. *Journal of Psychology and Christianity, 24*(1), 65–67.

Cook, R. (2011). Incidents and injury within the hippotherapy milieu: Four years of safety study data on risk, risk management, and occurrences. *Scientific and Educational Journal of Therapeutic Riding, 57*–66.

Corring, D., Lundberg, E., & Rudnick, A. (2013). Therapeutic horseback riding for ACT patients with schizophrenia. *Community Mental Health Journal, 49*(1), 121–126.

Cushing, J.L., & Williams, J.D. (1995). The wild mustang program: A case study in facilitated inmate therapy. *Journal of Offender Rehabilitation, 22*(3–4), 95–112.

Cuypers, K., De Ridder, K., & Strandheim, A. (2011). The effect of therapeutic horseback riding on 5 children with attention deficit hyperactivity disorder: A pilot study. *Journal of Alternative and Complementary Medicine, 17*(10), 901–908.

Dabelko-Schoeny, H., Phillips, G., Darrough, E., DeAnna, S., Jarden, M., Johnson, D., & Lorch, G. (2014). Equine-assisted interaction for people with dementia. *Anthrozoos, 27*(1), 141–155.

de Araújo, T.B., De Oliveira, R.J., Martins, W.R., De Moura Pereira, M., Copetti, F., & Safons, M.P. (2013). Effects of hippotherapy on mobility, strength and balance in elderly. *Archives of Gerontology and Geriatrics, 56*(3), 478–481.

de Araújo, T.B., Silva, N.A., Costa, J.N., Pereira, M.M., & Safons, M.P. (2011). Effect of equine-assisted therapy on the postural balance of the elderly. *Brazilian Journal of Physical Therapy, 15*(5), 414–419.

Deaton, C. (2005). Humanizing prisons with animals: A closer look at "cell dogs" and horse programs in correctional institutions. *Journal of Correctional Education, 56*(1), 46–62.

Debuse, D., Chandler, C., & Gibb, C. (2005). An exploration of German and British physiotherapists' views on the effects of hippotherapy and their measurement. *Physiotherapy Theory and Practice, 21*(4), 219–242.

Debuse, D., Gibb, C., & Chandler, C. (2009). Effects of hippotherapy on people with cerebral palsy from the users' perspective: a qualitative study. *Physiotherapy Theory and Practice, 25*(3), 174–192. http://doi.org/10.1080/09593980902776662

Dell, C.A., Chalmers, D., Bresette, N., Swain, S., Rankin, D., & Hopkins, C. (2011). A healing space: The experiences of First Nations and Inuit youth with equine-assisted learning (EAL). *Child and Youth Care Forum, 40*(4), 319–336.

Dell, C.A., Chalmers, D., Dell, D., Sauve, E., & MacKinnon, T. (2008). Horse as healer: An examination of equine assisted learning in the healing of First Nations youth from solvent abuse. *Pimatisiwin: A Journal of Aboriginal and Indigenous Community Health, 6*(1), 81–106.

Drinkhouse, M., Birmingham, S., Fillman, R., & Jedlicka, H. (2012). Correlation of human and horse heart rates during equine-assisted therapy sessions with at-risk youths: A pilot study. *Journal of Student Research, 1*(3), 22–25.

Duncan, R.C., Critchley, S., & Marland, J. (2014). Can Praxis: A model of equine assisted learning (EAL) for PTSD. *Canadian Military Journal, 2*(14), 64–69.

Earles, J., Vernon, L., & Yetz, J. (2015). Equine-assisted therapy for anxiety and posttraumatic stress symptoms. *Journal of Traumatic Stress, 28*, 149–152.

El-Meniawy, G.H., & Thabet, N.S. (2012). Modulation of back geometry in children with spastic diplegic cerebral palsy via hippotherapy training. *Egyptian Journal of Medical Human Genetics, 13*(1), 63–71. http://doi.org/10.1016/j.ejmhg.2011.10.004

Encheff, J., Armstrong, C., Masterson, M., Fox, C., & Gribble, P. (2012). Hippotherapy effects on trunk, pelvic, and hip motion during ambulation in children with neurological impairments. *Pediatric Physical Therapy, 24*(3), 242–250.

Equine Assisted Growth and Learning Association (EAGALA). (2016). *How It Works.* Retrieved from: http://home.eagala.org/works

Ewing, C.A., MacDonald, P.M., Taylor, M., & Bowers, M.J. (2007). Equine-facilitated learning for youths with severe emotional disorders: A quantitative and qualitative study. *Child and Youth Care Forum, 36*(1), 59–72.

Ferruolo, D.M. (2015). Psychosocial equine program for veterans. *Social Work, 61*(1), 53–60.

Fershtman, J.L. (September 21, 2016). *Can You Release Equine Activity Liability Act Liabilities? The Answer May Surprise You.* Retrieved from: www.equinelawblog.com/release-equine-activity-liabilities

Fliers, E., Franke, B., Lambregts-rommelse, N., et al. (2009). Undertreatment of motor problems in children with ADHD. *Child and Adolescent Mental Health, 15*(2), 85–90.

Frank, A., McCloskey, S., & Dole, R.L. (2011). Effect of Hippotherapy on Perceived Self-competence and Participation in a Child With cerebral palsy. *Pediatric Physical Therapy, 23*, 301–308. http://doi.org/10.1097/PEP.0b013e318227caac

Frederick, K.E., Ivey Hatz, J., & Lanning, B. (2015). Not just horsing around: The impact of equine-assisted learning on levels of hope and depression in at-risk adolescents. *Community Mental Health Journal, 51*(7), 809–817.

Frewin, K., & Gardiner, B. (2005). New age or old sage? A review of equine assisted psychotherapy. *The Australian Journal of Counselling Psychology, 6*, 13–17.

Froeschle, J. (2009). Empowering abused women through equine assisted career therapy. *Journal of Creativity in Mental Health, 4*(2), 180–190.

Gabriels, R.L., Pan, Z., Dechant, B., Agnew, J.A., Brim, N., & Mesibov, G. (2015). Randomized controlled trial of therapeutic horseback riding in children and adolescents with autism spectrum disorder. *Journal of the American Academy of Child & Adolescent Psychiatry, 54*(7), 541–549.

Gencheva, N., Ivanova, I., & Stefanova, D. (2015). Evaluation of hippotherapy in the course of multiple sclerosis treatment. *Activities in Physical Education and Sport, 5*(2), 183–187.

Giagazoglou, P., Arabatzi, F., Dipla, K., Liga, M., & Kellis, E. (2012). Effect of a hippotherapy intervention program on static balance and strength in adolescents with intellectual disabilities. *Research in Developmental Disabilities, 33*(6), 2265–2270.

Giagazoglou, P., Arabatzi, F., Kellis, E., Liga, M., Karra, C., & Amiridis, I. (2013). Muscle reaction function of individuals with intellectual disabilities may be improved through therapeutic use of a horse. *Research in Developmental Disabilities, 34*(9), 2442–2448.

Gibbons, J.L., Cunningham, C.A., Paiz, L., Poelker, K.E., & Chajón, A. (2016). "Now, he will be the leader of the house": An equine intervention with at-risk Guatemalan youth. *International Journal of Adolescence and Youth, 10*(10), 1–15.

Glazer, H.R., Clark, M.D., & Stein, D.S. (2004). The impact of hippotherapy on grieving children. *Journal of Hospice & Palliative Nursing, 6*(3), 171–175.

Guerino, M.R., Briel, A.F., & Araújo, M., & das, G.R. (2015). Hippotherapy as a treatment for socialization after sexual abuse and emotional stress. *Journal of Physical Therapy Science, 27*(3), 959–962.

Håkanson, M., Möller, M., Lindström, I., & Mattsson, B. (2009). The horse as the healer: A study of riding in patients with back pain. *Journal of Bodywork and Movement Therapies, 13*(1), 43–52.

Hamill, D., Washington, K., White, O. R. (2007). The Effect of Hippotherapy on Postural Control in Sitting for Children with Cerebral Palsy. *Physical & Occupational Therapy in Pediatrics, 27*(4), 23–42.

Hammer, A., Nilsagård, Y., Forsberg, A., Pepa, H., Skargren, E., & Oberg, B. (2005). Evaluation of therapeutic riding (Sweden)/hippotherapy (United States): A single-subject experimental design study replicated in eleven patients with multiple sclerosis. *Physiotherapy Theory and Practice, 21*(1), 51–77.

Haylock, P.J., & Cantril, C.A. (2006). Healing with horses: Fostering recovery from cancer with horses as therapists. *Explore: The Journal of Science and Healing, 2*(3), 264–268.

Hemingway, A., Meek, R., & Hill, C.E. (2015). An exploration of an equine-facilitated learning intervention with young offenders. *Society & Animals, 23*(6), 544–568.

Holmes, C.M.P., Goodwin, D., Redhead, E.S., & Goymour, K.L. (2012). The benefits of equine-assisted activities: An exploratory study. *Child and Adolescent Social Work Journal, 29*(2), 111–122.

Homnick, D.N., Henning, K.M., Swain, C.V., & Homnick, T.D. (2013). Effect of therapeutic horseback riding on balance in community-dwelling older adults with balance deficits. *Journal of Alternative and Complementary Medicine, 19*(7), 622–626.

Homnick, T.D., Henning, K.M., Swain, C.V., & Homnick, D.N. (2015). The effect of therapeutic horseback riding on balance in community-dwelling older adults: A pilot study. *Journal of Applied Gerontology: The Official Journal of the Southern Gerontological Society, 34*(1), 118–126.

Honkavaara, M., Rintala, P. (2010). The Influence of Short Term, Intensive Hippotherapy on Gait in Children with Cerebral Palsy. *European Journal of Adapted Physical Activity, 3*(2), 29–36.

Hyun, G.J., Jung, T.-W., Park, J.H., et al. (2016). Changes in gait balance and brain connectivity in response to equine-assisted activity and training in children with attention deficit hyperactivity disorder. *The Journal of Alternative and Complementary Medicine, 22*(4), 286–293.

Jang, B., Song, J., Kim, J., Kim, S., Lee, J., Shin, H.Y., Kwon, J.Y., Kim, Y.-H., & Joung, Y.-S. (2015). Equine-assisted activities and therapy for treating children with attention-deficit/hyperactivity disorder. *Journal of Alternative and Complementary Medicine, 21*(9), 546–553.

Jenkins, S.R., & Digennaro Reed, F.D. (2013). An experimental analysis of the effects of therapeutic horseback riding on the behavior of children with autism. *Research in Autism Spectrum Disorders, 7*(6), 721–740.

Johansen, S.G., Arfwedson Wang, C.E., & Binder, P.-E. (2016). Facilitating change in a client's dysfunctional behavioural pattern with horse-aided psychotherapy: A case study. *Counselling & Psychotherapy Research, 16*(3), 222–231.

Johansen, S.G., & Malt, U.F. (2010). Development of a new therapeutic equine facilitated psychotherapy program for patients with mood and other psychiatric disorders. *Journal of Affective Disorders, 122*(2010), S44–S45.

Kaiser, L., Smith, K.A., Heleski, C.R., & Spence, L.J. (2006). Exploring the bond effects of a therapeutic riding program on at-risk and special education children. *Journal of the American Veterinary Medical Association, 228*(2), 46–52.

Kemp, K., Signal, T., Botros, H., Taylor, N., & Prentice, K. (2014). Equine facilitated therapy with children and adolescents who have been sexually abused: A program evaluation study. *Journal of Child and Family Studies, 23*, 558–566.

Kendall, E., & Maujean, A. (2015). Horse play: A brief psychological intervention for disengaged youths. *Journal of Creativity in Mental Health, 10*(1), 46–61.

Kendall, E., Maujean, A., Pepping, C.A., et al. (2015). A systematic review of the efficacy of equine-assisted interventions on psychological outcomes. *European Journal of Psychotherapy & Counselling, 2537*(17), 57–79.

Kern-Godal, A., Arnevik, E.A., Walderhaug, E., & Ravndal, E. (2015). Substance use disorder treatment retention and completion: A prospective study of EAT for young adults. *Addiction Science and Clinical Practice, 10*(21), 3–12.

Kern-Godal, A., Brenna, I.H., Arnevik, E.A., & Ravndal, E. (2016a). More than just a break from treatment: How substance use disorder patients experience the stable environment in horse-assisted therapy. *Substance Abuse: Research and Treatment, 10*, 99–108.

Kern-Godal, A., Brenna, I.H., Kogstad, N., Arnevik, E.A., & Ravndal, E. (2016b). Contribution of the patient horse relationship to substance use disorder treatment: Patients' experiences. *International Journal of Qualitative Studies on Health and Well-Being, 11*, 1–12.

Kim, H., Her, J.G., & Ko, J. (2014). Effect of horseback riding simulation machine training on trunk balance and gait of chronic stroke patients. *Journal of Physical Therapy Science, 26*(1), 29–32.

Kim, S.G., & Lee, C.-W. (2014). The effects of hippotherapy on elderly persons' static balance and gait. *Journal of Physical Therapy Science, 26*(1), 25–27.

Kim, S.G., & Lee, J.H. (2015). The effects of horse riding simulation exercise on muscle activation and limits of stability in the elderly. *Archives of Gerontology and Geriatrics, 60*(1), 62–65.

Kim, S.G., Yuk, G.-C., & Gak, H. (2013). Effects of the horse riding simulator and ball exercises on balance of the elderly. *Journal of Physical Therapy Science, 25*(11), 1425–1428.

Kim, Y.-N., & Lee, D.-K. (2015). Effects of horse-riding simulation exercise on balance, gait, and activities of daily living in stroke patients. *Journal of Physical Therapy Science, 27*(3), 607–609.

Krejčí, E., Janura, M., & Svoboda, Z. (2015). The benefit of hippotherapy for improvement of attention and memory in children with cerebral palsy: A pilot study. *Acta Gymnica, 45*(1), 27–32. http://doi.org/10.5507/ag.2015.004

Kukull, W.A., & Ganguli, M.G. (2012). Generalizability: The trees, the forest, and the low-hanging fruit. *Neurology: The Official Journal of the American Academy of Neurology, 78*(23), 1886–1891.

Kulkarni-Lambore, S., McGuigan, A., Narula, N., Sepelak, K. (2001). Kinematic Gait Analysis of an Individual with Cerebral Palsy Before and After Hippotherapy. *Physical Therapy, 81*(5), A40–A41.

Kwon, J.Y., Chang, H.J., Lee, J.Y., Ha, Y., Lee, P.K., & Kim, Y.H. (2011). Effects of hippotherapy on gait parameters in children with bilateral spastic cerebral palsy. *Archives of Physical Medicine and Rehabilitation, 92*(5), 774–779. http://doi.org/10.1016/j.apmr.2010.11.031

Lac, V. (2016). Amy's Story: An existential-integrative equine-facilitated psychotherapy approach to anorexia nervosa. *Journal of Humanistic Psychology*, 1–12.

Lac, V., Marble, E., & Boie, I. (2013). Equine-assisted psychotherapy as a creative relational approach to treating clients with eating disorders. *Journal of Creativity in Mental Health*, 8(4), 483–498.

Lanning, B., Baier, M.E.M., Ivey-Hatz, J., Krenek, N., & Tubbs, J.D. (2014). Effects of equine assisted activities on autism spectrum disorder. *Journal of Autism and Developmental Disorders*, 44, 1897–1907.

Lanning, B., & Krenek, N. (2013). Guest Editorial: Examining effects of equine-assisted activities to help combat veterans improve quality of life. *Journal of Rehabilitation Research and Development*, 50(8), vii–xiii.

Lechner, H.E., Feldhaus, S., Gudmundsen, L., Hegemann, D., Michel, D., Zäch, G.A., & Knecht, H. (2003). The short-term effect of hippotherapy on spasticity in patients with spinal cord injury. *Spinal Cord: The Official Journal of the International Medical Society of Paraplegia*, 41(9), 502–505.

Lechner, H.E., Kakebeeke, T.H., Hegemann, D., & Baumberger, M. (2007). The effect of hippotherapy on spasticity and on mental well-being of persons with spinal cord injury. *Archives of Physical Medicine and Rehabilitation*, 88(10), 1241–1248.

Lee, P.T., Dakin, E., & Mclure, M. (2016). Narrative synthesis of equine-assisted psychotherapy literature: Current knowledge and future research directions. *Health and Social Care in the Community*, 24(3), 225–246.

Lentini, J.A., & Knox, M. (2009). A qualitative and quantitative review of equine facilitated psychotherapy (EFP) with children and adolescents. *The Open Complementary Medicine Journal*, 1, 51–57.

Lentini, J.A., & Knox, M.S. (2015). Equine-facilitated psychotherapy with children and adolescents: An update and literature review. *Journal of Creativity in Mental Health*, 10(3), 278–305.

Lindroth, J.L., Sullivan, J.L., & Silkwood-Sherer, D. (2015). Does hippotherapy effect use of sensory information for balance in people with multiple sclerosis? *Physiotherapy Theory & Practice*, 31(8), 575–581.

MacKinnon, J.R., Noh, S., Laliberte, D., Allan, D.E., & Lariviere, J. (1995). Therapeutic horseback riding: A review of literature. *Physical & Occupational Therapy in Pediatrics*, 15(1), 1–15.

Manikowska, F., Jóźwiak, M., Idzior, M., Chen, P.-J. B., & Tarnowski, D. (2013). The effect of a hippotherapy session on spatiotemporal parameters of gait in children with cerebral palsy—pilot study. *Ortopedia, Traumatologia, Rehabilitacja*, 15(3), 253–257. http://doi.org/10.5604/15093492.1058420

Maujean, A., Kendall, E., Lillan, R., Sharp, T., & Pringle, G. (2013). Connecting for health: Playing with horses as a therapeutic tool. *Journal of Community Psychology*, 41(4), 515–522.

McCullough, L., Risley-Curtiss, C., & Rorke, J. (2015). Equine facilitated psychotherapy: A pilot study of effect on posttraumatic stress symptoms in maltreated youth. *Journal of Infant, Child & Adolescent Psychotherapy*, 14(2), 158–173.

McGee, M.C., & Reese, N.B. (2009). Immediate effects of a hippotherapy session on gait parameters in children with spastic cerebral palsy. *Pediatric Physical Therapy: The Official Publication of the Section on Pediatrics of the American Physical Therapy Association*, 21(2), 212–8.

McGibbon, N.H., Andrade, C.K., Widener, G., Cintas, H.L. (1998). Effect of an equine-movement therapy program on gait, energy expenditure, and motor function in children with spastic cerebral palsy: a pilot study. *Developmental Medicine and Child Neurology*, *40*, 754–762.

McGibbon, N.H., Benda, W., Duncan, B.R., & Silkwood-Sherer, D. (2009). Immediate and Long-Term Effects of Hippotherapy on Symmetry of Adductor Muscle Activity and Functional Ability in Children With Spastic Cerebral Palsy. *Archives of Physical Medicine and Rehabilitation*, *90*(6), 966–974. http://doi.org/10.1016/j.apmr.2009.01.011

Mehra, B. (2002). Bias in qualitative research: Voices from an online classroom. *The Qualitative Report*, *7*(1), 1–19.

Meinersmann, K.M., Bradberry, J., & Roberts, F.B. (2008). Equine-facilitated psychotherapy with adult female survivors of abuse. *Journal of Psychosocial Nursing and Mental Health Services*, *46*(12), 36–42.

Memishevikj, H., & Hodzhikj, S. (2010). The effects of equine-assisted therapy in improving the psycho-social functioning of children with autism. *Journal of Special Education and Rehabilitation*, *11*, 57–67.

Menezes, K.M., Copetti, F., Wiest, M.J., Trevisan, C.M., & Silveira, A.F. (2013). Effect of hippotherapy on the postural stability of patients with multiple sclerosis: A preliminary study. *Fisioterapia E Pesquisa*, *1000*(4), 43–49.

Munoz-Lasa, S., Ferriero, G., Valero, R., Gomez-Muniz, F., Rabini, A., & Varela, E. (2011). Effect of therapeutic horseback riding on balance and gait of people with multiple sclerosis. *Giornale Italiano Di Medicina Del Lavoro Ed Ergonomia*, *33*(4), 462–467.

Nervick, D., & Parent-Nichols, J. (2012). Hippotherapy effects on trunk, pelvic, and hip motion during ambulation in children with neurological impairments. *Pediatric Physical Therapy*, *24*(3), 251.

Nevins, R., Finch, S., Hickling, E.J., & Barnett, S.D. (2013). The Saratoga WarHorse project: A case study of the treatment of psychological distress in a veteran of Operation Iraqi Freedom. *Advances in Mind-Body Medicine*, *27*(4), 22–25.

Newton-Cromwell, S.A., McSpadden, B.D., & Johnson, R. (2015). Incorporating experiential learning for equine-assisted activities and therapies with an in-house equine therapy program for veterans. *Journal of Equine Veterinary Science*, *35*(5), 458.

Nurenberg, J.R., Schleifer, S., Carson, S., Tsang, J., Montalvo, C., & Chou, K. (2013). Equine-facilitated group psychotherapy with chronic psychiatric inpatients: Two controlled studies. *European Psychiatry*, *28*, 1.

Nurenberg, J.R., Schleifer, S.J., Shaffer, T.M., et al. (2015). Animal-assisted therapy with chronic psychiatric inpatients: Equine-assisted psychotherapy and aggressive behavior. *Psychiatric Services*, *66*(1), 80–86.

Oh, H.W., Lee, M.G., Jang, J.Y., Jin, J.J., Cha, J.Y., Jin, Y.Y., & Jee, Y.S. (2014). Time-effects of horse simulator exercise on psychophysiological responses in men with chronic low back pain. *Isokinetics and Exercise Science*, *22*(2), 153–163.

Oh, Y., Seo, H., Jang, B., Song, J., Lee, J., Jeong, B., Kim, Y., Kwon, J., & Joung, Y. (2015). Therapeutic effect of 12 weeks equine assisted activities and therapies (EAA/T) in children with attention deficit hyperactivity disorder. *European Child & Adolescent Psychiatry*, *24*(1), 171–172.

Park, J., Lee, S., Lee, J., & Lee, D. (2013). The effects of horseback riding simulator exercise on postural balance of chronic stroke patients. *Journal of Physical Therapy Science*, *25*(9), 1169–1172.

Park, J.H., Shurtleff, T., Engsberg, J., Rafferty, S., You, J.Y., You, I.Y., & You, S.H. (2014). Comparison between the robo-horse and real horse movements for hippotherapy. *Bio-Medical Materials and Engineering*, *24*(6), 2603–2610. http://doi.org/10.3233/BME-141076

Pauw, J. (2000). Therapeutic horseback riding studies: Problems experienced by researchers. *Physiotherapy*, *86*(10), 523–527.

Porter-Wenzlaff, L. (2007). Finding their voice: Developing emotional, cognitive, and behavioral congruence in female abuse survivors through equine-facilitated psychotherapy. *Explore: The Journal of Science and Healing*, *3*(5), 529–534.

Professional Association of Therapeutic Horsemanship International (PATH Intl.). (2016). *Learn about EAAT*. Retrieved from: www.pathintl.org/resources-education/resources/eaat/27-resources/general/194-eaat-benefits

Ribeiro, M.F., Espindula, A.P., Ferreira, A.A., Ferraz, M.L.F., Souza, L.A.P.S., Diniz, L.H., & Teixeira, V.D.P.A. (2015). Electromyographic evaluation of lower limbs in individuals with Down syndrome in hippotherapy. *Physiotherapy*, *101*(2), e1279–e1280.

Rooney, P. (2005). Researching from the inside: Does it compromise validity? A discussion. *Dublin Institute of Technology*, *3*(3), 1–19.

Rosenbaum, P. (2009). A randomized controlled trial of the impact of therapeutic horse riding on the quality of life, health, and function of children with cerebral palsy. *Developmental Medicine & Child Neurology*, *51*, 89–91.

Saggers, B., & Strachan, J. (2016). Horsing around: Using equine facilitated learning to support the development of social-emotional competence of students at risk of school failure. *Child & Youth Services*, *37*(3), 231–252.

Scheidhacker, M., Friedrich, D., & Bender, W. (2002). About the treatment of anxiety disorders by psychotherapeutic riding: Long-term observations and results of an experimental clinical study. *Krankenhauspsychiatrie*, *13*(4), 145–152.

Schlosser, R. (2006). The role of systematic reviews in evidence-based practice, research and development. *Focus: A Publication of the National Center for the Dissemination of Disability Research*, *15*, 321–322.

Schroeder, K., & Stroud, D. (2015). Equine-facilitated group work for women survivors of interpersonal violence. *The Journal for Specialists in Group Work*, *3922*, 1–22.

Schultz, P.N., Remick-Barlow, G.A., & Bobbins, L. (2007). Equine-assisted psychotherapy: A mental health promotion/intervention modality for children who have experienced infra-family violence. *Health and Social Care in the Community*, *15*(3), 265–271.

Selby, A., & Smith-Osborne, A. (2013). A systematic review of effectiveness of complementary and adjunct therapies and interventions involving equines. *Health Psychology*, *32*(4), 418–432.

Seredova, M., Maskova, A., Mrstinova, M., & Volicer, L. (2016). Effects of hippotherapy on well-being of patients with schizophrenia. *Archives of Neuroscience*, *3*(4), 1–5.

Sharpe, H. (2014). Equine-facilitated counselling and women with eating disorders: Articulating bodily. *Canadian Journal of Counselling and Psychotherapy*, *48*(2), 127–152.

Shurtleff, T.L., & Engsberg, J.R. (2010). Changes in trunk and head stability in children with cerebral palsy after hippotherapy: a pilot study. *Physical & Occupational Therapy in Pediatrics*, *30*(2), 150–63. http://doi.org/10.3109/01942630903517223

Shurtleff, T., Engsberg. J (2012). Long-term effects of hippotheray on one child with cerebral palsy: a research case study. *British Journal of Occupational Therapy*, *75*(8), 359–366.

Shurtleff, T.L., Standeven, J.W., & Engsberg, J.R. (2009). Changes in Dynamic Trunk/Head Stability and Functional Reach After Hippotherapy. *Archives of Physical Medicine and Rehabilitation*, *90*(7), 1185–1195. http://doi.org/10.1016/j.apmr.2009.01.026

Signal, T., Taylor, N., Botros, H., Prentice, K., & Lazarus, K. (2013). Whispering to horses: Childhood sexual abuse, depression and the efficacy of equine facilitated therapy. *SAANZ Journal*, *5*(1), 24–32.

Silkwood-Sherer, D., & Warmbier, H. (2007). Effects of hippotherapy on postural stability, in persons with multiple sclerosis: A pilot study. *Journal of Neurologic Physical Therapy*, *31*(2), 77–84.

Smith-Osborne, A., & Selby, A. (2010). Implications of the literature on equine-assisted activities for use as a complementary intervention in social work practice with children and adolescents. *Child and Adolescent Social Work Journal*, *27*, 291–307.

Snider, L., Korner-Bitensky, N., Kammann, C., Warner, S., & Saleh, M. (2007). Horseback riding as therapy for children with cerebral palsy: Is there evidence of its effectiveness? *Physical & Occupational Therapy in Pediatrics*, *27*(2), 5–23.

Sterba, J.A. (2007). Does horseback riding therapy or therapist-directed hippotherapy rehabilitate children with cerebral palsy? *Developmental Medicine and Child Neurology*, *49*(1), 68–73.

Substance Abuse and Mental Health Services Administration (SAMHSA). (2016). *Critical Issues Facing Veterans and Military Families*. Retrieved from: www.samhsa.gov/veterans-military-families/critical-issues

Sung, Y.H., Kim, C.J., Yu, B.K., & Kim, K.M. (2013). A hippotherapy simulator is effective to shift weight bearing toward the affected side during gait in patients with stroke. *Neuro Rehabilitation*, *33*(3), 407–412.

Sunwoo, H., Chang, W.H., Kwon, J.-Y., Kim, T.-W., Lee, J.-Y., & Kim, Y.-H. (2012). Hippotherapy in adult patients with chronic brain disorders: A pilot study. *Annals of Rehabilitation Medicine*, *36*(6), 756–761.

Symington, A. (2012). Grief and horses: Putting the pieces together. *Journal of Creativity in Mental Health*, *7*, 165–174.

Taylor, R.R., Kielhofner, G., Smith, C., Butler, S., Cahill, S.M., Ciukaj, M.D., & Gehman, M. (2009). Volitional Change in Children With Autism: A Single-Case Design Study of the Impact of Hippotherapy on Motivation. *Occupational Therapy in Mental Health*, *25*, 192–200.

Thompson, J.R., Iacobucci, V., & Varney, R. (2012). Giddyup! Or whoa nelly! Making sense of benefit claims on websites of equine programs for children with disabilities. *Journal of Developmental and Physical Disabilities*, *24*, 373–390.

Trotter, K.S., Chandler, C.K., Goodwin-Bond, D., & Casey. (2008). A comparative study of the efficacy of group equine assisted counseling with at-risk children and adolescents. *Journal of Creativity in Mental Health*, *3*, 254–284.

Tseng, S.-H., Chen, H.-C., & Tam, K.-W. (2012). Systematic review and meta-analysis of the effect of equine assisted activities and therapies on gross motor outcome in children with cerebral palsy. *Disability and Rehabilitation*, *35*, 1–11.

Waite, C., & Bourke, L. (2013). "It's different with a horse": Horses as a tool for engagement in a horse therapy program for marginalised young people. *Youth Studies Australia*, *32*(4), 13–21.

Walson, H. (2003). *Detailed Discussion of the Equine Activity Liability Act*. Retrieved from: www.animallaw.info/article/detailed-discussion-equine-activity-liability-act

Wang, G., Ma, R., Qiao, G., Wada, K., Aizawa, Y., & Satoh, T. (2015). The effect of riding as an alternative treatment for children with cerebral palsy: A systematic review and meta-analysis. *Integrative Medicine International*, *1*(4), 211–222.

Wehofer, L., Goodson, N., & Shurtleff, T.L. (2013). Equine assisted activities and therapies: A case study of an older adult. *Physical & Occupational Therapy in Geriatrics*, *31*(1), 71–87.

Whalen, N.C., & Case-Smith, J. (2012). Therapeutic effects of horseback riding therapy on gross motor function in children with cerebral palsy: A systematic review. *Physical & Occupational Therapy in Pediatrics*, *32*(3), 229–242.

Whittlesey-Jerome, W.K. (2014). Adding equine-assisted psychotherapy to conventional treatments: A pilot study exploring ways to increase adult female self-efficacy among victims of interpersonal violence. *The Practitioner Scholar: Journal of Counseling and Professional Psychology, 3,* 82–101.

Wilkie, K.D., Germain, S., & Theule, J. (2016). Evaluating the efficacy of equine therapy among at-risk youth: A meta-analysis. *Anthrozoos, 29,* 377–393.

Wilson, C.C., & Barker, S.B. (2003). Challenges in designing human-animal interaction research. *American Behavioral Scientist, 47*(1), 16–28.

Wilson, K., Buultjens, M., Monfries, M., & Karimi, L. (2015). Equine-assisted psychotherapy for adolescents experiencing depression and/or anxiety: A therapist's perspective. *Clinical Child Psychology and Psychiatry,* 1–18. doi: 10.1177/1359104515572379

Yokoyama, M., Kaname, T., Tabata, M., Hotta, K., Shimizu, R., Kamiya, K., . . . Masuda, T. (2013). Hippotherapy to improve hypertonia caused by an autonomic imbalance in children with spastic cerebral palsy. *Kitasato Medical Journal, 43*(November 2012), 67–73.

Yoo, J.-H., Kim, S.-E., Lee, M.-G., Jin, J.-J., Hong, J., Choi, Y.-T., et al. (2014). The effect of horse simulator riding on visual analogue scale, body composition and trunk strength in the patients with chronic low back pain. *International Journal of Clinical Practice, 68*(8), 941–949.

Yoo, J.-H., Oh, Y., Jang, B., Song, J., Kim, J., et al. (2016). The effects of equine-assisted activities and therapy on resting-state brain function in attention-deficit/hyperactivity disorder: A pilot study. *Clinical Psychopharmacology and Neuroscience: The Official Scientific Journal of the Korean College of Neuropsychopharmacology, 14*(4), 357.

Yorke, J., Adams, C., & Coady, N. (2008). Therapeutic value of equine-human bonding in recovery from trauma. *Anthrozoös, 21*(1), 17–30.

Yorke, J., Nugent, W., Strand, E., Bolen, R., New, J., & Davis, C. (2013). Equine-assisted therapy and its impact on cortisol levels of children and horses: A pilot study and meta-analysis. *Early Child Development and Care, 183*(7), 874–894.

Zadnikar, M., & Kastrin, A. (2011). Effects of hippotherapy and therapeutic horseback riding on postural control or balance in children with cerebral palsy: A meta-analysis. *Developmental Medicine and Child Neurology, 53*(8), 684–691.

5   The Clinical Practice of Equine-Assisted Therapy

☐ Conducting Therapy in a Non-Conventional Setting

Although equine-assisted therapy is considered a novel or emerging treatment, it is not a separate or isolated form of therapy (Ekholm Fry, 2013; Pham & Bitonte, 2016). If licensed professionals choose to use an emerging treatment, or see patients in a non-conventional setting, the laws, ethics, and boundaries associated with their professional healthcare practice and licensure do not change (Becker, 2010; Ekholm Fry, 2013).

The validity of non-conventional therapy settings is demonstrated by the use of exposure therapy to treat phobias and anxieties (Abramowitz, et al., 2012), community-based occupational therapy and mental health counseling (Boyd-Franklin & Bry, 2001; Snider, et al., 2007; Kronenberg, et al., 2010; Scaffa & Reitz, 2013; Westbrook, 2014), and wilderness or adventure therapies used to address addiction, mental health issues, self-esteem, and self-confidence in youth, veterans, and women (Powch, 1994; Gass, et al., 2012; Bettmann, et al., 2013; McGeeney, 2016; Joyce & Dietrich, 2016).

Specific to equine-assisted therapy, the non-conventional farm setting is considered an important and beneficial part of the treatment milieu (Vidrine, et al., 2002; Bizub, et al., 2003; Chardonnens, 2009; Bachi, et al., 2011; Berget & Braastad, 2011; Ekholm Fry, 2013; Carlsson, et al., 2014).

Like any type of treatment (conventional or novel), patients seek equine-assisted therapy for the purpose of addressing clinical issues and achieving treatment goals. Professionals are responsible for adhering to conventional healthcare practices even when providing a novel treatment, or working in a non-conventional setting.

☐ The Right Patient

Not all patients are appropriate for equine-assisted therapy. Licensed healthcare professionals are responsible for using the results of current research along with their clinical knowledge, training, and expertise to decide which treatment best serves the presenting condition and the specific individual. These professionals must determine which patients are best suited for this emerging treatment and at what point in therapy the treatment would be most effective.

Key questions a therapist should consider when determining if equine-assisted therapy is an appropriate treatment include:

- What clinical rational supports the use of equine-assisted therapy for this patient's condition?
- Is there empirical evidence to support the use of equine-assisted therapy for this patient's condition?
- Has the patient been evaluated for any possible precautions and contraindications?
- What treatment goals will equine-assisted therapy specifically address? And, how will incorporating horses and the farm milieu meet those goals more effectively than another, less costly or logistically challenging approach?
- Do the benefits associated with equine-assisted therapy for this condition outweigh the risks involved?
- Does the patient seem interested in equine-assisted therapy? And does he/she like being outside, or have an interest in horses?
- Does the family have the financial resources and time to support the use of equine-assisted therapy?
- Can equine-assisted therapy be delivered in a consistent manner based upon the patient's situation?
- Does the patient (or his/her parents, referral source, etc.) understand the investigational nature of equine-assisted therapy, and is he/she willing to sign a consent form to participate in this type of novel treatment?

Although professionals may be inclined to rely upon their own experiences of equine-assisted therapy and its impact on different patients, they are also responsible for knowing which benefits can be supported by empirical study and which cannot. Precautions and contraindications and the inherent risk of the treatment also complicate matters, and make careful assessment and evaluation on the part of the licensed professional even more important (Tseng, et al., 2012).

Clinical Indications

Many benefits claims related to equine-assisted therapy are advertised by providers and national associations. In some cases, the benefits mentioned are supported only by limited research, and in others the benefits may not be supported by any empirical research whatsoever. The widespread use of anecdotal reports applied in place of empirical evidence, or citing research that isn't transferable to the type of therapy offered, can mislead consumers into believing equine-assisted therapy is a "proven" treatment approach.

Conditions like ADHD, muscular dystrophy, spina bifida, and depression are widely reported to be effectively treated by equine-assisted therapy. However, current research does not support these claims. Other populations like veterans or active military personnel and autism are commonly treated using hippotherapy, and in many cases professionals suggest this practice is strongly supported by current research. This is inaccurate, as not a single research project published in a peer-reviewed journal could be located at the time of writing this book that investigated the use of hippotherapy for veterans or active military personnel, and out of the 24 published research articles studying the use of an equine-assisted interaction for individuals with autism, only three used hippotherapy.

A vast majority of the current research investigates the use of non-clinical equine-assisted interactions like adaptive riding or equine-assisted learning used to address or even "treat" serious medical conditions like autism and combat-related PTSD. It is impossible to assume a non-therapy method will produce the same or even similar results as a therapy service. Therefore, professionals cannot in good faith use the results of a study conducted using a non-therapy method provided by a non-licensed paraprofessional to support their own clinical decision making.

Given the lack of conclusive evidence, and the investigational nature of equine-assisted therapy, it is not yet possible to state with any certainty that equine-assisted therapy is clinically indicated for a specific population. However, it is helpful for professionals to have a clear understanding of which populations or conditions have been empirically studied. Professionals interested in providing any form of equine-assisted therapy are urged to do so with caution, carefully evaluating their patients for any signs that the treatment may be causing harm, or not producing the desired results. It is also recommended that providers are clear in their marketing materials, and indicate which benefits claims are empirically based, and which are anecdotal.

The following is a list of conditions or populations that have been empirically investigated using a documented form of therapy with outcomes published in a peer-reviewed journal. This list does not include all the studies conducted using a non-therapy method like adaptive riding or equine-assisted learning. Detailed information about these studies can be found in Chapter Four of this book:

- Addictions or chemical dependency (three studies/equine-assisted mental health)
- Anxiety (one study/equine-assisted mental health)
- At-risk youth (eight studies/equine-assisted mental health)
- Autism (three studies/hippotherapy)

- Cerebral palsy (24 live horse studies/hippotherapy)
- Down syndrome (three studies/hippotherapy)
- Eating disorders (four studies/equine-assisted mental health)
- Elderly populations (four live horse studies/hippotherapy)
- Grief (one hippotherapy study/one equine-assisted mental health study)
- Intellectual disabilities (two studies/hippotherapy)
- Multiple sclerosis (five studies/hippotherapy)
- Neurological conditions (four studies/hippotherapy)
- Non-combat PTSD, trauma, and abuse (13 equine-assisted mental health studies/one hippotherapy study)
- Psychiatric conditions or mental illness (five studies/equine-assisted mental health)
- Self-harming behaviors (two studies/equine-assisted mental health)
- Spinal cord injury (two studies/hippotherapy)
- Stroke (two live horse studies/hippotherapy)
- Veterans or active military personnel (three studies/equine-assisted mental health)

Precautions and Contraindications

Equine-assisted therapy presents unique circumstances and additional risks not found in other clinical settings (Cook, 2011). Precautions and contraindications for the use of equine-assisted therapy are numerous, and are based upon the individual circumstances, the condition, the specific patient, and the training and licensure of the provider.

It is advised that professionals read the American Hippotherapy Association Inc.'s (AHA) "Best Practice for Use of Hippotherapy by Occupational Therapy, Physical Therapy, and Speech-Language Pathology Professionals" (AHA, 2017) and the PATH Intl. "Precautions and Contraindications," gain consultation from experienced medical and mental health professionals, and develop their own set of precautions and contraindications given the services they provide, the conditions they treat, and the treatment setting. However, AHA and PATH Intl. provide the following precautions and contraindications to help guide the ethical use of the treatment (PATH Intl., 2016; AHA, 2017):

Precautions May Include

- Age (under 3 or elderly)
- Gross obesity
- Height and weight
- History of animal abuse
- History of fire setting
- History of seizure disorder
- Joint mobility limitation

- Medication side effects
- Migraines
- Stress-induced reactive airway disease (asthma)
- Suspected current or past physical, sexual, and/or emotional abuse

Contraindications May Include

- Actively dangerous to self or others (suicidal, homicidal, aggressive)
- Actively delirious, demented, dissociative, psychotic, or severely confused (including severe delusion involving horses)
- Acute herniated disc with or without nerve root compression
- Actively substance abusing
- Atlantoaxial instability (AAI)—a displacement of the C1 vertebra in relation to the C2 vertebra as seen on x-ray or computed tomography of significant amount (generally agreed to be greater than 4 mm for a child), with or without neurologic signs as assessed by a qualified physician; this condition is seen with diagnoses which have ligamentous laxity such as Down syndrome or juvenile rheumatoid arthritis
- Chiari II malformation with neurologic symptoms
- Coxa arthrosis—degeneration of the hip joint; the femoral head is flattened and functions like a hinge joint rather than as a ball and socket joint. Sitting on the horse puts extreme stress on the joint.
- Grand mal seizures—uncontrolled by medications
- Hemophilia with a recent history of bleeding episodes
- Indwelling urethral catheters
- Medical conditions during acute exacerbations (rheumatoid arthritis, herniated nucleus pulposis, multiple sclerosis, diabetes, etc.)
- Open wounds over a weight-bearing surface
- Pathologic fractures without successful treatment of the underlying pathology (e.g. severe osteoporosis, osteogenesis imperfecta, bone tumor, etc.)
- Tethered cord with symptoms
- Unstable spine or joints including unstable internal hardware

Informed Consent

If the results of careful assessment suggest that equine-assisted therapy may be a useful treatment for the patient, it is essential that the patient (or his/her parent/guardian) is provided with full disclosure regarding the evidence (or lack thereof) supporting the intervention and its potential risks (Tseng, et al., 2012). Patients also have a right to understand what treatment may be like, and what unique characteristics or circumstances they may encounter. Additional costs and travel time should be addressed, and the licensed professional has a responsibility to consider if this additional cost or time might cause undue stress or harm to the patient or his/her parent/guardian, or limit the effectiveness of treatment in any way.

Once all of the information has been presented, an informed decision can be made by the patient (or his/her parent/guardian) regarding whether or not to consent to treatment. This is a critical legal and ethical step to conducting treatment. Consent indicates the patient understands the risks and benefits of the service, and is willing to actively engage in the treatment process.

Right Patient, Wrong Time?

Through careful assessment a licensed professional may identify a patient who would be well served by equine-assisted therapy, but the next question to be asked is, "Is now the right time?"

Take for example, a child with cerebral palsy. Although the patient appears to meet all necessary criteria and seems like a good fit, the therapist must take into consideration the timing of the treatment. Hippotherapy is known to be physically challenging (Debuse, et al., 2009), and the therapist may want to see the patient in an office setting until he/she has built up a level of strength, and then introduce him/her to the farm environment. Also, during treatment, the patient may have setbacks and the office setting could be more suited to help him/her regain strength before returning to equine-assisted therapy.

In the case of mental health professionals, working with horses can be provocative (Karol & Tac, 2007), and in some cases the patient may not be ready for the possible unintended disclosure which equine-assisted therapy can invoke. The professional may wish to see the patient in the office until the patient is emotionally and mentally prepared, and skilled enough to manage the outcomes of such disclosure.

Finally, at any time during the use of equine-assisted therapy, a licensed professional may realize the intervention isn't right for the patient at the time, and transition the patient back to an office setting. Sometimes patients need less stimuli and require the safety and comfort of an office setting, or they may need complete confidentiality that cannot be guaranteed in the dynamic farm environment.

☐ The Right Type of Treatment

Once care has been established with the appropriate licensed healthcare professional, and the licensed professional has evaluated the patient to determine if including horses and the farm milieu is a good option for the patient, it is time to determine what model or method will best address the patient's treatment goals.

Each treatment model is different, and may be more or less effective based upon the type of therapy it is paired with and the population or condition treated. Research and publication related to these different treatment strategies and models of equine-assisted therapy is still in its infancy, but a few researchers and authors have tackled the challenge, attempting to define, describe, and clarify the theoretical or philosophical foundations and practical applications of different forms of equine-assisted therapy (Engel & MacKinnon, 2007; Karol & Tac, 2007; Hallberg, 2008; Latella & Langford, 2008; Kirby, 2010, Bachi, 2013; Brandt, 2013; Cook, 2013; Carlsson, et al., 2014; Notgrass & Pettinelli, 2015; Thomas & Lytle, 2016; Kirby, 2016).

Continued study and rigorous research is still needed to build upon existing concepts and to establish unified, comprehensive, theoretical frameworks and practical applications for the various treatment models used. Even with this lack of research, professionals have a responsibility to be as knowledgeable as possible about the different treatment options and use their best clinical judgement when choosing to include horses in human healthcare.

The upcoming section briefly introduces readers to hippotherapy, equine-facilitated psychotherapy, the EAGALA model of equine-assisted psychotherapy, and equine-assisted counseling. These emerging models are most commonly referenced in the literature, although it is assumed that over time new models will develop and these will morph and change. Readers are urged to learn more about each of these models, and additional resources are provided in each section to help in this effort.

Hippotherapy

Hippotherapy describes the way in which licensed physical, occupational, and speech therapists incorporate equine movement and the farm milieu into their therapy sessions. According to the AHA, these professionals "use clinical reasoning in the purposeful manipulation of equine movement to engage sensory, neuromotor, and cognitive systems to achieve functional outcomes" (AHA, 2016).

Hippotherapy is not to be confused with an adaptive riding lesson. Rather, hippotherapy consists of treatment exercises and activities that take place while the patient is mounted on the horse, usually focusing on improving balance, posture, and gross motor function, and increasing sensory integration, neurologic function, neuromuscular coordination, or motor learning (Benda, et al., 2003; Lechner, et al., 2007; Macauley & Gutierrez, 2004; Latella & Langford, 2008; McGibbon, et al., 2009; Angoules, et al., 2015). In most cases, patients do not control the direction or pace of the horse during hippotherapy (Lechner, et al., 2007; Shurtleff, et al., 2009; Encheff, et al., 2012; Ajzenman, 2013), and most activities take place at the walk in an enclosed arena (Lechner, et al., 2007; Cook, 2014).

Licensed physical, occupational, or speech therapists conduct the therapy session, and are typically supported by horse handlers who control and direct the horse, and side walkers who support the patient during the mounted segment of the session. The horse may be led through obstacles or patterns (like a figure eight or a serpentine) or asked to change direction, length of stride, or tempo (Shurtleff, et al., 2009; Encheff, et al., 2012; Ekholm Fry, 2013; Ajzenman, 2013). The therapist may manually intervene, helping the patient through stretches, exercises, or activities that take place while mounted on the horse (Lechner, et al., 2003). Regular equipment like bareback pads, halters, lead ropes, and riding helmets are used along with adaptive equipment such as safety stirrups and surcingles with handles (Encheff, et al., 2012; Cook, 2014).

Hippotherapy may also be used in conjunction with farm milieu activities that include horse care, grooming, and social interaction (Shurtleff, et al., 2009; Angoules, et al., 2015; AHA, 2016). Although use of the farm milieu is referenced as a part of hippotherapy (Shurtleff, et al., 2009; AHA, 2016), it is of note that the use of farm-based activities is not well documented in research nor in the training of licensed physical, occupational, or speech therapists.

Due to the similarities in training and application, it can be difficult to distinguish between the use of hippotherapy for physical, occupational, or speech therapy (Shurtleff, et al., 2009). However, each of these professions apply the treatment somewhat differently. For example, a speech therapist might use hippotherapy to address social and communication issues while the physical therapist focuses on restoring function and the occupational therapist works on daily living skills and visual or fine motor skills and movement (Personal communication with Rebecca Cook, January 20, 2017). There is much more work to be done establishing how these different professions incorporate horses and use hippotherapy.

Resources

Many physical, occupational, or speech therapists who provide hippotherapy in the United States receive training through the AHA and are certified by the credentialing process of the American Hippotherapy Certification Board (AHCB). This process is considered the gold standard within the equine-assisted therapy industry, and is widely recognized.

To date, few manuals or books have been written about the clinical practice of hippotherapy as provided by the distinct professions of physical, occupational, and speech therapy. The following books were identified as resources specific to hippotherapy, but demonstrate the lack of specificity about the type of therapy used.

- Cook, R. (2013). *Brown Pony Series: Book One: Introduction to hippotherapy*. CreateSpace Independent Publishing Platform.

- Cook, R. (2014). *Brown Pony Series: Book Two: Risk management & safety in hippotherapy.* CreateSpace Independent Publishing Platform.
- Cook, R. (2014). *Brown Pony Series: Book Four: The business of hippotherapy.* CreateSpace Independent Publishing Platform.
- Cook, R. (2015). *Brown Pony Series: Book Three: Considering hippotherapy in your career plans.* CreateSpace Independent Publishing Platform.
- Cook, R. (2016). *Incorporating games in hippotherapy: Companion book to the Brown Pony Series.* CreateSpace Independent Publishing Platform.
- Engel, B. & MacKinnon, J.R. (2007). *Enhancing human occupation through hippotherapy: A guide for occupational therapy.* Bethesda, MD: AOTA Press.
- Spink, J. (1993). *Development riding therapy.* Communication Skill Builders.

Equine-Facilitated Psychotherapy

Equine-facilitated psychotherapy is provided by licensed mental health professionals who either work in tandem with an equine specialist, or who are "dually trained." This term indicates the professional is a licensed mental health provider with horse experience and specialty training in equine-facilitated psychotherapy.

The model is loosely organized around key principles that include viewing the horse as a sentient co-facilitator whose free-form behaviors and interactions provide therapeutic fodder (Hallberg, 2008; Ford, 2013; Brandt, 2013). Use of feedback provided by the horse and opportunities for metaphor enhance the therapeutic process and help bring unconscious thoughts, feelings, and responses into consciousness (Rothe, et al., 2005; Karol & Tac, 2007; Hallberg, 2008; Bachi, et al., 2011; Bachi, 2013; Brandt, 2013).

Another key principle of equine-facilitated psychotherapy is the importance of the relationship between the patient and the horse (Karol & Tac, 2007; Hallberg, 2008; Bachi, et al., 2011; Bachi, 2013). The patient is encouraged to develop a deep relationship with the horse, and engage creatively without pre-scripted activities or tasks. Commonly, patients are invited to observe the horses at liberty in an arena or a pasture, engage in spontaneous activities like touching, grooming, leading, or engaging with a horse at liberty to practice communication and develop relationship. Patients may even paint upon the horse as a form of creative expression. Patients learn about equine communication and behavior, and are taught basic horsemanship skills to help ensure safety and respect for both parties, and in some cases, mounted work might be included as a part of the session (Vidrine, et al., 2002; Karol & Tac, 2007; Hallberg, 2008; Bachi, et al., 2011; Brandt, 2013; McCullough, et al., 2015).

Generally, there is a strong focus on present-moment awareness (Karol & Tac, 2007; Hallberg, 2008) and the integration of the mind-body-spirit connection (Hallberg, 2008; Bachi, et al., 2011). Breathing, meditation, and mindfulness practices are commonly included.

Music, drawing, painting, and other creative arts are used adjunctively (Hallberg, 2008; Ford, 2013), and depth or insight-oriented psychotherapeutic approaches pair nicely. Emerging distinctions within the model include Gestalt Equine Psychotherapy (Kirby, 2010, Lac, 2014) and Equine-Facilitated Body and Emotion-Oriented psychotherapy (Johansen, et al., 2014).

Since equine-facilitated psychotherapy is insight-oriented, and mostly guided by the non-manualized, non-scripted interactions between the patient and the horse, it tends to move at the patient's pace of self-discovery and could be considered a long-term approach to psychotherapy. This model may be well suited for individuals dealing with trauma, abuse, anxiety, and low self-esteem who are seeking increased self-awareness and self-actualization.

Since risk mitigation strategies like teaching patients about basic horsemanship skills and educating them about equine communication and behavior are commonly used in equine-facilitated psychotherapy, the risks associated with the model are lessoned. However, along with the previously mentioned precautions and contraindications, there are other specific considerations to take into account.

Individuals who are not actively dissociated or psychotic, but who are dealing with schizophrenia or schizoaffective disorder, may be served by equine-facilitated psychotherapy, but the depth-oriented activities that are typically included in the model may be precautionary, as they could prompt breaks from reality (Brandt, 2013). Also, individuals with intellectual disabilities may not benefit from the abstract concepts or activities common to equine-facilitated psychotherapy. Other patients who are seeking a brief, more action-oriented form of counseling may also not be suited for the model.

Resources

Individuals interested in offering equine-facilitated psychotherapy commonly receive training from Eponaquest, Adventure in Awareness™, the Human-Equine Alliances for Learning (HEAL), the Equine Psychotherapy Institute, and the Human-Equine Relational Development Institute (HERD). Training programs that focus on Gestalt Equine Psychotherapy like the Gestalt Equine Institute of the Rockies may also be relatable. Although some of these trainings, and the books referenced here, may focus on experiential learning or use different terminology, many of the foundational principles are commonly found in equine-facilitated psychotherapy.

Here is a list of books related to equine-facilitated psychotherapy:

- Buzel, A.H. (2016). *Beyond words: The healing power of horses.* Bloomington, IN: AuthorHouse.
- Dunning, A. (2017). *The horse leads the way: Honoring the true role of the horse in equine facilitated practice.* Bishopscastle, UK: YouCaxton Publications.
- Kirby, M. (2016). *An introduction to equine assisted psychotherapy: Principles, theory, and practice of the Equine Psychotherapy Institute Model.* Bloomington, IN: Balboa Press AU.
- Kohanov, L. (2001). *The Tao of Equus: A woman's journey of healing & transformation through the way of the horse.* Novato, CA: New World Library.
- Kohanov, L. (2003). *Riding between the worlds: Expanding our potential through the way of the horse.* Novato, CA: New World Library.
- Lac, V. (2017). *Equine-facilitated psychotherapy and learning: The Human-Equine Relational Development (HERD) Approach.* Cambridge, MA: Academic Press.
- Hallberg, L. (2008). *Walking the way of the horse: Exploring the power of the horse-human relationship.* Bloomington, IN: Iuniverse.
- Rector, B. (2005). *Learning with the help of horses.* Bloomington, IN: AuthorHouse.
- Shambo, L. (2013). *The listening heart: The limbic path beyond office therapy.* Chehalis, WA: Human-Equine Alliances for Learning (HEAL).

The EAGALA Model of Equine-Assisted Psychotherapy

The EAGALA model of equine-assisted psychotherapy is offered by mental health professionals who work in tandem with an "equine specialist." Both must be EAGALA certified and follow the EAGALA model.

This model is defined by a manualized approach that includes non-mounted, non-horsemanship activities and a specific facilitation style similar to that of a "ropes" or challenge course (Hallberg, 2008; Drinkhouse, et al., 2012; Gergely, 2012; Notgrass & Pettinelli, 2015). In this model, a primary focus is on the process of achieving or accomplishing goals or tasks that include horses (Schultz, et al., 2007; Ford, 2013). In some cases, the horse is considered a therapeutic tool whose responses and actions provide the patients with opportunities for transference, learning, and self-reflection (Schultz, et al., 2007; Gergely, 2012).

The model is action-oriented, in many ways aligning with principles of cognitive behavioral therapy, adventure-based therapy, and experiential education (Notgrass & Pettinelli, 2015). However, it is non-directive in nature (Notgrass & Pettinelli, 2015; Thomas & Lytle, 2016) and does not include teaching skills. Patients are given tasks like haltering a horse or moving a group of loose horses, but a "hands off" approach is used by the facilitators who provide as little information or direction as possible about how to accomplish the task (Notgrass & Pettinelli, 2015; Thomas & Lytle, 2016; EAGALA, 2016). Facilitators use a specific experiential processing strategy that includes carefully observing the patients in their attempts to accomplish the task, and after the designated time allotted for the task, presenting selected observations using objective language (Gergely, 2012). During the debrief, patients have the opportunity for reflection and to generalize their learning (Drinkhouse, et al., 2012). In many cases this model is provided in a group format.

The EAGALA model does not include teaching horsemanship, horse communication, or horse safety protocols, and uses ground-only activities. EAGALA suggests this makes the model "both safe and effective" (EAGALA, 2016). This statement is in direct opposition to the results of research related to equine injuries which state understanding equine communication, behavior, and psychology—and providing safety training—are two of the most effective ways to reduce the risk of equine inflicted injury (Hausberger, et al., 2008; Cuenca, et al., 2009; Hawson, et al., 2010; Cook, 2011; Merkies, et al., 2014; Carmichael, et al., 2014).

Linda Liestman, an equine insurance broker, adds an important perspective:

> Over the past couple years we are beginning to see incidents that cause us concern and we are trying to determine how to deal with this before it becomes a problem. The problems we are seeing occur as therapy moves towards patients/participants being on the ground with horses, and attempting to do something with the horse, such as move the horse around, single a horse from a group, halter a horse, lead a horse, make the horse negotiate an obstacle, etc. without being given safety training or pre-instruction.
>
> (personal communication, May 26, 2016)

She goes on to provide a recent example, "A girl was knocked down when she was told to approach the horse with a halter and figure out how to put the halter on the horse with no safety instruction given" (personal communication, May 26, 2016). Linda provided multiple examples of other insurance claims she is currently addressing that involve participants getting kicked, stepped on, or knocked over during ground-based therapy sessions (personal communication, June 6, 2016). She notes that the accident rate for adaptive riding, hippotherapy, observation-based equine-facilitated psychotherapy, and general riding are acceptably low, with few accidents reported (personal communication, May 26, 2016). Debi DeTurk Peloso of Markel Insurance corroborates, stating that adaptive riding, hippotherapy, and equine-facilitated psychotherapy provided by PATH Intl.-certified individuals are well within the acceptable risk margins, and haven't been subject to a rate increase since 1999 (personal communication, September 16, 2016).

The research results of Hausberger, et al. (2008); Hawson, et al. (2010); and Carmichael, et al. (2014) support the findings of Liestman, showing that serious accidents occur commonly on the ground. Carmichael, et al. (2014) discovered that although injury patterns were different between mounted and non-mounted activities, the likelihood of serious trauma was the same. The researchers concluded, "Horses are dangerous to riders and handlers, as evidenced by equal rates of head injury" (p. 1482).

Given these reports, without safety adaptations the EAGALA model of equine-assisted therapy may not be advisable for fragile populations like small children, the elderly, or those with physical conditions that could be made life-threatening if they were kicked or knocked over by a horse.

The EAGALA model of equine-assisted psychotherapy can also be evocative and the activities may simultaneously raise frustration levels and highlight dysfunctional or maladaptive patterns of behavior (Drinkhouse, et al., 2012). This can be highly effective with some populations, especially "at-risk" youth, families, couples, or groups, while other populations may not respond well to this therapeutic approach.

Resources

Although EAGALA is the only entity allowed to provide a certificate of completion in its training model, other organizations may provide training that is methodologically similar to the EAGALA model. Horse Sense of the Carolinas is one such example, offering training, continuing education opportunities, and program manuals.

Here is a list of books related to the EAGALA model of equine-assisted psychotherapy:

- Hallberg, L. (2008). *Walking the way of the horse: Exploring the power of the horse-human relationship*. Bloomington, IN: Iuniverse.
- Nussen, J. (2012). *Soul recovery: Equine assisted activities for healing from abuse by others, loss of others & loss of self*. CreateSpace Independent Publishing Platform.
- Knapp, S. (2013). *More than a mirror: Horses, humans & therapeutic practices*. Marshall, NC: Horse Sense of the Carolinas, Inc.
- Mandrell, P. J. (2006). *Introduction to equine-assisted psychotherapy*. Maitland, FL: Xulon Press.
- Parent, I.B. (2016). *The fundamentals of equine assisted trauma therapy: With practical examples from working with members of the armed forces*. CreateSpace Independent Publishing Platform.
- Parent, I.B. (2016). *Teamwork in equine assisted teams*. CreateSpace Independent Publishing Platform.
- Perkins, B.L. (2016). *Counseling in nature with at-risk adolescents: Equine assisted psychotherapy and low rope techniques*. CreateSpace Independent Publishing Platform.

- Thomas, L. & Lytle, M. (2016). *Transforming therapy through horses: Case stories teaching the EAGALA model in action*. CreateSpace Independent Publishing Platform.

Equine-Assisted Counseling

Although equine-assisted counseling is the least developed of the three models of equine-assisted mental health, it is an emerging practice that shows promise and deserves continued investigation. Equine-assisted counseling appears to be a practical, problem-solving, skills-based, present-moment approach to mental health treatment that is closely aligned with the principles of choice and reality therapies (Hallberg, 2008; Trotter, et al., 2008; Cameron & Robey, 2013).

Equine-assisted counseling focuses on present and future goals and the process of developing the skills necessary to achieve those goals (Hallberg, 2008). The relationship between the horse and the patient becomes a fertile teaching ground where patients can practice new skills and witness their own challenges and successes (Hallberg, 2008; Trotter, et al., 2008; Cameron & Robey, 2013). Patients address issues of relationship, control, taking action, and being responsible for their own behaviors, thoughts, and feelings. They learn to make changes in their lives through personal evaluation, planning, and practice (Cameron & Robey, 2013).

Rather than using "ropes" or challenge course-like activities as in the EAGALA model of equine-assisted psychotherapy, equine-assisted counseling is likely to use horsemanship skill building activities including grooming, leading, learning to care for horses, or riding (Hallberg, 2008; Trotter, et al., 2008; Cameron & Robey, 2013). Similarly to equine-facilitated psychotherapy, the inclusion of horsemanship skills helps to reduce the risk associated with the model. These activities foster relationship between the horse and the patient, and increase independence and self-efficacy, guiding the patient away from reliance or dependence upon the therapist.

Since equine-assisted counseling is present-moment focused, it does not necessitate that patients investigate their history or engage in depth-oriented psychotherapy. As such, this type of therapy may not be suited for those in the initial/mid-stages of dealing with past trauma and abuse. However, in later stages of recovery from trauma, this approach may be much more applicable.

Generally, equine-assisted counseling is likely a good match for patients who enjoy a practical skills-oriented approach that involves setting goals, making plans, and working hard to accomplish their desired outcome. This approach may be brief or short-term in nature, with patients seeking out guidance to address a specific goal and discontinuing services once that goal has been reached.

Resources

Since this model is developing, no specific trainings could be identified and few books detail this approach. However, these three resources may be of help to learn more about the model:

- Burgon, H. (2014). *Equine-assisted therapy and learning with at-risk young people.* London, UK: Palgrave Macmillan.
- Hallberg, L. (2008). *Walking the way of the horse: Exploring the power of the horse-human relationship.* Bloomington, IN: Iuniverse.
- Trotter, K.S. (2011). *Harnessing the power of equine assisted counseling: Adding animal assisted therapy to your practice.* New York, NY: Routledge.

☐ The Right Setting

Even though equine-assisted therapy takes place in a non-conventional setting like a barn, farm, or riding stable, the facility still must to be viewed as a healthcare establishment that provides a professional service.

The National Institute of Building Sciences provides guidance for healthcare facilities, stating:

> The facility conveys a message to patients, visitors, volunteers, vendors, and staff. Ideally, that message is one that conveys welcoming, caring, comfort, and compassion, commitment to patient well-being and safety, where stress is relieved, refuge is provided, respect is reciprocated, competence is symbolized, way-finding is facilitated, and families are accommodated.
>
> (Carr, 2014, para. 1)

Along with ensuring the equine-assisted therapy facility feels welcoming, safe, and comfortable, the facility must also operate under the same legal and ethical safety perimeters as would any conventional healthcare facility. Program directors or other staff who manage the clinical services that take place at the facility are, in essence, healthcare administrators. This means they must be trained to understand, adapt, and implement healthcare laws, standards, ethics, policies, procedures, and protocols in the equine-assisted therapy setting.

Facility Considerations

The equine-assisted therapy setting is unique as it combines aspects of a farm with a healthcare environment where people receive treatment for physical and mental health conditions. This complicated dynamic necessitates careful risk assessment and risk management with special attention paid to issues of safety, confidentiality, accessibility, hygiene, and professionalism.

The care, upkeep, and appearance of a healthcare facility is important for patient wellbeing and for the reputation of the program or provider. Facilities should meet basic conventional healthcare standards which include general upkeep, life safety, confidentiality, and recordkeeping considerations.

Probably the biggest struggle healthcare providers face when dealing with a non-conventional setting is the ability to protect patient confidentiality and assert appropriate clinical boundaries (Becker, 2010; Bachi, et al., 2011).

The juxtaposition of a confidential healthcare service that takes place in an open setting, or even at a public facility where non-therapy services are also provided, can cause challenges for licensed professionals. Lack of designated confidential farm-based treatment areas, the difficulty in maintaining acoustical and visual privacy during treatment, and the way in which confidential patient information is shared and stored can pose opportunities for unintentional breaches of confidentiality.

Although licensed professionals providing equine-assisted therapy may have patients sign a confidentiality waiver which acknowledges the provider cannot guarantee the confidentiality of the patient while at the farm, this action does not abdicate the professional's responsibility to use every means possible to maintain patient confidentiality.

Although each professional may have different requirements related to patient confidentiality during treatment, all healthcare providers utilizing the farm environment have an important responsibility to safeguard patient confidentiality. Professionals are urged to consider the following questions when evaluating the facility for equine-assisted therapy use:

- Does the facility appear well maintained and cared for? Are the animals healthy? Is the treatment equipment up to date and safe?
- Are the treatment spaces private and protected from public areas?
- Is there acoustical and visual privacy from public spaces, including waiting areas, driveways, pedestrian paths, and main roads?
- Is there a private area to conduct treatment team meetings or meet with patients or parents?
- Where are patient records stored, and how are they handled? Do these practices meet standards of the Health Insurance Portability and Accountability Act (HIPAA)?
- How is patient and visitor movement managed while on site?
- Does the facility have all of the spaces needed for the specific type of therapy (i.e. outdoor/indoor arenas, small working spaces, fenced pasture, sitting areas, private therapy rooms or outdoor spaces, a sensory trail, etc.)
- Is there a professional, comfortable, and welcoming waiting area for patients, parents, and caregivers?
- Is there an accessible bathroom?
- Does the facility meet basic healthcare facility requirements like having lighted exit signs, fire extinguishers, fire alarms, sprinklers, posted

emergency information, an evacuation plan, and a locked cabinet for animal medication storage?

- Is there enough parking?
- Can patients easily find their way around the facility? Are private and public areas well marked?
- Does the facility meet requirements of the Americans With Disabilities (ADA) Act?
- Is the facility fully fenced with a gated entrance? If not, how are visitors checked in and monitored?

The PATH Intl. standards also provide a helpful and comprehensive resource when considering a facility's appropriateness. They can be accessed online at www.pathintl.org.

Personnel Considerations

People are a vital part of any clinical setting. How they present themselves and the way they interact with patients plays an important role in professionalizing the setting and making patients feel safe, comfortable, and welcomed. Providing equine-assisted therapy is not the same as offering riding lessons or other, non-therapy, equine services. Differentiating between therapy and non-therapy services is ethically and legally important, and how the staff present themselves can help patients identify they are receiving a healthcare service.

Just as in conventional healthcare settings, the providers, staff, or volunteers working at an equine-assisted therapy program have a responsibility to act and dress professionally and consider how their demeanor may be perceived by patients. Although the farm milieu can afford therapists the ability to connect more authentically with their patients, boundary violations are also more prevalent (Becker, 2010; Bachi, et al., 2011). Therapists, staff, and volunteers walk a fine line between appearing too casual and therefore risking unintentional boundary violations, or seeming too rigid and formal.

Non-licensed staff employed at programs that offer equine-assisted therapy and even the volunteers who assist with services should be trained and educated about healthcare practices just as if they worked in a conventional healthcare setting. This will help to foster greater awareness about the importance of adhering to conventional healthcare practices, laws, and ethics.

☐ Designing the Equine-Assisted Therapy Session

Assuming care has already been established with a patient, a treatment plan is in place, and the results of careful evaluation suggest that equine-assisted therapy is an appropriate treatment option, it is time to begin contemplating the design of the equine-assisted therapy session.

Develop Session Goals

The first step in designing an equine-assisted therapy session is to carefully review the patient's treatment plan and determine which treatment goals will be addressed during the session. This process necessitates that licensed professionals use clinical reasoning coupled with research results—and the values, preferences, or individual limitations of their patients—in an effort to provide the best "evidence-based" approach possible (Sackett, et al., 2000).

Setting session goals is an important part of the patient-professional collaborative process. The best treatment plans are likely the result of a collaborative effort between the licensed professional and the patient or the patient's parent or guardian (Coulter, 2011). If patients or their parents/guardians (if the patient is too young or doesn't have the cognitive ability) feel empowered by the treatment process, they are more likely to engage and work harder to achieve their treatment goals. Talking through these goals before the session begins, and discussing the outcomes at the end of the session, can help the patient (or parents) feel more engaged and invested in treatment. This process can also help professionals evaluate the effectiveness of the treatment on a session-by-session basis, and make changes to the treatment plan as necessary.

Both long-term treatment goals and shorter-term session goals should be written in a manner consistent with whatever form of conventional therapy the professional offers. For example, a long-term occupational therapy goal could read "Demonstrate improved endurance and strength for postural control and upper extremity function by maintaining position for 4 minutes with verbal cues." Each session is composed of specific activities conducted while mounted on a horse designed to help to achieve this goal. It is important each of these activities is worded clinically, not as an equine activity. For instance, a session or short-term goal might read, "The patient will be able to push himself erect from a prone position with little assistance and maintain the position for 2 minutes."

Similarly, a mental health goal could read, "Decrease anxiety symptoms and demonstrate increased ability to function independently." A corresponding short-term goal could read, "The patient will be able to follow a simple set of directions and engage in a solo activity for 5 minutes with little additional contact with the therapist." The activity conducted to address this goal includes teaching the patient how to groom a horse, and then practice grooming alone with the therapist at a safe distance observing.

The task of the therapist is to match clinical goals with appropriate equine activities. This is one of the key areas in which specialized training in equine-assisted therapy is necessary for a professional to be considered competent.

Determine the Context

Dependent upon the presenting issues of the patient and the associated treatment goals, the licensed professional must determine what context therapy will take place. Would group or individual therapy be most effective? What is the right dose (length of session, frequency, and duration of treatment) of equine-assisted therapy for the condition and the service? These important decisions can alter the effectiveness of treatment.

Individual vs. Group

The AHA (2010) states, "Hippotherapy is a one-on-one treatment and generally occurs until the client meets discharge criteria" (p. 1). Although physical, occupational, and speech therapists may use other farm-based activities which could include a group approach, research does indicate that typically physical, occupational, and speech therapists see patients individually, whereas mental health professionals are more likely to see patients both individually and in a group context (Stroud & Hallberg, 2016).

The choice to see a patient individually or in a group context should be made based upon clinical reasoning and the presenting needs of the patient, not because either approach is easier or more cost/time-effective for the therapist. Many patients require the privacy and complete attention of the therapist, and thus individual therapy is the appropriate choice. However, in some cases patients would benefit from supported interactions with peers and learning from the experiences of others. In this case, a group context might be indicated. But it is important to remember that not every patient is suited for group therapy, and not every treatment model supports the group context.

Providing therapy in a group context is a nuanced specialization, and conducting groups with horses is even more specialized (Schroeder & Stroud, 2015). Licensed professionals considering offering equine-assisted therapy groups are advised to obtain additional training and supervision in group facilitation and group dynamics, and ensure they can maintain the safety of the group while working with equines.

Finally, if a group context is chosen, the number of patients per group is important to consider both for clinical reasons and to address the staff-to-animal-to-patient ratios. When providing groups, the training requirements for staff and animals are different as are the facility needs. Licensed professionals must take all of this into account prior to offering group sessions, and make sure they have enough trained staff or volunteers to support the group format, and that their animals and facility are appropriate for offering groups.

Session Length, Frequency, and Duration of Treatment

Establishing therapeutic dosing for any treatment is a science that combines many factors, and necessitates formal (and well-designed) dose-response studies, through evaluation of existing research results, and ongoing patient observation and titration of the treatment (FDA, 1994).

Healthcare professionals who recommend any treatment are expected to carefully monitor their patients to determine the effectiveness of the dose. If the dose is effective, the patients will show notable improvement in symptomology without severe side effects. Along with ensuring the patient can tolerate the treatment without side effects, healthcare professionals must also evaluate the responsiveness of their patients and titrate the treatment accordingly.

Little research has been done to date to establish the proper dose of the various equine-assisted therapy services based upon condition or stage in treatment. This is a critical step in gaining creditability for the equine-assisted therapy industry (Vohnout, 2011; Holm, et al., 2014; Berg & Causey, 2014; Kendell, et al., 2015).

At present, the variations in possible dosing are notable ranging from 4–40 sessions of different lengths and types (Whalen & Case-Smith, 2012; Tseng, et al., 2012; Park, et al., 2014; Kendall, et al., 2015; Nurenberg, et al., 2015). Literature suggests that sessions range in length from 5 minutes to 120 minutes, depending upon the type of service and the context (group vs. individual). According to research, hippotherapy sessions are most commonly 30–45 minutes in length and could take place once or twice a week (Champagne & Dugas, 2010; Cook, 2011; Vohnout, 2011; Whalen & Case-Smith, 2012; Park, et al., 2014). Individual psychotherapy or counseling ranges between 45–60 minutes in length and is more likely to take place once per week (Gresham, 2014; Stroud & Hallberg, 2016). Group psychotherapy or counseling appears to be more time-intensive ranging from 90–120 minutes in length (Schroeder & Stroud, 2015; Stroud & Hallberg, 2016). It is likely this wide variation may be causing some of the mixed and inconclusive research findings (Kendall, et al., 2015).

Given the state of therapeutic dosing and equine-assisted therapy, licensed professionals are urged to follow best practice guidelines for the specific clinical intervention they use, and carefully observe how their patients tolerate treatment. Based upon these observations, professionals may make adjustments to session length, frequency, and duration.

Choose the Appropriate Activity

Once the goals and the session context have been established, it is time to decide what types of activities will best help the patient to achieve these goals. This step is critical in demonstrating that equine-assisted therapy is being used intentionally, not just because the therapist likes the setting or personally enjoys horses.

Designing treatment activities is a skill that develops through education, training, and experience. The professional must learn to apply specific equine activities using clinical reasoning to address long-term treatment goals, as well as short-term session goals. The therapist is responsible for understanding the potential impact these activities might have on the patient, and for determining which activities to use at what stage in treatment. In this author's experience, those new to equine-assisted therapy may design activities that are too complex or difficult for the patient's stage in treatment, or include too many activities for one session. This usually occurs because the professional is excited to try new activities, and concerned about keeping the patient engaged. Many times, instead of being engaged, the patient may become fatigued, overwhelmed, or frustrated.

Physical, occupational, and speech therapists tend to be highly conscious of fatiguing their patients and take active steps to ensure they do not ask too much during the course of one session (El-Meniawy & Thabet, 2012; Silkwood-Sherer, et al., 2012; Homnick, et al., 2013; Baik, et al., 2014; Gencheva, et al., 2015). Hippotherapy and other equine or farm-based activities can be more strenuous than in-office techniques, and patients may be more likely to complete these activities without noticing they are tired, overwhelmed, or in pain. This can be both an advantage and a concern when providing equine-assisted therapy.

For skilled mental health professionals, one simple activity like observing a horse or learning to touch a horse can produce weeks of therapeutic fodder. If a session has too many activities planned, the nuances or subtleties that could emerge from any one of those activities may go unnoticed, and instead, maladaptive patterns might be exhibited as patients feel pushed or overstimulated (Drinkhouse, et al., 2012). Also related to equine-assisted mental health, professionals have numerous approaches or models to choose from, but picking the right one for each individual patient is very important. For example, if a patient presents with a high level of arousal, a history of sexual assault, and challenges with focus and attention, and the treatment goal is to decrease hyperarousal, an EAGALA model activity that involves chasing or moving loose horses in a group context may not be suited. Instead, an individual equine-facilitated psychotherapy session involving an activity that focuses on quiet, calming, and meditative grooming while practicing deep breathing is a choice that can be supported by clinical evidence (King, 2016; Creswell, et al., 2016).

Licensed professionals who provide equine-assisted therapy are typically used to—and likely comfortable with—being outdoors in the natural environment. Many patients who attend equine-assisted therapy do not have the same history or experience. Just spending time outside can be tiring or can even feel overwhelming for some patients. This, coupled with the intensity of the treatment activities, is important to take into account when designing equine or farm activities. Giving patients space to rest, to sit, or to relax in a comfortable position can be a helpful strategy to combat fatigue or sensory overload.

Choose Staff and Animal Partners

Given the session goals, the contextual decisions, and the activities used to address the goals, the next step in designing a session is to determine the personnel needs for the session, including animals. This decision relies upon understanding the functionality and personality of the patient, the amount of time in treatment, the treatment goals intended to be addressed by the session, and the activities utilized.

Choosing Staff

As addressed in earlier sections of this book, licensed professionals have a responsibility to uphold the dignity of their patients (ACA, 2016; APA, 2016; AOTA, 2016; APTA, 2016; NASW, 2016) and to keep them safe (both emotionally and physically) during therapy. Although various training and membership associations have detailed requirements about the staff that must be included during an equine-assisted therapy session, in some cases these requirements may not take into consideration the larger ethical concerns.

Patients have a right to choose how their private healthcare information is shared, and with whom (ACA, 2016; APA, 2016; AOTA, 2016; APTA, 2016; ASHA, 2016; NASW, 2016). Licensed professionals must gain the patient's prior approval before bringing another person into a confidential therapy session or sharing information with such an individual. At any point, the patient can request a change to who is present or how confidential healthcare information is shared.

It is advised that licensed healthcare professionals spend time discussing the possible staffing scenarios, and even introduce the patient to the staff or volunteers who might be present. It is important that the professional gives the patient a chance to decide if the inclusion of these individuals feels safe to him/her prior to conducting the session. Also, throughout the duration of the service, the professional should check in with the patient privately to see if he/she feels differently as treatment progresses.

There are significant differences in staffing models between hippotherapy and the different forms of equine-assisted mental health. During hippotherapy, multiple staff and/or interns or volunteers may assist the licensed healthcare provider in the roles of horse handler and side walkers. The licensed healthcare professional is clearly in charge of the session, providing clinical direction to the patient and the staff/volunteers/interns, or may even step in and physically manipulate the patient's body to enhance treatment outcomes. During the mounted portion of the session, the therapist is likely to focus on guiding the patient through hands-on activities designed to address functional goals, and may give specific directions to the side walkers or the horse handler. It is common for the therapist to use time either before or after the session to meet with the patient and/

or family members alone in a confidential office space to discuss health-related issues, provide activities or exercises to do at home, or discuss progress and set goals.

In contrast, the various models of equine-assisted mental health have different ways in which licensed healthcare providers include other staff, volunteers, or interns. In some cases, the licensed professional works directly with a non-licensed "equine specialist" who is present during most or all of the session. Unlike hippotherapy, in which the licensed professional remains clearly in charge of the therapy session and oversees the staff and volunteers, equine specialists are commonly viewed as a partner with equal but different responsibilities for the clinical session.

As such, the role of the "equine specialist" may include designing and facilitating the equine-assisted activities, attending to the welfare of the horse or horses, and keeping the patient physically safe during the session. It is common for the licensed mental health professional to share confidential patient information with the equine specialist in order to help him/her to achieve these tasks effectively.

This role evolved because many licensed mental health professionals are not trained in equine physiology, psychology, or behavior, and in some cases receive little training in the application of the equine interaction. This led to concerns by the equine community that licensed mental health professionals would not be able to attend to the needs of the horses, or keep the patients safe during a session. In the models mentioned previously, the licensed mental health professional may take an observer role, watching the interactions occurring between the horse, the patient, and the equine specialist, and stepping in only to facilitate the processing portion of the session, or add clinical interpretation. In other cases, the licensed mental health professional works closely with the equine specialist, co-facilitating the experience. In either of these situations, due to the dynamic nature of equine-assisted mental health, it is possible, if not likely, that the therapist will discuss deeply personal psychotherapeutic issues with the patient in front of the equine specialist (Lee, et al., 2016), and in some cases the equine specialist may even comment or add to the discussion.

The relationship between the equine specialist and the licensed therapist is complicated and deserves much greater research (Lee, et al., 2016). The roles of the two individuals appear confusing, and the interaction is fraught with possible ethical boundary violations. One suggestion to help remedy this situation is for licensed mental health professionals to gain more training, education, and experience working with horses and facilitating the equine-assisted mental health session. This would allow licensed mental health professionals to guide the direction of the session based upon clinical goals, use clinical reasoning to choose activities, and decide when it is appropriate to include another person in a session.

If the licensed mental health professional needs safety support during a portion of the session, the role of the horseperson can remain clearly that of an assistant who follows the direction of the clinician. This helps to address ethical issues created by a non-licensed person potentially influencing the direction of a clinical session. If the licensed mental health professional feels a co-facilitator is necessary, as in the case of a group or family session, he or she should work with another licensed mental health professional or Master's level intern in counseling or social work.

Obviously, the equine-assisted therapy industry has some growing to do related to how it handles the inclusion of additional non-licensed individuals in confidential therapy sessions. However, ensuring that the patient feels safe and comfortable is the first and most important step for licensed professionals to take. This includes making sure their patients (or the parents) understand it is their right to choose if additional people are included in the therapy session. Based upon this information, the therapist may have to modify the service, or may even determine that equine-assisted therapy isn't the appropriate intervention at the time.

Choosing Animal Partners

The process of selecting equine partners takes clinical reasoning, thought, and intention (Anderson, et al., 1999; Matsuura, et al., 2008; Moisa, et al., 2012; Janura, et al., 2012). The physiological, psychological, and behavioral characteristics of the horse have a great impact on the patient. Licensed professionals can intentionally use these attributes to enhance the treatment, and animal selection is made based upon pre-existing knowledge about the patient's condition, the treatment goals, and the activities used.

In most cases, physical, occupational, and speech therapists carefully choose a specific horse for the session based upon the clinical needs of the patient and the confirmation, temperament, and personality of the horse. Mental health professionals may use similar clinical reasoning when pairing patients and horses, or may use the "mutual choosing" approach in which patients and horses choose each other with little intervention by the mental health professional. The number of horses who will participate, and how they will participate, is also an important consideration.

In some cases, other animals will be included in therapy sessions. This should occur only after the professional is additionally trained to work with the species and the specific animal.

Licensed professionals learn to make these clinical decisions after specialized training, education, and experience, and may use ongoing supervision as a tool to enhance their skills and knowledge.

Identify the Specific Farm Setting

Given all the factors just discussed, the licensed professional will then decide what farm setting best supports the session. This could be an arena, a smaller pen, a pasture, a sensory trail, or a few chairs near the horses.

Once the setting has been identified, the professional should check the area to make sure it is safe and all necessary equipment is present and in good working order. As a part of this preparation, licensed professionals may want to consider how the setting can be made as comfortable and professional as possible. Evaluating for confidentiality issues and mitigating any concerns is an important step to creating a safe and professional setting. Considering how the patient will be welcomed into the space can also help elevate the professionalism of the service, and set the tone for the session.

Prepare Staff and Volunteers

Another essential step in setting up an equine-assisted therapy session involves preparing any staff or volunteers who will be helping with the session. This includes a brief review of the patient(s) attending, the treatment goals, the activities that will be conducted, the animals who may participate, the setting that will be used, and most importantly, what the roles are of each of the staff or volunteers.

Preparing staff and volunteers also helps with retention issues. Staff and volunteers who do not feel they are properly briefed and know what is expected of them may become frustrated or disenfranchised, and may eventually seek out other volunteer opportunities (Dollard, et al., 2003). The more prepared the staff and volunteers, the more capable, competent, and independent they will become. A prepared staff is a confident staff, and they will help the service run smoothly, and allow the professional to focus more intently upon the patient.

Following a session, it is also important to take a moment to debrief with the staff and volunteers. This offers an opportunity for staff or volunteers to ask questions and voice concerns, and for the professional to offer feedback and direction for upcoming sessions. In many cases, the staff or volunteers may see things the professional missed, and this information can be helpful in developing a deeper understanding of the patient and his/her needs.

Some licensed professionals who work with the same staff or volunteers all day or even for half of a day may do one briefing in the morning for all upcoming patients, and a debrief before lunch or at the end of the day. Others chose to do briefings and debriefings every session. Although briefings and debriefings with staff and volunteers takes extra time, having a well-prepared staff speaks volumes about the professionalism of the service.

Prepare Yourself

The final step in designing an equine-assisted therapy session involves the professional themselves. So often this step is the one that is forgotten or left undone. Licensed professionals are urged to take a moment prior to welcoming the patient into the session to ground and center, check in with themselves, and review their plan for the upcoming patient. This process allows the professional the time to identify how they are feeling, and gives them a chance to move out of their role as organizer and into their role as a healthcare provider. This can be invaluable as it is easy to lose sight of this role when attempting to manage staff and volunteers, deal with horse or facility issues, and prepare logistically for a day at the farm.

In some cases, this time of personal preparedness can take place while staff and volunteers are preparing the horses and getting themselves ready for the session. This can be a nice ritual for all involved. It allows everyone the time to step into their roles and prepare before the patients arrive. This way, when the patients do arrive they are more likely to experience a sense of harmony and order rather than the chaotic energy of people trying to get ready for the session.

With all the moving parts involved in offering equine-assisted therapy, it is easy to rush through to the moment of seeing the patient. But, each one of the steps included here supports the effectiveness of the service, and enhances the professionalism of the industry.

☐ Conclusion

The complexity of providing equine-assisted therapy is not to be discounted or overlooked. The treatment environment is dynamic and nuanced, and presents both opportunities and challenges that are not present in a conventional treatment setting. Knowing how to use these opportunities while mitigating the risks takes skill gained through training, experience, and support.

As the industry advances, professionals will refine their knowledge and expertise, becoming more and more capable and effective in helping patients reach their individual treatment goals through the use of equine-assisted therapy.

☐ References

Abramowitz, J.S., Deacon, B.J., & Whiteside, S.P.H. (2012). *Exposure therapy for anxiety: Principles and practice* (1st edition). New York, NY: The Guilford Press.

Ajzenman, H.F. (2013). Effect of hippotherapy on motor control, adaptive behaviors, and participation in children with autism spectrum disorder: A pilot study. *American Journal of Occupational Therapy, 67*(6), 653–663.

American Counseling Association (ACA). (2016). *ACA Code of Ethics*. Retrieved from: www.counseling.org/resources/aca-code-of-ethics.pdf

American Hippotherapy Association, Inc. (AHA). (2010). *Hippotherapy vs. Therapeutic Riding*. Retrieved from: http://windrushfarm.org/downloads/american.pdf

American Hippotherapy Association, Inc. (AHA). (2016). Retrieved from: www.american hippotherapyassociation.org/

American Hippotherapy Association, Inc. (AHA). (2017). *Best Practices for the Use of Hippotherapy by Occupational Therapy, Physical Therapy, and Speech-Language Pathology Professionals*. Retrieved from: www.americanhippotherapyassociation.org/wp-content/uploads/2015/02/Final-2017-Best-Practice.pdf

American Occupational Therapy Association (AOTA). (2016). *Occupational Therapy Code of Ethics, 2015*. Retrieved from: www.aota.org/-/media/corporate/files/practice/ethics/code-of-ethics.pdf

American Physical Therapy Association (APTA). (2016). *Code of Ethics for a Physical Therapist*. Retrieved from: www.apta.org/uploadedFiles/APTAorg/About_Us/Policies/Ethics/CodeofEthics.pdf

American Psychological Association (APA). (2016). *Ethical Principles of Psychologists and Code of Conduct*. Retrieved from: www.apa.org/ethics/code/principles.pdf

American Speech-Language-Hearing Association (ASHA). (2016). *Code of Ethics*. Retrieved from: www.asha.org/Code-of-Ethics/

Anderson, M.K., Friend, T.H., Evans, W.J., & Bushong, D.M. (1999). Behavioral assessment of horses in therapeutic riding programs. *Applied Animal Behaviour Science, 63*, 11–24.

Angoules, A., Koukoulas, D., Balakatounis, K., Kapari, I., & Matsouki, E. (2015). A review of efficacy of hippotherapy for the treatment of musculoskeletal disorders. *British Journal of Medicine and Medical Research, 8*(4), 289–297.

Bachi, K. (2013). Application of attachment theory to equine-facilitated psychotherapy. *Journal of Contemporary Psychotherapy, 43*(3), 187–196.

Bachi, K., Terkel, J., & Teichman, M. (2011). Equine-facilitated psychotherapy for at-risk adolescents: The influence on self-image, self-control and trust. *Clinical Child Psychology and Psychiatry, 17*(2), 298–312.

Baik, K., Byeun, J.-K., & Baek, J.-K. (2014). The effects of horseback riding participation on the muscle tone and range of motion for children with spastic cerebral palsy. *Journal of Exercise Rehabilitation, 10*(5), 265–270.

Becker, S. (2010). Wilderness therapy: Ethical considerations for mental health professionals. *Child and Youth Care Forum, 39*(1), 47–61.

Benda, W., McGibbon, N.H., & Grant, K.L. (2003). Improvements in muscle symmetry in children with cerebral palsy after equine-assisted therapy (hippotherapy). *Journal of Alternative and Complementary Medicine, 9*(6), 817–825.

Berg, E.L., & Causey, A. (2014). The life-changing power of the horse: Equine-assisted activities and therapies in the U.S. *Animal Frontiers, 4*, 72–75.

Berget, B., & Braastad, B.O. (2011). Animal-assisted therapy with farm animals for persons with psychiatric disorders. *Ann Ist Super Sanità, 47*(4), 384–390.

Bettmann, J.E., Russell, K.C., & Parry, K.J. (2013). How substance abuse recovery skills, readiness to change and symptom reduction impact change processes in wilderness therapy participants. *Journal of Child and Family Studies, 22*(8), 1039–1050.

Bizub, A., Joy, A., & Davidson, L. (2003). "It's like being in another world": Demonstrating the benefits of therapeutic horseback riding for individuals with psychiatric disability. *Psychiatric Rehabilitation Journal, 26*(4), 377–384.

Boyd-Franklin, N., & Bry, B.H. (2001). *Reaching out in family therapy: Home-based, school, and community interventions* (1st edition). New York, NY: The Guilford Press.

Brandt, C. (2013). Equine-facilitated psychotherapy as a complementary treatment intervention. *Practitioner Scholar: Journal of Counseling & Professional Psychology, 2*(1), 23–42.

Cameron, J., & Robey, P. (2013). The horse power of choice theory. *International Journal of Choice Theory and Reality Therapy, 32*(1), 87–99.

Carlsson, C., Ranta, D.N., & Traeen, B. (2014). Equine assisted social work as a mean for authentic relations between clients and staff. *Human-Animal Interaction Bulletin, 2*(1), 19–38.

Carmichael, S.P., Davenport, D.L., Kearney, P.A., & Bernard, A.C. (2014). On and off the horse: Mechanisms and patterns of injury in mounted and unmounted equestrians. *Injury: International Journal of the Care of the Injured, 45*(9), 1479–1483.

Carr, R.F. (2014). *Health Care Facilities.* Retrieved from: www.wbdg.org/building-types/health-care-facilities

Champagne, D., & Dugas, C. (2010). Improving gross motor function and postural control with hippotherapy in children with Down syndrome: Case reports. *Physiotherapy Theory and Practice, 26*(8), 564–571.

Chardonnens, E. (2009). The use of animals as co-therapists on a farm: The child-horse bond in person-centred equine-assisted psychotherapy. *Person-Centered & Experiential Psychotherapies, 8*(4), 319–332.

Cook, R. (2011). Incidents and injury within the hippotherapy milieu: Four years of safety study data on risk, risk management, and occurrences. *Scientific and Educational Journal of Therapeutic Riding,* 57–66.

Cook, R. (2013). *Introduction to hippotherapy.* Publisher: Rebecca Cook.

Cook, R. (2014). *Risk management and safety in hippotherapy.* Publisher: Rebecca Cook.

Coulter, A. (2011). *Engaging patients in healthcare.* London, UK: Open University Press.

Creswell, D., Taren, A.A., Lindsay, E.K., Greco, C.M., & Gianaros, P.J. (2016). Alterations in resting-state functional connectivity link mindfulness meditation with reduced interleukin-6: A randomized controlled trial. *Biological Psychiatry, 80*(1), 53–61.

Cuenca, A.G., Wiggins, A., Chen, M.K., Kays, D.W., Islam, S., & Beierle, E.A. (2009). Equestrian injuries in children. *Journal of Pediatric Surgery, 44*(1), 148–150.

Debuse, D., Gibb, C., & Chandler, C. (2009). Effects of hippotherapy on people with cerebral palsy from the users' perspective: A qualitative study. *Physiotherapy Theory and Practice, 25*(3), 174–192.

Dollard, M., Winefield, H.R., & Winefield, A.H. (2003). *Occupational stress in the service professions.* New York, NY: CRC Press.

Drinkhouse, M., Birmingham, S.S.W., Fillman, R., & Jedlicka, H. (2012). Correlation of human and horse heart rates during equine-assisted therapy sessions with at-risk youths: A pilot study. *Journal of Student Research, 1*(3), 22–25.

Ekholm Fry, N. (2013). Equine-assisted therapy: An overview. In M. Grassberger, R.A. Sherma, O.S. Gileva, C.M.H. Kim, & K.Y. Mumcuoglu (Eds.), *Biotherapy: History, principles, and practice* (pp. 255–258). Netherlands: Springer.

El-Meniawy, G.H., & Thabet, N.S. (2012). Modulation of back geometry in children with spastic diplegic cerebral palsy via hippotherapy training. *Egyptian Journal of Medical Human Genetics, 13*(1), 63–71.

Encheff, J., Armstrong, C., Masterson, M., Fox, C., & Gribble, P. (2012). Hippotherapy effects on trunk, pelvic, and hip motion during ambulation in children with neurological impairments. *Pediatric Physical Therapy, 24*(3), 242–250.

Engel, B.T., & MacKinnon, J.R. (2007). *Enhancing human occupation through hippotherapy: A guide for occupational therapy* (1st edition). Bethesda, MD: AOTA Press.

Equine Assisted Growth and Learning Association (EAGALA). (2016). Retrieved from: www.eagala.org

Food and Drug Administration (FDA). (1994). *Guideline for Industry: Dose Response Information to Support Drug Registration.* Retrieved from: www.fda.gov/downloads/drugs/guidancecomplianceregulatoryinformation/guidances/ucm073115.pdf

Ford, C. (2013). Dancing with horses: Combining dance/movement therapy and equine facilitated psychotherapy. *American Journal of Dance Therapy, 35*(2), 93–117.

Gass, M.A., Gillis, H.L., & Russell, K.C. (2012). *Adventure therapy: Theory, research, and practice* (1st edition). New York, NY: Routledge.

Gencheva, N., Ivanova, I., & Stefanova, D. (2015). Evaluation of hippotherapy in the course of multiple sclerosis treatment. *Activities in Physical Education and Sport, 5*(2), 183–187.

Gergely, E.J. (2012). *Equine-assisted psychotherapy: A descriptive study.* Self-published thesis.

Gresham, H. (2014). *Practice patterns of equine assisted psychotherapists.* Self-published thesis.

Hallberg, L. (2008). *Walking the way of the horse: Exploring the power of the horse-human relationship.* Bloomington, IL: iUniverse.

Hausberger, M., Roche, H., Henry, S., & Visser, K.E. (2008). A review of the human-horse relationship. *Applied Animal Behaviour Science, 109*(1), 1–24.

Hawson, L.A., McLean, A.N., & McGreevy, P.D. (2010). The roles of equine ethology and applied learning theory in horse-related human injuries. *Journal of Veterinary Behavior: Clinical Applications and Research, 5*(6), 324–338.

Holm, M.B., Baird, J.M., Kim, Y.J., et al. (2014). Therapeutic horseback riding outcomes of parent-identified goals for children with autism spectrum disorder: An ABA' multiple case design examining dosing and generalization. *Journal of Autism and Developmental Disorders, 44*(4), 937–947.

Homnick, D.N., Henning, K.M., Swain, C.V., & Homnick, T.D. (2013). Effect of therapeutic horseback riding on balance in community-dwelling older adults with balance deficits. *Journal Alternative Complementary Medicine, 19*(7), 622–626.

Janura, M., Svoboda, Z., Dvorakova, T., et al. (2012). The variability of a horse's movement at walk in hippotherapy. *Kinesiology, 44*(2), 148–154.

Johansen, S.G., Arfwedson Wang, C.E., Binder, P.-E., & Malt, U.F. (2014). Equine-facilitated body and emotion-oriented psychotherapy designed for adolescents and adults not responding to mainstream treatment: A structured program. *Journal of Psychotherapy Integration, 24*(4), 323–335.

Joyce, S., & Dietrich, Z. (2016). Promoting resilience among veterans using wilderness therapy. *Wilderness & Environmental Medicine, 27*(3), 427–427.

Karol, J., & Tac, N. (2007). Applying a traditional individual psychotherapy model to equine-facilitated psychotherapy (EFP): Theory and method. *Clinical Child Psychology and Psychiatry, 12*(1), 77–90.

Kendall, E., Maujean, A., Pepping, C.A., Downes, M., Lakhani, A., Byrne, J., & Macfarlane, K. (2015). A systematic review of the efficacy of equine-assisted interventions on psychological outcomes. *European Journal of Psychotherapy & Counselling, 2537*(17), 57–79.

King, A. (2016). Altered default mode network (dmn) resting state functional connectivity following a mindfulness-based exposure therapy for posttraumatic stress disorder (ptsd) in combat. *Depression and Anxiety, 33*(4), 289–299.

Kirby, M. (2010). Gestalt equine psychotherapy. *Gestalt Journal of Australia and New Zealand, 6*(2), 60–68.

Kirby, M. (2016). *An introduction to equine assisted psychotherapy: Principles, theory, and practice of the Equine Psychotherapy Institute model.* Bloomington, IN: Balboa Press Au.

Kronenberg, F., Pollard, N., & Sakellariou, D. (2010). *Occupational therapies without borders—Towards an ecology of occupation-based practices* (2nd edition). London, UK: Jessica Kingsley Publishers.

Lac, V. (2014). Horsing around: Gestalt equine psychotherapy as humanistic play therapy. *Journal of Humanistic Psychology,* 1–16.

Latella, D., & Langford, S. (2008). Hippotherapy: An effective approach to occupational therapy intervention. *Occupational Therapy Practice, 13*(2), 16–20.

Lechner, H.E., Feldhaus, S., Gudmundsen, L., et al. (2003). The short-term effect of hippotherapy on spasticity in patients with spinal cord injury. *Spinal Cord: The Official Journal of the International Medical Society of Paraplegia, 41*(9), 502–505.

Lechner, H.E., Kakebeeke, T.H., Hegemann, D., & Baumberger, M. (2007). The effect of hippotherapy on spasticity and on mental well-being of persons with spinal cord injury. *Archives of Physical Medicine and Rehabilitation, 88*(10), 1241–1248.

Lee, P.T., Dakin, E., & Mclure, M. (2016). Narrative synthesis of equine-assisted psychotherapy literature: Current knowledge and future research directions. *Health and Social Care in the Community, 24*(3), 225–246.

Macauley, B.L., & Gutierrez, K.M. (2004). The effectiveness of hippotherapy for children with language-learning disabilities. *Communication Disorders Quarterly, 25*(4), 205–217.

Matsuura, A., Ohta, E., Ueda, K., Nakatsuji, H., & Kondo, S. (2008). Influence of equine conformation on rider oscillation and evaluation of horses for therapeutic riding. *Journal of Equine Science, 19*(1), 9–18.

McCullough, L., Risley-Curtiss, C., & Rorke, J. (2015). Equine facilitated psychotherapy: A pilot study of effect on posttraumatic stress symptoms in maltreated youth. *Journal of Infant, Child, and Adolescent Psychotherapy, 14*(2), 158–173.

McGeeney, A. (2016). *With nature in mind: The ecotherapy manual for mental health professionals.* London, UK: Jessica Kingsley Publishers.

McGibbon, N.H., Benda, W., Duncan, B.R., & Silkwood-Sherer, D. (2009). Immediate and long-term effects of hippotherapy on symmetry of adductor muscle activity and functional ability in children with spastic cerebral palsy. *Archives of Physical Medicine and Rehabilitation, 90*(6), 966–974.

Merkies, K., Sievers, A., Zakrajsek, E., Macgregor, H., Bergeron, R., & König Von Borstel, U. (2014). Preliminary results suggest an influence of psychological and physiological stress in humans on horse heart rate and behavior. *Journal of Veterinary Behavior: Clinical Applications and Research, 9*, 242–247.

Moisa, C.M., Barabasi, J., & Papuc, I. (2012). Selection methods for horses used in hippotherapy. *Bulletin UASMV, Veterinary Medicine, 69*(1–2), 156–163.

National Association of Social Workers (NASW). (2016). *Code of Ethics of the National Association of Social Workers.* Retrieved from: www.socialworkers.org/pubs/Code/code.asp

Notgrass, C.G., & Pettinelli, J.D. (2015). Equine assisted psychotherapy: The Equine Assisted Growth and Learning Association's model overview of equine-based modalities. *Journal of Experiential Education, 38*(2), 162–174.

Nurenberg, J.R., Schleifer, S.J., Shaffer, T., Yellin, M., Desai, P.J., Amin, R., Bouchard, A., & Montalvo, C. (2015). Animal-assisted therapy with chronic psychiatric inpatients: Equine-assisted psychotherapy and aggressive behavior. *Psychiatric Services in Advance, 66*(1), 80–86.

Park, E.S., Rha, D.W., Shin, J.S., Kim, S., & Jung, S. (2014). Effects of hippotherapy on gross motor function and functional performance of children with cerebral palsy. *Yonsei Medical Journal, 55*(6), 1736–1742.

Pham, C., & Bitonte, R. (2016). Hippotherapy: Remuneration issues impair the offering of this therapeutic strategy at Southern California rehabilitation centers. *NeuroRehabilitation, 38*(4), 411–417.

Powch, I.G. (1994). Wilderness therapy: What makes it empowering for women? *Women & Therapy, 15*(3–4), 11–27.

Professional Association of Therapeutic Horsemanship International (PATH Intl.). (2016). *Precautions and Contraindications*. Retrieved from: www.pathintl.org/resources-education/resources/eaat/203-precautions-and-contraindications

Rothe, E., Vega, B., Torres, R., Soler, S., & Pazos, R. (2005). From kids and horses: Equine facilitated psychotherapy for children. *International Journal of Clinical and Health Psychology, 5*(2), 373–383.

Sackett, D.L., Straus, E.S., Richardson, S.W., Rosenberg, W., & Haynes, B.R. (2000). *Evidence-based medicine: How to practice and teach EBM* (2nd edition). London, UK: Churchill Livingstone.

Scaffa, M.E., & Reitz, M.S. (2013). *Occupational therapy in community-based practice settings* (2nd edition). Philadelphia, PA: P.A. Davis Company.

Schroeder, K., & Stroud, D. (2015). Equine-facilitated group work for women survivors of interpersonal violence. *The Journal for Specialists in Group Work, 3922*, 1–22.

Schultz, P.N., Remick-Barlow, G.A., & Bobbins, L. (2007). Equine-assisted psychotherapy: A mental health promotion/intervention modality for children who have experienced infra-family violence. *Health and Social Care in the Community, 15*(3), 265–271.

Shurtleff, T.L., Standeven, J.W., & Engsberg, J.R. (2009). Changes in dynamic trunk/head stability and functional reach after hippotherapy. *Archives of Physical Medicine and Rehabilitation, 90*(7), 1185–1195.

Silkwood-Sherer, D.J., Killian, C.B., Long, T.M., & Martin, K.S. (2012). Hippotherapy—an intervention to habilitate balance deficits in children with movement disorders: A clinical trial. *Physical Therapy, 92*(5), 707–717.

Snider, L., Korner-Bitensky, N., Kammann, C., Warner, S., & Saleh, M. (2007). Horseback riding as therapy for children with cerebral palsy: Is there evidence of its effectiveness? *Physical & Occupational Therapy in Pediatrics, 27*(2), 5–23.

Stroud, D., & Hallberg, L. (2016). [Horses in healthcare: An international assessment of the professional practice of equine-assisted therapy]. Unpublished raw data.

Thomas, L., & Lytle, M. (2016). *Transforming therapy through horses: Case stories teaching the EAGALA model in action*. CreateSpace Independent Publishing Platform.

Trotter, K.S., Chandler, C.K., & Goodwin-Bond, D.C. (2008). A comparative study of the efficacy of group equine assisted counseling with at-risk children and adolescents. *Journal of Creativity in Mental Health, 3*, 254–284.

Tseng, S.-H., Chen, H.-C., & Tam, K.-W. (2012). Systematic review and meta-analysis of the effect of equine assisted activities and therapies on gross motor outcome in children with cerebral palsy. *Disability and Rehabilitation, 35*, 1–11.

Vidrine, M., Owen-Smith, P., & Faulkner, P. (2002). Equine-facilitated group psychotherapy: Applications for therapeutic vaulting. *Issues in Mental Health Nursing, 23*(6), 587–603.

Vohnout, M.A. (2011). *Increasing public awareness of the benefits of hippotherapy: An advocacy plan*. Self-published thesis.

Westbrook, L.R. (2014). *Community and in-home behavioral health treatment* (1st edition). New York, NY: Routledge.

Whalen, N.C., & Case-Smith, J. (2012). Therapeutic effects of horseback riding therapy on gross motor function in children with cerebral palsy: A systematic review. *Physical & Occupational Therapy in Pediatrics, 32*(3), 229–242.

6   The Business of Providing Equine-Assisted Therapy Services

☐   Practice Patterns of Professionals Providing Equine-Assisted Therapy

As the industry of equine-assisted therapy continues to grow and develop, it would benefit greatly from increased self-study in the form of national and international cross-sectional professional practice surveys. By collaborating in a process of objective information gathering, the industry will be better able to understand, define, articulate, value, and advocate for its unique role within the healthcare system. Understanding the demographics, business practices, and economics of an industry will help individual professionals and the industry as a whole make informed decisions about its future.

To date, what little is known about the practice patterns of professionals providing equine-assisted therapy comes from a few small-scale independent research projects, and the membership statistics of professional associations (Cerquozzi, et al., 2007; McConnell, 2010; Cook, 2011; Gresham, 2014; Cook, 2014; PATH Intl., 2015; Stroud & Hallberg, 2016).

Unfortunately, other than Stroud & Hallberg's (2016) survey, the majority of statistical data is limited to specific professions (Cerquozzi, et al., 2007; McConnell, 2010; Gresham, 2014) or combines membership data from both licensed and non-licensed providers, making it impossible to separate therapy services from non-therapy services (PATH Intl., 2015). However, it is still helpful to review the information available, and begin looking for trends and patterns that will inform professional practice.

Who Are They?

Stroud & Hallberg's (2016) research includes the first cross-sectional international survey aimed at understanding the characteristics and practice patterns of professionals who provide some form of equine-assisted therapy. The results of this study help the industry take shape, showing a majority of providers are white (92%) women (93%) with an average age of 48, who practice in over 50 countries around the world using equine-assisted therapy to address a wide range of conditions including but not limited to anxiety, depression, trauma, autism, learning disabilities, multiple sclerosis, and cerebral palsy. Sixty-four percent of providers hold a Master's degree or higher, and 58% are licensed. Collectively these providers average 8.39 years of clinical experience in their respective fields, and a majority report over 20 years of prior horse experience. Of the 252 respondents, 66% are mental health professionals, 23% are physical therapists, 15% are occupational therapists, and 9% are speech therapists (Stroud & Hallberg, 2016).

Cook (2014) corroborates, reporting a majority (27.7%) of her survey respondents hold 9–15 years of experience providing hippotherapy, and an additional 13.8% have 16 or more years of experience providing services. Cook cites the American Hippotherapy Association, Inc.'s (AHA) membership statistics for 2013 (n = 765) which show 41% of members are physical therapists, 35% are occupational therapists, and 16% are speech therapists.

Although Gresham's (2014) thesis research was limited by a small sample size, her findings were also consistent with those of Stroud & Hallberg (2016) in some areas. She discovered that a majority of professionals providing equine-assisted therapy (equine-assisted/facilitated psychotherapy specifically) were white (90%) and female (93%), with an average age of 49.

Where and How Do They Practice?

Cook (2014) reports 53.2% of physical, occupational, and speech therapists who responded to her survey state they provide equine-assisted therapy at a PATH Intl. facility. She also notes that 36.2% of respondents identified they were employees, 33% provide equine-assisted therapy services in private practice, and 27.7% state they work contractually. It is not clear from Cook's findings if those who report being employees work full-time or part-time.

Stroud & Hallberg (2016) discovered that 67% of physical therapists who responded to the survey reported working at a non-profit center, while 53% of survey respondents use the private practice model. Mental health professionals use the private practice model the most, followed by speech therapists, occupational therapists, and lastly physical therapists. Therapists reported providing services primarily at a shared or collaborative private equine facility (29%), at a public horse boarding facility (25%), or at their own homes (23%).

Of the 252 respondents to Stroud & Hallberg's survey, just under 1 in 5 (19%) of these highly qualified professionals report working full-time in a paid position providing equine-assisted therapy (Stroud & Hallberg, 2016). This is supported by Gresham (2014), whose survey respondents report providing services on a part-time basis, documenting an average of 10.5 patient contact hours per week.

How Are They Funded?

According to PATH Intl.'s (2015) statistics, its member centers obtain 20% of their funding through individual donations, 19% from fundraisers, and 16% from in-kind donations. An additional 19% of all funding comes from participant fees. These statistics do not delineate between equine-assisted therapy practices and adaptive riding centers. Therefore, it is hard to determine what revenue streams are most common for licensed healthcare providers who work at PATH Intl. centers.

Stroud & Hallberg (2016) found 63% of their survey respondents identified "private pay" as their most common source of payment. Only 27% reported receiving insurance reimbursement, with a majority of these professionals being occupational therapists (83%). A smaller percentage of mental health professionals (47%) and physical therapists (38%) also report receiving insurance reimbursement. Funds from grants, donations, or contracts were the least likely source of income.

Based upon Stroud & Hallberg's data, occupational therapists tend to charge the most for their services (average of $130 per hour), receive insurance reimbursement more frequently than other professionals (2–4 times more likely [83%]), retain the highest net pay percentage (74%), and are the only providers of equine-assisted therapy who indicated they felt their practices were financially sustainable (Stroud & Hallberg, 2016).

Overall, the majority (43%) of Stroud & Hallberg's respondents reported they did not believe their equine-assisted therapy practice was financially sustainable. One respondent commented, "Financial viability is extremely difficult in our EAT field due to the cost of equines compared to the income from private pay." Another states, "The overhead for running these types of programs is very expensive. Nobody ever talks about this side of things" (Stroud & Hallberg, 2016).

☐ Business Models

As in any other industry, there are multiple ways professionals can design and operate their businesses. The business model a professional chooses affects expenses and revenue streams. Therefore, it is important to understand the functions of the different models and choose the model most suited for the individual business or professional practice.

The Non-Profit Model

In the United States, non-profit 501(c)(3) organizations are tax exempt and require specific operating practices, policies, and bylaws. "Nonprofit is a designation given by the IRS to describe organizations that are allowed to make a profit but that are prohibited from distributing their profits or earnings to those in control of the organizations" (Zietlow, et al., 2007,

p. 2). These organizations can apply for tax-exempt status from the IRS, and if approved are not required to pay federal income taxes, most state income taxes, and in many cases other taxes like sales tax or property tax.

Non-profit organizations cannot distribute corporate income to share-holders. Instead, profits must remain within corporate accounts in the form of salaries and other payables such as operational expenses to run the business, or as retained earnings that can be used for investments made for and by the organization to fulfill its stated mission. If the non-profit closes, all remaining funds are re-distributed to other tax-exempt organizations or the government and no individual or group of stakeholders personally benefits.

Non-profits are sometimes misunderstood simply because of the term "non-profit." Many believe these organizations make little or no income, and rely mostly on the goodwill of charitable donors. This is a misnomer, as non-profits are free to charge for their services, assuming this action is supported by their mission and vision (Gray, et al., 2004). Depending upon the mission and the services provided, the organization may offer a sliding scale payment plan, or include a statement related to offering services regardless of ability to pay. Non-profits also obtain funds both from charitable contributions and from grants. Those who donate to a non-profit with the federal tax-exempt designation of a 501(c)(3) can claim a tax deduction for this donation. This is an incentive for charitable giving, and these donations help non-profits to accomplish their missions and visions.

Non-profits are not owned; rather, they are governed by a volunteer (and usually unpaid) board of directors and managed by a professional staff. In many cases, non-profits are founded by an individual who person-ally believes in the vision and mission of the organization. This individual may remain on the board, or may be hired as the executive director of the organization. It is important to remember the founder does not own the organization, and if hired as the executive director, still answers to the board of directors. The dynamics of an unpaid, and many times inexpe-rienced, volunteer board of directors providing oversight for staff who are usually experts in their industry can prove complicated, and necessitates thoughtful facilitation (Renz, 2010).

These types of organizations are further complicated as they have two distinct functions; providing services (as per their mission), and man-aging fundraising efforts. The two branches have different stakeholders with separate needs. Each branch requires different marketing techniques, strategic planning, and staff skills. In many cases, one of these branches is stronger than the other, potentially causing challenges with long-term sustainability.

Philosophically, non-profit organizations are mission driven, and as the Non-Profit Finance Fund (2016) states, "Most of us would prefer to think about mission rather than the bottom line" (para. 1). It is common that people who found non-profits do so because of a passionate desire to help those in need, not necessarily because of their business and financial training or expertise.

The non-profit sector is likely to be significantly affected during times of economic hardship (Non-Profit Finance Fund, 2011). Funding sources are less forthcoming, and established revenue streams may decrease or cease altogether. Of the nearly 2,000 non-profits surveyed in 2011, only 19% of these organizations reported having enough savings to provide them with a six-month buffer, while 28% reported having one month or less of cash on hand to cover operating expenses. The majority (32%) report having only 2–3 months of cash available (Non-Profit Finance Fund, 2011). At the same time as organizations face financial fragility, they report an increased demand for free or discounted services.

Given the complications of non-profit management and fiscal stability, it is no wonder Fichman & Levinthal (1991) document that non-profits run the risk of closing their doors after the "honeymoon" period is over. A honeymoon period refers to the start-up phase when an organization may rely upon the personal assets of founders and stakeholders, and the goodwill and positivity of the community to launch the non-profit forward. After the start-up assets dwindle, the organization may be unprepared to raise the funds necessary to continue functioning. In some cases, during this "honeymoon" period, the organization's leaders are focused on providing services and not on the long-term sustainability of the business.

Although undocumented, personal observations and conversations with many providers of equine-assisted therapy support Fichman & Levinthal's theory, suggesting an emerging pattern of non-profit equine-assisted therapy organizations closing after 5–10 years of operation. Different skills are needed as the organization ages, and the founder may not have the necessarily skills to move the organization forward. Also, the energy and effort needed to start and grow a non-profit can be immense, and if good transition planning isn't done, the organization may die when the founder or founding team exits (Adams, 2005).

Learning how to run a successful and financially viable business is key to long-term sustainability. Since so many equine-assisted therapy programs use a non-profit model, additional training and support in the areas of non-profit business management and fiscal planning could help increase long-term sustainability and might decrease center closures.

The Private Practice Model

In the private practice model, the licensed professional owns his or her own business and (in the United States) chooses whatever federal tax structure he or she deems appropriate to protect his or her assets such as a limited liability corporation (LLC) or a professional limited liability corporation (PLLC). The licensed professional is solely responsible for the oversight and management of his or her own business, both developing business practices and managing the business which includes budgeting, billing, payables, accounting and tax reporting, maintaining and protecting patient records, and providing clinical services in accordance with healthcare laws and ethical codes. There is no oversight beyond federal, state, and local laws.

In the United States, those in private practice generally do not receive charitable donations, as there is no tax advantage for the person donating. This can be a limiting factor, but all expenses related to the business are tax deductible for the business owner, and this is of great benefit to those offering equine-assisted therapy.

The private practice business model allows for the greatest flexibility and individuality. Professionals can be nimble and responsive to changes in healthcare trends or the economy. Within their scope of practice, they determine what services to offer, how much to charge for the services, and how they would like to allocate their resources. They also choose the location they would like to conduct their services which could include working out of their own property, renting space, or contracting with another facility. In other cases, group private practices are established that share resources like a facility, horses, and volunteers or staff. Members of the group practice pay a percentage of their earnings to use these resources but continue to operate as sole proprietors of their own businesses.

The primary disadvantages of private practice include a lack of support or oversight when it comes to business management and clinical decision making. Some professionals in private practice do not set their businesses up as independent entities like an LLC or PLLC, or mismanage their finances, and thus put their personal assets at risk. Others do not obtain the correct liability insurance, don't report their income accurately, or provide services outside of their scope of practice, and consequently deal with legal issues. Much of this can be resolved by identifying a cohort of other professionals in private practice and setting up peer supervision meetings on a regular basis. These meetings provide an opportunity to discuss clinical issues that may arise, and also to support one another in the challenges of running one's own business.

The Hospital or Treatment Center Model

In some cases, equine-assisted therapy may be used in a hospital or treatment center. Providers work as part of the treatment team and patients are referred to services based upon identified need or the design of the program (e.g. all patients receive one equine session at the beginning and end of their treatment). The hospital or treatment center assumes the cost of the equine facility and the horses themselves, and the professional is paid for his/her clinical services.

In this model, non-therapy methods may also be used in conjunction with conventional treatment approaches. All non-therapy providers are supervised by licensed professionals to ensure ethical provision of services.

The hospital/treatment center model is advantageous to professionals, as they are not responsible for any of the overhead costs associated with providing equine-assisted therapy. However, the disadvantages can come in the form of professionals having little control over the setting, the animal care, and/or the administration of the services.

Embracing Conventional Healthcare: The Clinic Model

At present, the industry of equine-assisted activities and therapies does not usually follow the typical clinic model established by conventional healthcare providers.

In conventional healthcare settings, patients come to a clinic where they receive services from a myriad of both independently licensed and non-independently licensed (but supervised) providers. Those with advanced degrees and licenses may supervise a cadre of other people, like medical assistants, residents, and interns or students. This model of medical hierarchy helps to ensure the safety and wellbeing of the patients, the coherence of the team's treatment approach, provides clear distinction between the roles and duties of the various team members, and decreases patient costs.

In this system, providers without independent licensure can be a valuable part of the healthcare team, and everyone works together to provide the best care possible for the patients. All services rendered are considered an important part of the treatment plan, and some may be reimbursable by insurance while others may be paid for out of pocket.

If the equine-assisted therapy industry were to follow suit, patients could be admitted under the umbrella of the clinic, and could be evaluated and assessed on site by a licensed professional. Once the evaluation was complete, services would be determined based upon presenting need and a treatment plan initiated that could include physical therapy, occupational therapy, speech therapy, or mental health therapy, and even non-therapy life enhancement or life skills-building services like adaptive riding or equine-assisted learning. All providers would work as part of the collaborative team and non-licensed individuals could be supervised by licensed professionals. Clinic policies and procedures related to facility, patient care, patient recordkeeping, and patient billing would be standardized and follow ethical and legal requirements.

In this model professionals could either be staff, and paid hourly or salaried, or they could be independent contractors, providing services at a set rate. The clinic would be responsible for all expenses, including marketing, collections, facility and animal care, and all administrative costs. Clinics could operate as for-profit businesses or use a non-profit model.

☐ Revenue Streams

For any service to be sustainable and accessible, those providing it must be able to make a living wage, and those receiving it must be able to afford it. Identifying and understanding consumer-friendly, sustainable revenue streams is essential for the equine-assisted therapy industry.

Pham & Bitonte (2016) provide an important perspective on this topic. These researchers investigated why more rehabilitation centers in California were not using equine-assisted therapy. Although 85% of the centers who responded reported a familiarity with hippotherapy and its benefits, only 17.5% offered hippotherapy services to their patients. This led the researchers to question what was causing this phenomenon. They learned that 62.5% of respondents stated the lack of insurance reimbursement as the primary issue impairing the utilization of hippotherapy. Second to insurance reimbursement issues was the inability of patients to pay out of pocket for this expensive service (45%). This was followed by financial concerns voiced by clinics related to providing or supporting equine-assisted therapy (37.5%), and equally noted was the lack of trained therapists available to provide the service (37.5%) (Pham & Bitonte, 2016). Accessibility issues were also reported, as commonly patients must drive long distances to receive services.

Insurance Reimbursement

Insurance reimbursement is the cornerstone of most successful healthcare practices in the United States. As evidenced by Pham & Bitonte's (2016) research, lack of insurance reimbursement for equine-assisted therapy directly affects patients' ability to access the treatment. If a treatment is not reimbursable by insurance, many patients cannot afford to pay for it, and professionals either cannot offer the treatment or are faced with discounting costs to make the treatment more accessible. The second of these options can result in a public perception that the treatment is more affordable than it really is, and providers are faced with cutting costs, supplementing their income, or attempting to attract new clientele or charitable donations to offset the high operating expenses.

The topic of insurance reimbursement related to equine-assisted therapy is complicated. Although licensed healthcare professionals are mostly allowed to use whatever treatment activities, strategies, tools, or approaches best fit the needs of their patients, address presenting conditions, and support the treatment goals, there are some cases when novel or emerging treatments are not reimbursed by insurance.

Generally, insurance companies only reimburse after a treatment is deemed "evidence-based." In recent conversations with Blue Cross Blue Shield Regence, this was made clear by a representative who stated, "'Equine' or 'Hippo' therapy is considered investigational by Regence. Any related claims should be denied as non-covered" (personal correspondence, October 5, 2016). Given the results of current research and systematic reviews, it is clear why insurance companies may choose to deny coverage for equine-assisted therapy. Other than possibly children with cerebral palsy, there is limited (if any) conclusive, high-quality empirical research findings that support equine-assisted therapy as an evidence-based practice for specific populations insured by these companies.

To make matters worse, hippotherapy and the various models of equine-assisted mental health are commonly confused with separate or stand-alone services, when in fact they fall into the category of treatment activities or approaches employed during the provision of a regulated (and conventional) form of healthcare like physical, occupational, or speech therapy, or psychology, counseling, psychotherapy, or social work. This confusion further confuses and alarms insurance companies. The lack of differentiation between therapy and non-therapy services, the fact that there is no standardization in the training and qualifications for providers, and the issues with terminology have only worsened the problem.

The AHA's task force on insurance reimbursement continues to educate both providers and insurance companies about this important distinction. This task force also helps to educate its members about proper use of terminology and billing practices, reminding licensed professionals, "Under no circumstance should a therapist try to bill for services and attempt to hide the fact they are doing hippotherapy from the payer which would be fraudulent" (Casady, 2012, p. 6). The task force also recommends individual therapists contact their patients' insurance companies to talk with them prior to providing equine-assisted therapy.

Physical, occupational, and speech therapists use specific billing codes that best describe the treatment provided, like therapeutic exercise, therapeutic activity, neuromuscular education, or sensory integrative activities. According to the AHA, hippotherapy can fall under one of these already established categories if documented correctly (AHA, 2017). This can make insurance billing somewhat easier for these professionals.

Licensed mental health professionals face a grayer area regarding insurance billing. Unlike physical, occupational, or speech therapists, licensed mental health professionals do not have CPT (Current Procedural Terminology) codes for specific treatment procedures. Other than a diagnostic evaluation, a crisis code, and an interactive complexity add-on code, CPT codes for psychotherapy identify only the length of the psychotherapy session and whether it is individual, family/couples, or group. Licensed mental health professionals choose what approach or technique to use during the session based upon presenting patient issues and their own training and education. However, insurance companies can review treatment plans at any time and determine if the services provided meet a "medical necessity," if the approach is a proven or evidence-based treatment consistent with the best standard of care, and if it is the most cost-effective treatment for the patient's symptoms. Due to the lack of conclusive research specific to various conditions commonly treated by psychotherapy and the added cost of equine-assisted psychotherapy, insurance companies are likely to deny claims that state equine-assisted psychotherapy was utilized.

While physical, occupational, and speech therapists are supported by the AHA, which provides outreach and advocacy for its members, licensed mental health professionals lack a national association specific to their profession and dedicated to the advocacy of all licensed mental health professionals who provide equine-assisted mental health regardless of methodological approach. This limits licensed mental health professionals in their negotiations with insurance companies and state licensing boards.

The industry of equine-assisted therapy seems torn about how to move forward with insurance reimbursement. Some people believe separate billing codes should be established for the various types of equine-assisted therapy, while others think the intervention should be considered a treatment strategy used during the provision of a conventional form of therapy, and therefore does not necessitate separate billing codes.

Probably the most compelling reason to advocate for separate billing codes is directly related to revenue. At present, most licensed professionals use standard CPT billing codes, and thus are not able to charge more for an equine-assisted therapy session than a non-equine-assisted therapy session. As Gresham (2014) notes, most mental health professionals charge between $85–$116 per equine-assisted psychotherapy session, which is in alignment with (if not somewhat lower than) typical insurance reimburse rates for non-equine individual, group, or family/couples counseling.

If new codes were created, costs could be negotiated that might actually cover the expense of the service, and professionals could make a living wage rather than providing the service at a loss or as a hobby or passion, and patients would not have to pay additionally out of pocket for a "barn fee." But, for this to occur it is likely the industry of equine-assisted therapy would have to prove, through conclusive research results, that equine-assisted therapy treats specific populations more effectively, or works more quickly than other in-office strategies.

Unfortunately, insurance fraud is common among healthcare providers (Coalition against Insurance Fraud, 2016). This is not usually because of malicious intent, but rather due to a lack of education and knowledge, and a desire to help their patients (Hyman, 2002). Thus, it is very important that licensed professionals providing equine-assisted therapy be extremely careful about how they bill, and discuss any questions they may have with the insurance companies they work with, or with knowledgable legal aid.

Private Pay

Working with insurance companies can be trying, and jumping through the hoops required to be reimbursed for services has only gotten more complicated. Claims made for equine-assisted therapy may be denied due to the investigational nature of the treatment and patient confidentiality is also harder to protect than in times past. For these and other reasons, many professionals have chosen to use the private pay system.

This system has a number of advantages and disadvantages. It is certainly a far easier system of collections than insurance reimbursement, which requires a different billing and accounting system and very careful documentation. In theory, professionals using a private pay system can charge whatever they like, and provide services in whatever manner they deem appropriate since they are not under contract with an insurance company. This can be lucrative and successful when targeting a niche population, but may not transfer to the larger demographic.

However, the private pay model can also be disadvantageous to the industry as a whole. One of the benefits of insurance reimbursement is the standardization of healthcare fees. Of course, this has its own limitations and issues, but lack of standardized fees can lead to professionals either charging far more than what the service costs to provide, or charging less. For example, if one equine-assisted therapy provider charges $50 for a session while another charges $130, and both seem to offer the same service and have similar experience, the patient is likely to go to the provider who charges less money. Over time, this drives down the cost of services, makes the profession less financially viable, and brings into question the clinical value of the treatment.

Pham & Bitonte's (2016) research further highlights the disadvantage of the private pay system. These researchers note that if patients must pay for the service out of their own pocket rather than using health insurance, they may not be able to afford the service. This can lead to providers discounting services, only seeing a specific demographic, or seeing patients less often than their condition indicates they should.

Heather Ajzenman points out that private pay fees should be based on normal and customary reimbursement rates and recommends using Medicaid as the standard (personal communication, June 25, 2017). The challenge with this approach is that Medicaid rates vary state-to-state and thus don't provide nation-wide standardization. Even private insurance companies tend to reimburse differently based upon the state in which a consumer lives.

Finally, licensed professionals who have contracts with insurance companies but would prefer to accept only cash may not be allowed to do so based upon the contractual agreements they have in place with insurance companies. Also, there are laws related to whether or not a professional who has contracts with insurance companies can charge a different rate for cash-paying patients than those who use insurance. It is very important that professionals follow legal and ethical practices related to accepting cash payments.

Contracts

Some providers of equine-assisted therapy supplement their other revenue streams by seeking and obtaining contracts to provide services to various populations. Common examples include licensed mental health professionals who provide contractual equine-assisted mental health services to residential treatment centers, or physical therapists who work contractually for hospitals or clinics who send patients for hippotherapy.

These contracts can be lucrative and mutually beneficial, and provide financial stability for the professional. The licensed professional benefits because he or she can negotiate a set rate for services, and rely upon the revenue over the duration of the contract. These services can also offer the possibility to work with populations who could not pay for services on their own, but who may benefit greatly from work with horses. This can provide exciting opportunities for increased experience and professional growth.

The program contracting with the licensed professional benefits because its patients receive equine-assisted therapy without having any of the overhead associated with an equine facility, caring for horses, or the other expenses related to the business. Patients and staff alike who attend equine-assisted therapy programs report enjoying the time at the farm, and feeling refreshed and rejuvenated (Carlsson, et al., 2014).

It is of great importance when considering offering contractual programs that the logistics of providing this type of service are carefully considered and attended to. Scheduling, prep time, forms, transportation, program staff involvement, patient management, patient-to-staff ratios, and session documentation commonly cause challenges for equine-assisted therapy providers, and require thought and planning.

In this author's experience, those newer to equine-assisted therapy or unfamiliar with negotiating contracts may start out by setting unrealistic expectations for the contract including allowing too many patients to attend sessions, not identifying appropriate staff-to-patient ratios, not setting clear boundaries related to rules and expectations, or charging too little to be able to effectively staff the sessions.

Charitable Contributions

PATH Intl. reports its centers obtain a significant percentage (at least 55%) of their revenue from charitable contributions (PATH Intl., 2015). Since most of their member centers are non-profit organizations, this is not surprising. The funds from charitable giving are vital to the ongoing financial success of non-profits. They offset operating expenses, pay for patient services, and provide the resources for capital improvements.

For professionals who operate in a private practice setting, charitable contributions count for a very small percentage of their revenue. Physical therapists indicate receiving more revenue from grants and donations than other professionals (Stroud & Hallberg, 2016), possibly because of their close association with non-profit adaptive riding centers.

Like physical therapists, other licensed professionals who work at non-profit centers may also benefit from charitable giving in a number of ways. They may pay a reduced rent for use of the facility since the expenses of the animals and the facility are offset by grants, donations, or in-kind giving. They may also be paid to provide services that are covered by funds obtained through grants or donations. Finally, they may be able to apply for specific grants in a collaborative effort with the non-profit center.

☐ Expenses and Operational Needs

There is no question equine-assisted therapy is costly to provide. Exactly how much is challenging to say as evidenced by PATH Intl. statistics that report budget sizes ranging from $999 to over $1 million annually (PATH Intl., 2015).

There are many variables to consider depending upon the size of the program or the practice. A private practice could take place at someone else's facility and the provider may only pay a small session fee, whereas a program could have a large facility including indoor and outdoor arenas, offices, therapy rooms, pastures, barns, and multiple staff and horses.

Stroud & Hallberg (2016) discovered many of their survey respondents were "unsure" about the actual cost of providing equine-assisted therapy. One wrote, "Great question-don't have this data," and another responded, "Oops, haven't calculated that."

In some cases, survey respondents suggested the expense was equal or greater to the income. One respondent wrote:

> By the time I add in my cost to travel to barn, pay to have insurance billed, time to coordinate with ES [equine specialist], I'm not making any money doing this. It's actually costing me money in that it takes me away from the office during hours I could be seeing clients (without added costs). I do this because I enjoy it and believe it is beneficial.
> (Stroud & Hallberg, 2016)

Given Stroud & Hallberg's survey results and those of Gresham's (2014) survey, the emerging pattern seems to show that many providers of equine-assisted therapy offer their services on a part-time and sometimes pro-bono basis. One might even suggest providers consider equine-assisted therapy a hobby, passion, or labor of love. Although there is nothing inherently wrong with offering services as a hobby or because of a passionate belief in the effectiveness of the treatment, financial insecurity and lack of business acumen can have an effect on patients.

If professionals offering equine-assisted therapy don't craft realistic budgets or think strategically about the design and implementation of their businesses, they may find themselves unable to continue providing services. This can occur because they are not making enough money to sustain themselves and the business, or to pay for the facility and other operating expenses. Of course, if the business fails, this affects patients as they will no longer be able to receive services.

The following information is provided in order to help professionals think strategically and plan for the needs and expenses related to providing equine-assisted therapy.

Facilities

The possibilities for facility use are many and expenses vary greatly between the different options. Professionals can choose between contracting with other equine-assisted services providers, renting space, using their own property, or building/buying a facility. These choices provide flexibility and opportunity for professionals at all stages of practice.

Renting Use of Space

Some professionals identify a facility and make arrangements to rent a portion of the space or pay for use of the space by the session. In this author's experience, professionals could expect to pay anywhere from $2,000 per month for use of a large amount of space where they board their own horses and staff their own services to around $25 per hour-long session. For per-hour rental agreements, it is common for the rate to include the horse(s) and use of a designated space (arena, round pen, outdoor areas, and sometimes even an indoor office). In some cases, volunteers are identified by the facility to assist with the session. If an equine specialist or adaptive riding instructor is required, the professional will usually pay additionally for this support.

Professionals are urged to consider the following questions when looking to rent shared space:

* Are the horses and the facility cared for and treated in a manner that is ethical and aligns with your personal beliefs?
* Does the facility meet your clinical needs? Will you be able to provide services safely and ethically? Will your patients feel comfortable and safe here?

- Will you be able to protect the confidentiality of your patients at this facility?
- Do you get along with the owners/managers, other staff, or volunteers? Can you see yourself working here?

Using Personal Property

For professionals who own their own horse property, using it to provide equine-assisted therapy services can be a very positive arrangement. However, it is important to consider all aspects of this arrangement. Professionals may consider asking the following questions:

- How would you feel about bringing patients to your home? How would your family feel? Your neighbors? Will this impact what populations you will be comfortable serving?
- Who else lives on the property, and can you protect the confidentiality of your patients from family members or possible visitors?
- How do you feel about working with your personal horses? Have you considered issues of transference? Do you think you can separate your personal relationship with the horses from your professional relationship? If so, how?
- Is your property zoned to be able to provide equine-assisted therapy? Is it accessible for patients, and how far will they have to travel?
- Is there enough parking? Where will patients wait? Is there an accessible bathroom that isn't in your home?

For those who provide equine-assisted therapy as a private practice, a percentage of the facility costs, expenses of horse care, and facility maintenance can be written off as a business expense. This can be a significant draw to using one's own property. For those who run a non-profit organization but operate out of their own homes, it is advisable the non-profit organization contract with the owner of the property, identifying a specific area to rent, determining the cost, and signing a rental agreement. Regardless of which model is used, it is important to talk with a tax accountant about setting this arrangement up in a legal manner.

Building or Buying a Facility

Certainly, the most expensive of all options is purchasing or designing and building an equine-assisted therapy facility. An equine-assisted therapy facility can require drastically different infrastructure depending upon what type of service is offered, where the practice or program is located, and what the climate is like. Extensive planning and consultation is recommended for anyone interested in buying or building an equine-assisted therapy facility.

Horse Ownership

The cost of horse ownership must be carefully considered and planned for. Purchasing or obtaining horses can be an expensive undertaking, but it pales in comparison to the costs associated with caring for horses over their lifespan.

The University of Maine reports the average cost of horse ownership in the United States is $3,876 per horse per year. This breaks down to roughly $200–$300 per month per horse (University of Maine, 2012). A more recent estimate provided by the University of Minnesota Horse Extension suggests the cost of owning one horse is closer to $6,400 per horse per year, or $533 per month (Christie, 2016).

These estimates include:

- Hay
- Grain
- Veterinary care and medication
- Farrier services
- Bedding
- Pasture maintenance
- Building maintenance
- Training (very little funds are allocated to this area)

The estimates do not include the expense of boarding a horse, or all of the equipment that goes with horse ownership like halters, lead ropes, grooming tools, bareback pads, saddles, bridles, and veterinary supplies, or barn equipment like waterers or water buckets, pooper scoopers, wheelbarrows, tractors, and arena equipment. Alternative healthcare options for the horses like acupuncture, chiropractic care, or supplements that may help to prevent burnout and keep horses healthier and happier throughout their working lives are also not included.

Between 2006–2011, the American Veterinary Medical Association reported the population of "pet horses" (the group most commonly associated with equine-assisted therapy) decreased from 7.3 million to 4.9 million (Burns, 2013). This is most likely due to the increasing expense associated with horse ownership. Although no data has been published, this may be a significant contributing factor to why some programs have been forced to shut their doors. Those providing equine-assisted therapy certainly feel the financial stress of horse ownership. One possible option to reduce this stress is to increase the number of collaborative environments where professionals come together to share resources including facilities and horses.

The Farm Milieu: A Cost Savings

Recently, providers of equine-assisted therapy have recognized the benefits of offering multi-species interactions (Chardonnens, 2009). Not all patients are interested in working with horses, and some may feel more comfortable interacting with other species of animal, especially when first starting at the farm. At any time during farm-based services, different species offer new opportunities for self-reflection, social interaction, and practicing (or learning) new skills (Berget & Braastad, 2011).

In stark contrast to the costs associated with horse ownership, according to various sources, caring for three chickens may run about $25 per month (Backyard Chickens, 2016) and the University of Minnesota suggests 10 goats could cost upwards of $850 per year or $71 per month (Kaiser, 2008). The ASPCA notes that a dog costs an estimated $695 per year or $58 per month to care for (ASPCA, 2016).

Intentionally, using the farm milieu can drastically reduce the cost of providing equine-assisted therapy services. If providers have the option to work with small animals like chickens, goats, cats, or dogs, or offer nature-based experiences like gardening or excursions around the property, session costs can be significantly reduced. In this model, the number of horses and personnel needed to operate is lessened, as not every session involves extra help or includes working directly with horses.

This approach has the potential to decrease the amount of space needed for the facility, opening up options to provide services in more urban areas and making services more accessible for more people. Using other non-equine activities means that multiple sessions could take place at once, even if a facility only has one arena. For example, a physical therapist could use the treatment room and transition out to work with a horse in the arena while the mental health professional sets up chairs under a tree by the goat enclosure. That therapy session involves engaging with the goats, taking a walk, and doing quiet reflective journaling rather than working with horses.

Of course, if a professional is interested in including other species, he or she is responsible for obtaining the necessary training, education, and supervision needed to understand the unique characteristics of the breed and the individual animal. It is also critical the professional learns appropriate activities and treatment strategies to use with the various species.

Liability Insurance

Although professionals maintain their own malpractice insurance, providing equine-assisted therapy necessitates a different type of liability insurance specific to the service. This type of insurance covers accidents associated with the treatment method. Insurance policies can be obtained through a variety of sources. Dependent upon the professional's membership association, he or she may receive discounts or be eligible for different policies.

The costs of equine liability insurance are dependent upon the type of service provided, the number of patients served, the number of horses, the size and type of the facility, and the amount of staff. A rough estimate is anywhere between $900–$2,000 per year for a start-up program (personal communication with Debi DeTurk Peloso, February 1, 2017). Common insurance providers are Markel Insurance, Equisure, ARK International Group, Agri-Risk, and American Equine Insurance Group.

Along with equine liability insurance, other types of insurance may be required. General liability insurance; property insurance; care, custody, and control coverage; worker's compensation insurance; and directors and officer's liability insurance are other forms of insurance that may be necessary. It is important for professionals to identify an insurance agent to work with to ensure their needs are met.

Administrative Expenses

Similarly to all other expenses, the cost of running a business depends completely on the business type and size. The administrative expenses of running a small private practice are completely different than those of a center or clinic.

It is good to remember that even if a professional runs a private practice from their home, and uses their personal cell phone, shares internet with the household, or uses their own computer and printer, a percentage of these expenses can be deducted each year.

Here are some general areas to consider when developing an administrative budget:

- Marketing and public relations expenses
- Printing, copying, and mailing
- Office supplies
- Therapy supplies
- Insurance billing
- Phone and internet
- Patient recordkeeping system
- Tax preparation, accounting, and financial advising
- Travel expenses
- Meals and entertainment
- Continuing education and training expenses
- Volunteer, staff, and/or donor incentives and recognition
- Volunteer and staff training
- Professional dues and subscriptions
- Professional license fees

Personnel

The costs of paying for a facility, caring for horses, and supporting the administrative needs of a business can be great, but the cost of hiring qualified staff and paying a professional wage can be even greater. Even if a program relies upon more volunteers or interns than paid staff, time and money must be allocated for recruitment, training, and ongoing management of the volunteers (Conners, 1995; Cook, 2011).

Unlike most forms of therapy, the existing models of equine-assisted therapy require the presence of multiple staff or volunteers in any given session. This can be a deterrent and a significant limiting factor for those interested in equine-assisted therapy.

For example, EAGALA requires both an "equine specialist" and a mental health professional during all sessions, even when working with a single participant (EAGALA, 2016). PATH Intl. also supports the use of an "equine specialist" working in conjunction with a licensed mental health professional (PATH Intl., 2016). Similarly, during a hippotherapy session, a licensed therapist leads the session and in many cases, three additional staff, interns, or volunteers are present per patient (Cook, 2014).

Although these staffing models were created with the safety and wellbeing of the patients and the horses in mind, the inclusion of so many people raises significant financial, administrative, and even ethical concerns. Including additional non-licensed, non-clinical personnel in a therapy session is not always clinically appropriate, and is certainly costly and/or time consuming, leading to possible issues with the long-term sustainability of the industry.

This topic is complicated and deserves careful consideration. However, it seems there could be room for other models of providing services that require less personnel when utilizing certain activities or working with specific populations.

☐ Other Business Considerations

Along with identifying a business model, developing revenue streams, planning for operational needs, and accounting for expenses, there are a few other important steps to consider prior to incorporating horses and the farm milieu in a therapy practice.

Creating a Business Plan and a Strategic Plan

Vision, preparedness, forward thinking, and regular reviews help businesses stay focused on goals and create long-term financial success (Zietlow, et al., 2007). Regardless of how big or small the business, creating a strategic plan and a business plan is good practice.

Business Plan

A business plan provides an overview of the business and justifies the validity of the business through careful planning, projections, and market research. An important component to the business plan is developing a pro forma—a picture of what the financial statements will look like if all assumptions hold true. This means the organization must identify its revenue streams, be aware of all of its expenses, and understand the marketplace.

Key points of a business plan:

- Program description and descriptions of services.
- Administrative plan including location, relationships with other businesses, personnel types and biographies, a risk management plan, and insurance needs.
- Market and S.W.O.T. (strengths, weaknesses, opportunities, and threats) analysis including target markets, competition, market trends, and results of market research.
- Marketing plan that includes brand identification and a brand platform (detailing the look and feel of the business and the consumer experience); points of differentiation; service pricing; and advertising, PR, and networking strategies.
- Financials including a full pro forma.

In some cases, the marketing plan is included in the business plan, and in others they are two separate documents. The marketing plan is as essential as the business plan for the overall success of the business. In essence, the marketing plan unites the vision for the business with a cohesive brand platform that demonstrates congruence between the vision, the services offered, the strategies for successful business operations, and the market identity of the business.

Strategic Planning

A strategic plan is a process of envisioning the future and putting this vision into broadly defined goals, objectives, and actionable steps.

Strategic planning is a collaborative, inclusive process. It involves everyone who has a stake in the business. For a professional in private practice, this could include a significant other or family members who might be affected by the operations of the business. For larger programs or centers, this involves the board of directors (if there is one) and staff, volunteers, or donors.

Key points of the strategic planning process:

- It is important that as many stakeholders as possible are included and involved in the process, and those who are not present should be notified of the results.
- Strategic planning should not be used as an opportunity for the leaders of an organization to tell their employees what they have decided to do. Rather, it is an opportunity for constituents to have a voice and a say in the direction of the organization.

- Dependent upon the size of the organization, strategic planning can be done together or in smaller groups and the information compiled and reviewed.
- Once consensus is formed, the outcomes should be published in an easy-to-access manner.
- Once the plan has been developed, don't change it mid-way. Make sure that the goals the group identifies and agrees upon are followed through. STICK WITH THE PLAN!
- Strategic planning should be done about every 1–3 years for new organizations, and every 3–5 years for more established organizations.

Developing Policies and Procedures

Regardless of the size of a business, it is important to document the policies and procedures that will be used while operating the business and providing services. Policies and procedures clarify operating practices that support the vision, mission, and culture of the business.

Even for those in private practice, documenting policies and procedures can be very helpful. Most types of professionals are required to create an informed consent and/or professional disclosure statement and must develop policies for this document especially related to billing and collections, information storing, confidentiality, and the policies specific to working with horses or coming to the farm. Policies and procedures should help to reduce risk and increase the quality of services provided.

PATH Intl. offers a comprehensive guide to developing policies and procedures for equine-assisted activities and therapies. Depending on the type of services offered, some of the recommended policies and procedures may not be needed—but nonetheless, it is a valuable resource for anyone providing equine-assisted therapy.

Designing Forms

Once policies and procedures have been established, it is usually clear what forms must be created. Each profession has different forms that are standard, and the work with horses necessitates additional paperwork. Well-crafted forms in alignment with the businesses brand platform demonstrate professionalism, competence, and consistency. It is recommended that professionals consult with a lawyer familiar with healthcare forms and liability releases to ensure each form meets the legal requirements for the state in which the business is located.

Below is a list of some of the common forms needed to provide equine-assisted therapy:

- Patient intake form (includes billing information)
- Patient release of information form

- Medical release form
- Client's rights statement
- Notice of privacy practices document
- Informed consent for equine-assisted therapy
- Professional disclosure form
- Equine-assisted therapy release of liability form
- Statement of financial responsibility and/or sliding scale payment plan form
- Volunteer release forms
- Volunteer time sheets
- Horse care logs
- Facility logs
- Incident reports (physical and psychological)
- Administrative forms

☐ Conclusion

Developing greater business acumen is a critical step in moving equine-assisted therapy from a hobby, passion, or labor of love to a sustainable, widely utilized, and respected type of treatment. Although the concept of business acumen sounds somewhat cold, unpleasant and impersonal, having strong abilities in this area is really just about leadership, vision, and fiscal management. Those with business acumen are likely to tune into the marketplace, understand the needs of consumers, consider the big picture, look for opportunities for collaborative relationships and growth, and provide great customer service while maintaining their bottom line (Cope, 2012).

The industry of equine-assisted therapy seems ripe for a critical focus on how to evolve in a more fiscally sound and business-savvy direction. Many creative options exist, and engaging in this transformative process will not only help the professionals to create more sustainable businesses—it will help patients have greater access to services.

☐ References

Adams, T. (2005). Founder transitions: Creating good endings and new beginnings. *Executive Transitions*. Retrieved from: www.aecf.org/m/resourcedoc/AECF-FounderTransitions-2005-Full.pdf

American Society for the Prevention of Cruelty to Animals (ASPCA). (2016). Retrieved from: www.aspca.org/

Backyard Chickens. (2016). *How Much Does It Cost to Raise Backyard Chickens?* Retrieved from: www.backyardchickens.com/a/how-much-does-it-cost-to-raise-backyard-chickens

Berget, B., & Braastad, B.O. (2011). Animal-assisted therapy with farm animals for persons with psychiatric disorders. *Ann Ist Super Sanità, 47*(4), 384–390.

Burns, K. (February 1, 2013). *Vital Statistics*. JAVMA News. Retrieved from: www.avma.org/news/javmanews/pages/130201a.aspx

Carlsson, C., Ranta, D.N., & Traeen, B. (2014). Equine assisted social work as a mean for authentic relations between clients and staff. *Human-Animal Interaction Bulletin, 2*(1), 19–38.

Casady, R. (2012). Insurance task force report. *Hippotherapy: The Official Publication of the American Hippotherapy Association*, Summer, 6–8.

Cerquozzi, C., Cerquozzi, E., Darragh, A., & Miller-Kuhaneck, H. (2007). An exploratory survey of occupational therapists' role in hippotherapy. *American Occupational Therapy Association's Developmental Disabilities Special Interest Section Quarterly, 30*(3), 1–4.

Chardonnens, E. (2009). The use of animals as co-therapists on a farm: The child—horse bond in person-centered equine-assisted psychotherapy. *Person-Centered and Experiential Psychotherapies, 8*(4), 319–332.

Christie, J. (2016). *The Cost of Horse Ownership.* Retrieved from: www.extension.umn.edu/agriculture/horse/care/the-cost-of-horse-ownership/

Coalition against Insurance Fraud. (2016). *By the Numbers: Fraud Statistics.* Retrieved from: www.insurancefraud.org/statistics.htm#13

Conners, T.D. (1995). *The volunteer management handbook.* San Francisco, CA: John Wiley & Sons.

Cook, R. (2011). Incidents and injury within the hippotherapy milieu: Four years of safety study data on risk, risk management, and occurrences. *Scientific and Educational Journal of Therapeutic Riding*, 57–66.

Cook, R. (2014). *Risk management and safety in hippotherapy.* Publisher: Rebecca Cook.

Cope, K. (2012). *Seeing the big picture: Business acumen to build your credibility, career, and company.* Austin, TX: Greenleaf Book Group Press.

Equine Assisted Growth and Learning Association (EAGALA). (2016). Retrieved from: www.eagala.org/

Fichman, M., & Levinthal, D.A. (1991). Honeymoons and the liability of adolescence: A new perspective on duration dependence in social and organizational relationships. *The Academy of Management Review, 16*(2), 442–468.

Gray, C.M., Weinberg, C., & Oster, S.M. (June 21, 2004). To fee or not to fee? (And related questions). *Non-Profit Quarterly.* Retrieved from: https://nonprofitquarterly.org/2004/06/21/to-fee-or-not-to-fee-and-related-questions/

Gresham, H. (2014). *Practice patterns of equine assisted psychotherapists.* Self-published thesis.

Hyman, D.A. (2002). HIPAA and health care fraud: An empirical perspective. *The Cato Journal, 22*(1), 151–178.

Kaiser, L.T. (May 2, 2008). *How Much Does It Cost to Raise Dairy Goats?* Retrieved from: www.extension.umn.edu/agriculture/dairy/business-tools-and-budgeting/cost-to-raise-dairy-goats/

McConnell, P.J. (2010). *National survey on equine assisted therapy: An exploratory study of current practitioners and programs.* Self-published dissertation.

Non-Profit Finance Fund. (2011). *2011 State of the Sector Survey.* Retrieved from: www.nonprofitfinancefund.org/sites/default/files/docs/2011/2011survey_brochure.pdf

Non-Profit Finance Fund. (2016). *Nonprofit Finance 101.* Retrieved from: www.nonprofitfinancefund.org/nonprofit-finance-101

Pham, C., & Bitonte, R. (2016). Hippotherapy: Remuneration issues impair the offering of this therapeutic strategy at Southern California rehabilitation centers. *NeuroRehabilitation, 38*(4), 411–417.

Professional Association of Therapeutic Horsemanship International (PATH Intl.). (2015). *2015 PATH Intl. Statistics.* Retrieved from: www.pathintl.org/images/pdf/about-narha/documents/2015-fact-sheet-web.pdf

Professional Association of Therapeutic Horsemanship International (PATH Intl.). (2016). Retrieved from: www.pathintl.org

Renz, D. (2010). *The Jossey-Bass handbook of nonprofit leadership and management* (3rd edition). San Francisco, CA: Jossey-Bass.

Stroud, D., & Hallberg, L. (2016). [Horses in healthcare: An international assessment of the professional practice of equine-assisted therapy]. Unpublished raw data.

University of Maine. (2012). *Guide to First-Time Horse Ownership*. Retrieved from: https://extension.umaine.edu/publications/1004e/

Zietlow, J., Hankin, J.A., & Seidner, A.G. (2007). *Financial management for nonprofit organizations: Policies and practices* (1st edition). Hoboken, NJ: Wiley Publishing.

7   The Ethics of Appropriating Horses for Human Wellbeing

☐ **The Five Freedoms**

Equine-assisted therapy provides a vocation for horses, in some cases saving them from abandonment or even death. It gives horses a purpose in a time when the future of the horse-human relationship is in flux. From the anecdotal reporting of the professionals providing equine-assisted therapy, for the most part, horses appear to enjoy the work.

However, when humans appropriate another species for the good of mankind, there are ethical considerations that must be attended to. The Five Freedoms (ASPCA, 2016) provide a first step in understanding ethical care. These principles were created in the United Kingdom as a response to livestock welfare, but were adopted over the years by the World Organization for Animal Health, the Royal Society for the Prevention of Cruelty to Animals, and the American Society for the Prevention of Cruelty to Animals (ASPCA).

The Five Freedoms are:

1. **Freedom from hunger or thirst** by ready access to fresh water and a diet to maintain full health and vigor
2. **Freedom from discomfort** by providing an appropriate environment including shelter and a comfortable resting area
3. **Freedom from pain, injury, or disease** by prevention or rapid diagnosis and treatment
4. **Freedom to express normal behavior** by providing sufficient space, proper facilities and company of the animal's own kind
5. **Freedom from fear and distress** by ensuring conditions and treatment which avoid mental suffering

Each of these five areas provides an opportunity for objective assessment. But, as researchers point out, objectively understanding equine welfare can be challenging (Anderson, et al., 1999; Popescu, et al., 2014; Lesimple, et al., 2014). Researchers identify that horse owners or handlers may be resistant to seeing indications of poor welfare, and that defensive attitudes can make it further difficult to change behaviors. Popescu, et al. (2014) propose that welfare assessment needs to be a tool not only for identifying problems, but also for supporting the positive actions of the owners or handlers. They hope that by doing this, horse owners or handlers may soften to the idea of ongoing assessment and support making critical changes that could positively impact the animal.

As Fazio, et al. (2013) state, "Despite remarkable amount of papers about the therapeutic horse-back riding wishing to analyse the therapeutic effects on human health, still very few studies focused on the impact of these activities on horses and their welfare" (p. 139). The results of the literature review conducted for this book support Fazio's statement. Only five peer-reviewed journal articles could be located specific to studying the wellbeing of horses working in equine-assisted therapy programs (O'Rourke, 2004; Kaiser, et al., 2006; Gehrke, et al., 2011; Fazio, et al., 2013; McKinney, et al., 2015). This is in stark contrast to the 227 articles published to date related to the conditions or populations served by equine-assisted interventions.

These studies show a general uncertainty about how horses may be affected, and it is clear researchers have work in front of them to determine which variables to study, and the best tools to measure those variables.

Regardless of the outcomes of research, professionals providing equine-assisted therapy have an important responsibility to find ways to assess (as objectively as possible) the horses they work with using the Five Freedoms, and to carefully consider all the factors that might influence equine wellbeing.

☐ Understanding Horses

To be able to objectively assess horses, one must first understand their behaviors and actions. A lack of scientifically-based ethological knowledge about horses coupled with little horse experience may lead professionals to be unable to assess the horses they work with, or to unknowingly engage with horses in a manner that results in negative physical or emotional responses (Merkies, et al., 2014).

People of all levels of horsemanship frequently misinterpret equine communication and behavior, commonly grounding their understanding of horses in information provided by horse trainers or books written by horse trainers, or on their own personal experiences. In most cases, this information is not derived from empirical scientific investigation.

Equitation science and rigorous ethological study provide a platform from which to better understand horses, and make informed decisions about how to engage with them. Included here are three topics that tend to be the least understood, or most misused, in the equine-assisted therapy realm.

Communication

Overarching all the following topics is the general issue of equine communication. As social animals, horses are highly communicative and synchronized as a herd, using visual, acoustical, tactile, or chemical communications to convey information (Goodwin, 1999; Waring, 2007; McGreevy, 2012).

Horses have a well-defined "language" which can be effectively understood by humans. Horses use communication in an attempt to diminish acts of actual (vs. perceived) aggression and violence. Typically, when all attempts at non-violent communications have been ignored, horses turn to more aggressive behaviors like biting, kicking, chasing, or striking. If humans are trained to understand the subtleties of equine communication, they are less likely to be injured because they will be responsive to the non-violent communications of the horse, and thus the horse will not be forced to escalate behaviors (Hausberger, et al., 2008; Cuenca, et al., 2009; Hawson, et al., 2010; Cook, 2011; Merkies, et al., 2014; Carmichael, et al., 2014; Starling, et al., 2016).

Horses use an assortment of vocal and non-verbal body-based actions to communicate including the noises they make, ear positions, facial expressions, use of head and leg gestures, and tail movements to subtly (and sometimes not so subtly) convey feelings, thoughts, and emotions (Hill, 2006; Waring, 2007; McGreevy, 2012).

This book cannot do justice to the depth of study and understanding ethologists have brought to equine communication and behavior (Goodwin, 1999; Brandt, 2004; Waring, 2007; Krueger, 2007; Warren-Smith & McGreevy, 2008; Goodwin, et al., 2009; McGreevy, et al., 2009; McGreevy, 2012; Henshall & McGreevy, 2014; Fureix, et al., 2015; Starling, et al., 2016). Providers of equine-assisted therapy should be trained to observe, interpret, and understand these critical communications. They are urged to pursue deeper investigation by reading books and research articles, and taking college or university courses.

Dominance

Goodwin (1999) points out, "As horses can establish an enduring social order, reinforcing the dominance relationship between individuals is of comparatively low importance and this must have implications for the human-horse relationship" (p. 17). For many years, horse people asserted that dominance over horses and the horse's corresponding submission was necessary to safely interact, but more in-depth scientific study shows this is not the case (Goodwin, 1999; Goodwin, et al., 2009; McGreevy, et al., 2009).

In fact, the concept of dominance is generally misused when transferred from humans to horses. In ethological terms, the term "dominance" relates to how horses use social structure and behavioral strategies to reduce the likelihood of violence and aggression between herd members (Waring, 2007; Henshall & McGreevy, 2014). Horses use ritualized posturing to assert themselves rather than engaging in actual acts of violence (Kaufmann, 1983; Henshall & McGreevy, 2014). Conversely, the human concept of dominance includes the use of controlling and aggressive actions with the intent to be viewed as more powerful than others, resulting in their submission. This is commonly misconstrued by humans as leadership.

When humans exert their type of dominance over horses, the horse is likely to understand the behaviors as aggression, and react by attempting to flee, using submissive (or appeasing) behaviors, avoiding, or in less frequent cases, responding with aggression. As Goodwin (1999) states, "If human individuals repeatedly attempt to reinforce their dominance over the horses in their charge, it should be recognised that the natural equine response is avoidance" (p. 17).

Leadership in horse herds is generally left to a female (mare), who typically uses a non-aggressive style to guide her herd to food and water and away from danger. In free-ranging herds, horses rely upon kinship, and they respect one another's space, thereby decreasing the need for shows of dominance (Goodwin, 1999). Use of aggression (when not a life-saving act) or controlling behaviors similar to the human construct of dominance are usually only exhibited in young horses or in bachelor herds.

In observing horse herds, one can watch as the herd (including the lead mare) distances from aggressive horses, preferring the company of those who respect their space, and don't push or chase them. This has implications for the horse-human relationship.

Fight, Flight, Freeze, Appease

Horses evolved as prey animals who rely primarily upon their ability to flee from predators to keep themselves safe (Starling, et al., 2016). The sympathetic nervous system alerts the fight, flight, freeze, appease pattern, and this system is activated when the horse feels fear, stress, confusion, or pain (Starling, et al., 2016; McDonnell, 2016). The first stage of this pattern is freezing, or ceasing all motion to check out the potential danger and assess what action is necessary. From this point, the horse may choose to submit (appease), run, or fight.

Humans activate the fight, flight, freeze, appease response when using certain training or engagement activities, particularly when they chase, confuse, or corner horses who cannot escape from the pressure. Horse trainers commonly use this as a way to assert their "leadership" or dominance over the horse, which leads to the horse's submissive or appeasing behaviors. In many cases this is considered a positive or effective way of bonding, communicating, or humanely interacting with horses (Henshall & McGreevy, 2014).

Henshall & McGreevy (2014) provide a description of "round penning" and an explanation provided by horse trainers as to its use:

> The horse is released into the round pen and is first chased away from the trainer by the application of aversive postural and auditory stimuli which elicit flight responses in the horse. This action is explained as the trainer assuming the role of the herd leader or alpha mare by banishing the horse from the protection of the "herd" or acting as a predator.
>
> (p. 3)

They go on to describe how the trainer forces the horse to "move its feet," as a technique to demonstrate higher social status or dominance over the horse. This activity is ceased when the horse lowers its head, turns inwards, and "licks and chews." These behaviors are described as "The horse showing respect for the trainer and signaling its desire to return to the vicinity of the trainer or safety of the herd" (Henshall & McGreevy, 2014, p. 3).

The researchers point out concerning flaws with this method. They remind readers that in the wild, "Chasing is usually of short duration and, during resource contests, usually ceases once sufficient distance between members of the dyad is achieved" (Henshall & McGreevy, 2014, p. 7). In a confined space like a round pen or arena where the horse cannot escape, horse trainers might chase the horse or require it to remain in a flight response for up to 15 minutes. Since the horse cannot remove itself, or gain sufficient distant from its pursuer, the sympathetic nervous system is triggered just as if the horse were experiencing a prolonged chase by a non-human predator.

As Dr. Leslie Steward points out, humans respond differently to a stressed or fearful animal and a calm and relaxed animal (Steward, 2017). In equine-assisted therapy, even if the human is told by the horse expert or therapist that the chasing activity is healthy and normal, the patient may respond to the horse's stress or fear by simultaneously experiencing discomfort or anxiety.

Equine reactions to stress are commonly misinterpreted by humans. Probably one of the most misunderstood is the licking-and-chewing response. Licking and chewing reflects a change in the autonomic nervous system, which results in salivation (Goodwin, 1999; McDonnell, 2016). For example, if a horse has been operating in a sympathetic state (fight, flight, freeze, appease) and the fear or pressure diminishes or is relieved, the horse will revert to a parasympathetic state (rest and restore). This transition stimulates the salivary glands, and results in licking-and-chewing, and sometimes swallowing (Goodwin, 1999; McDonnell, 2016). Yawning and stretching may also be attributed to the change between sympathetic and parasympathetic states.

Henshall & McGreevy (2014) suggest that licking and chewing during activities like round penning "may be of physiological [rather] than communicative origin and they constitute evidence of stress in the horse undergoing the technique" (p. 8). According to Warren-Smith & McGreevy (2008), "Head lowering and licking-and-chewing may also simply be a reflection of the physiological response to the presence of a potential predator" (p. 287).

McDonnell (2016) states:

> You asked whether this licking or chewing might mean processing. I have heard trainers comment at this moment that the horse is "chewing on a thought." It is usually in the context of working a horse by running it around in a round pen or pestering a horse to load into a trailer, then stopping to take a break and saying, "He's thinkin' about it." Whether scared or confused or excited from the running around or the trailer loading, the horse is in sympathetic mode.
>
> (para. 5)

Goodwin's (1999) research supports this statement. She suggests, "Licking-and-chewing may therefore prove to be a displacement activity or comfort behaviour, associated with conflicting motivations in the horse" (p. 18).

Evoking the fight, flight, freeze, appease response in horses is unlikely to do what horse trainers and others working with horses hope it will. In fact, according to Warren-Smith & McGreevy (2008):

> The benefits of chasing horses, especially in confined spaces, have been questioned (McLean, 2003) as it may serve only to enhance the flight response, which in the interest of safety should be avoided in all handling of nonhuman animals (Gonyou, 1995).
>
> (p. 287)

A majority of equine-related injury research supports Warren-Smith & McGreevy (2008), showing that accidents are more likely to occur when a horse is confused or afraid (Ball, et al., 2007; Hawson, et al., 2010; Merkies, et al., 2014; Starling, et al., 2016). Hawson, et al. (2010) report, "This study also found horse behavior to be the most significant factor in horse-related incidents and that the majority of case reports alluded to the horse showing a fear response" (p. 325). Starling, et al., (2016) agree, stating, "Research has suggested that horses displaying a fear response (either flight or fight) features prominently in horse-related injuries to humans" (p. 8).

Horses (like all animals) learn the most effectively from positive reinforcement. When horses feel safe, they can be curious and investigatory, and this leads to lasting behavioral change (Waring, 2007; Starling, et al., 2016). Training and interaction techniques that foster curiosity, investigation, and a sense of security and safety lead to long-lasting positive outcomes for both horses and the humans who engage with them. As Waring (2007) points out:

> When a horse is in an approach-withdrawal situation, fear can prevent or impede close investigation. Avoidance is typical. Thus an anxious horse may be repelled by slight or even imaginary barriers, such as a pool of water or an open doorway; whereas, when calm the same horse may approach, investigate, and proceed without incidence.
>
> (p. 95)

Conversely, if a horse experiences fear, trauma, confusion, or pain, specific neural circuits in the brain are activated that shifts the brain into fight, flight, freeze, appease mode. This causes the horse to be less receptive to learning, and more reactionary to future negative stimuli (Starling, et al., 2016). Even if the horse is appeasing and submissive, and responds by doing what the human requests, if he/she is acting out of fear, whatever lesson the human is trying to instill will be harder (if not impossible) to recall in different circumstances.

The Five Freedoms expressly state that animals should be free from fear or distress. It seems clear from all the research that activities which include pushing, chasing, cornering, or confusing horses induce the fight, flight, freeze, appease response. Equine-assisted therapy professionals are urged not to use these types of activities, and rather develop other means of engaging with horses that do not trigger this fear-based response.

Responses to Physical or Emotional Distress

Detecting physical pain in horses has been a growing concentration of research over the past decade (de Grauw & van Loon, 2016). Currently, assessment of facial expressions in horses seems to be a promising way to understand equine pain (Dalla Costa, et al., 2014; de Grauw & van Loon, 2016). Physical pain is difficult to assess even in other humans (Wenholz, 2004), and each individual human or animal has its own experience of pain which can make it hard to objectively assess. Horses are known to be stoic about pain, which can lead to further complications with detection and evaluation.

That being said, objective assessment is possible, and providers of equine-assisted therapy are urged to research the topic of equine assessment thoroughly and work closely with their veterinarians to develop objective assessment tools to use with their horses. A checklist of possible evaluation criteria is included at the end of this section. Providers are urged to establish a baseline for what "healthy" condition is for each horse, and then use the assessment regularly to evaluate their horses.

Emotional distress may be easier in some ways to evaluate, but more difficult for owners to accept. Studies have found that horses suffer from depressive symptoms due to an unhappy work environment, chronic stress, physical pain, or social isolation (Hausberger, et al., 2009; Fureix, et al., 2015). One study investigated how the work-related stressors of interpersonal conflicts, suppressed emotions, and physical constraints negatively impact a horse's mental state leading to behavioral problems (Hausberger, et al., 2009).

Hausberger, et al. (2009); McGreevy (2012); and Fureix, et al. (2015) report that horses who are under emotional distress are likely to present in a number of ways, from appearing withdrawn or depressed to engaging in stereotypic behaviors like cribbing, weaving, head shaking, tongue play, licking, wood chewing, pawing, kicking, or biting.

Assessing physical or emotional distress in horses comes down to knowing how to observe horses, set aside ego or personal agendas, and ask for help from a knowledgeable horseperson who does not spend time with the horse or horses in question. Outside assessment is key to evaluation, but the owner or caretaker must also be willing to consider the feedback provided.

The following criteria are important when assessing physical or emotional distress:

- Is the horse's temperature, pulse, and respiration (TPR) and capillary refill time (CRT) normal?
- What is the horse's body condition score? Is it in the normal range between 4–6? If not, what action needs to be taken?
- Is the horse eating, drinking, defecating, and urinating too much or too little?
- Is the horse redistributing weight frequently between his/her feet? Can the horse stand comfortably on all four feet, or is it shifting its weight and holding its body strangely?
- Is the horse obviously lame on any of its feet? Can the horse turn in a small circle and walk out sound? Is the horse sound at all gates? Is the horse sensitive to different types of footing?
- Does the horse move away from pressure exerted on his/her back?
- Are there signs of swelling or heat anywhere on the horse's body?
- Are there obvious wounds or other injuries?
- Is the horse laying down more or less than usual?
- Can the horse get up and lie down easily?
- Does the horse have normal gut sounds?
- Is the horse pawing the ground or biting at his/her barrel?
- Are the horse's eyes bright or dull?
- Are there wrinkles around the horse's eyes and corners of the mouth?
- Do the horse's ears go alert when something enters its space or can be seen from a distance?
- Does the horse seem excited by or interested in novel stimuli?
- Is the horse acting more agitated or aggressive?

- Is the horse isolating from others?
- Does the horse seem withdrawn or "shut down"?
- Is the horse displaying stereotypical behaviors like cribbing, weaving, head shaking, tongue play, licking, wood chewing, pawing, kicking, or biting?

☐ Respecting and Responding to the Needs of Horses

Human behavior has a direct impact on equine welfare (Lesimple, et al., 2010). This statement may sound simplistic and obvious, but it is important. Horse owners and caretakers make choices on a daily basis that impact the wellbeing of animals under their care.

Opinions abound in the horse industry regarding how to care for horses. It seems nearly every horseperson has a different approach, and believes their way of caring for horses is irrefutably correct. Once again, the scientific study of ethology is useful in developing and measuring humane horse care practices with less personal bias or opinion. The Five Freedoms also provide a general guideline to consider the essential components of equine welfare.

Providers of equine-assisted therapy have a vital responsibility to ensure that the horses they work with are physically and emotionally fit and able to engage in ethological behaviors that are inherent to the long-term health and wellbeing of the species.

Horse-Horse Companionship

Wild or feral horses rarely if ever live alone, as they rely upon each other for survival. They live in highly structured and stable matriarchal family groups or bachelor herds (Goodwin, 1999; Waring, 2007; McGreevy, et al., 2009; Henshall & McGreevy, 2014) and form long-lasting relationships with the other members of the herd.

Horses also develop "pair" bonds, in which two horses spend most of their time together, grazing, mutually grooming, playing, and resting (Goodwin, 1999; Waring, 2007). Horses enjoy engaging in all manner of comfort behaviors, many of which rely upon horse-to-horse relationships and the freedom to move.

Providing horses with the space to move freely and the time to be alone together without human contact is a critical aspect to equine wellbeing.

Grooming

Horses groom themselves and each other frequently. They use licking, nibbling, rolling, or itching themselves with their teeth or hooves or against a hard surface or tree branch (Waring, 2007). They seek out different areas within their environment to conduct some of these behaviors. For example, on a hot day, a horse might seek out a muddy, sandy, or otherwise cooler area to roll in, whereas after a cold night they may choose a nice patch of grass to lay down, roll around, and sunbathe. It is common to see horses do a full body shake once they have completed their grooming rituals. Many times, when one horse is rolling or sunbathing, a companion will stand watch to alert for danger.

Mutual grooming is common between horses, and usually involves standing face to face and using teeth to scratch around the withers, shoulders, back, or rump. One of the obvious purposes of mutual grooming is that it accesses parts of the body the horse could not easily reach by him/herself.

Humans can engage in the grooming process by using tools or their hands to rub or scratch the horse's body. Of course, each horse responds to grooming differently, and it is important to learn how individual horses like to be touched and groomed. Some have very sensitive skin, and don't enjoy touch in the same way as others.

Observing horses in a herd environment helps humans better understand which horses like contact, where they like to be touched, and how they communicate when something feels good or bad. Respectful trial and error is also important in developing human-horse grooming rituals. In some cases, humans assume all horses like grooming, and think it will foster deeper bonds. But, forcing a horse to withstand an activity that is uncomfortable or unpleasing to him/her is unlikely to foster a sense of connection or deepen the relationship. Instead, respectfully listening to the responses and reactions of the horse, and finding ways to adjust the activity to make it more comfortable for the horse will probably produce more positive outcomes.

Play

According to Waring (2007), "Play behavior seems to have a major role in the behavioral, social, and physiological development of equids" (p. 83). Horses play in a number of different ways. They run, buck, swerve, jump, hop, paw, strike, and kick. They may also pick up items in their mouths like brooms, hoses, or loose items laying around, or try to manipulate things with their mouths like door latches, light switches, or hooks. When they play together they rear, chase, nip, play fight, or run around just enjoying the fun of a good gallop. Horses need the space and opportunity to engage in these playful behaviors.

Although some humans believe they can effectively "play" with horses, this thinking is likely to be dangerous or at the least, confusing to horses. People are not horses, and although both species can come to understand each other, pretending to be a horse is not an effective way to communicate or engage with horses (Brandt, 2004; McGreevy, et al., 2009; Goodwin, et al., 2009; Henshall & McGreevy, 2014).

Although there is a proliferation of "games" that humans are taught to "play" with horses, the reality is these games are for humans, and are really training techniques or scripted ways for humans to engage with horses. The best way humans can support play in horses is to simply allow them to be horses, giving them plenty of space and time to be loose with other horses without human interference in a safe environment where they can play as much as they like.

Movement

Horse herds travel between various environments throughout the year based upon weather conditions and grazing opportunities (Waring, 2007). Depending on the season, they may spend more or less time eating, moving, or resting, but according to Hampson, et al. (2010), horses in the wild are likely to roam between 5–18 miles per day.

McGreevy (2012) adds additional detail, suggesting that free-ranging horses are likely to spend approximately 60% of their time eating, 20% standing, and 10% laying down (p. 18). This is very different from stalled horses, who spend 65% of their time standing, 15% laying down, and 15% eating (McGreevy, 2012, p. 18).

The freedom to move over distances is essential to equine wellbeing. Movement allows the digestive process to work naturally and mobilizes all other physical functions. Horses also use movement to seek sanctuary from weather, predators, and pests like biting flies and mosquitoes. Horses will abandon grazing territory simply to avoid the discomfort caused by these pests, sometimes traveling many miles to do so (McGreevy, 2012).

It is no wonder horses who are stalled or contained in smaller paddocks, arenas, or pens for long periods of time without adequate access to large turn-out (this means acres of space to roam), the companionship of other horses, and free-range feed develop stereotypical (or maladaptive) behaviors and health problems (Waring, 2007; McGreevy, 2012; Popescu, et al., 2014).

Shelter-Seeking

Horses seek shelter from adverse weather conditions, and move between different types of environments based upon the weather. If it is hot, they will seek shade and water. If it is buggy, they will move away from water sources and seek windy, drier, or otherwise protected conditions. They will help each other by standing head to tail and swishing their tails to keep the bugs off of one another. If it is cold, they will turn away from the elements and huddle together or seek more substantial shelter if conditions worsen.

When horses are appropriated by humans, it is the humans' responsibly to provide ample shelter. This can come in the form of covered run-in shelters or stalls. It is important to understand the herd dynamic and provide the appropriate amount of sheltered space. Horses who are higher on the social hierarchy may not allow horses lower in the social order to enter sheltered space. This can cause emotional stress and increase health risks for those horses, especially if they are older or sickly.

Exercise and Conditioning

Although there are a number of papers detailing optimal equine characteristics and selection for equine-assisted therapy (Anderson, et al., 1999; Ciesla, 2007; Matsuura, et al., 2008; Pluta, 2009; Moisa, et al., 2012; Pawelec, et al., 2014; Łojek, et al., 2015), there is a paucity of peer-reviewed research articles exploring the importance of exercise and conditioning for equine-assisted therapy horses.

This is unfortunate, as horses who work in equine-assisted physical, occupational, or speech therapy programs that offer hippotherapy, or any other program that offers mounted activities without an emphasis on proper riding position, are routinely expected to carry riders who are unbalanced and whose movements may alter the natural pattern of the horse's gait. In order to handle this disruption, horses must compensate by adjusting their stride and holding their bodies differently.

Lesimple, et al. (2010) studied the effects of riding technique on levels of pain in horses. The researchers state, "This set of data [implied] that improper riding postures may have a strong effect on horses' postures at work that may also lead to chronic vertebral problems" (p. 6). They learned that unbalanced, novice riders could induce "chronically altered welfare" (p. 6) if the riding instructor did not teach the student how to control their body posture.

These researchers also report that horses who are most negatively affected move with high, hollow necks. This causes chronic pain, and can lead to a variety of problem behaviors as well as depressive emotional states (Hausberger, et al., 2009; Lesimple, et al., 2010; Fureix, et al., 2015).

One of the remedies to this problem is exercise and proper conditioning conducted by an expert rider who is highly trained and knowledgeable (de Oliveira, et al., 2015). This regime should include stretching and bending, and encourage lateral flexion, head lowering, and long-loose strides. Strength- and endurance-building exercises are also important, as are fun outings in which the horse can experience new scenery and do something different (e.g. going on a trail ride, participating in a horse show, etc.). These types of off-site activities can help keep therapy horses fresh and engaged.

Ideally, horses used for hippotherapy or any other type of equine-assisted therapy that includes mounted work should be physically and emotionally fit, of prime age, supple, strong, and of a size, breed, and confirmation that can comfortably handle carrying unbalanced weight. Many programs that offer hippotherapy ensure their horses are fit and conditioned, since the quality of the horse's movement is a key therapeutic tool. But, in the case of adaptive riding programs and some equine-assisted mental health programs, these vital characteristics are not as commonly found. In many cases, horses are donated, and may be elderly, slightly lame, suffer from past traumas, and not in the best shape. Furthermore, volunteers may be recruited to exercise these horses who are not expert riders and may receive limited, if any, professional instruction.

Even for programs offering equine-assisted mental health, exercise and conditioning is very important. Just as with any human working in the helping industry, therapy animals need respite. They need a break from dealing with people's emotions and, just like people, exercise is a powerful remedy. Using their brains and challenging their bodies in different ways can help therapy horses by reducing the effects of stress on the body and the mind.

Sleeping, Eating, and Drinking

Since resting, eating, and drinking consume a great deal of the horse's daily life, these pursuits are important to understand and properly attend to. Horse caretakers commonly disagree upon the best practices for attending to these needs. In many cases, the opinions they hold are not based upon ethological knowledge, nor are they tempered by an understanding of the effects of domestication on the species. Furthermore, each horse is an individual with different needs and likes. In order to provide the best care possible, all of these factors must be taken into consideration.

Sleeping

In a pastured or free-ranging environment, horses sleep approximately 4–5 hours per 24-hour cycle. The majority of this time they stand up, although most horses lay down to sleep at least once per sleep cycle, and may spend up to 60 minutes in this position (Waring, 2007).

In a stalled environment without access to free-feed, horses are more likely to sleep longer, and lay down more. There are positive and negative aspects to this, and as Waring (2007) points out, every horse is different in his/her sleep needs. Each individual horse has a different sleep pattern. Some may be more comfortable sleeping at night while others prefer to sleep during the daytime. The season also plays an important role in sleep patterns. Waring (2007) notes that researchers have observed horses are less likely to lay down and more likely to graze during the nighttime than cattle or sheep.

Providers of equine-assisted therapy require their horses to be awake and alert for good portions of the daytime. It is important that horses get enough rest and relaxation time, as well as time to play, groom, and exercise. Thus, caregivers should carefully observe their horse herds, and determine how the horses function best given the constraints of working. This may take a process of trial and error to determine when they rest the most and best, and when they socialize, graze, play, and groom. This schedule may have to be adapted seasonally to account for changes in weather and daylight.

It is recommended by this author that providers of equine-assisted therapy have both stalls or private pens, and group turn-out spaces for horses to choose between. If stalls are provided, adequate bedding material is essential, as is proper hygiene and stall-cleaning practices. Some horses enjoy the security of a stall or private pen for portions of the day or night, while others may prefer to remain outdoors. Having private spaces for horses allows caregivers to monitor water intake and feed special supplements or medications as necessary, and it can give horses the opportunity to rest, relax, and eat unhindered if that is something they need or enjoy.

Generally, horses are clear communicators, and will make their needs heard. The best way to gain an understanding of the wants and needs of horses is through careful observation. For example, during summer, horses may want to come into their stalls or sheltered areas during the heat of the day to rest and escape the sun and the bugs. They may enjoy getting turned out later in the evening and lingering in pasture as the temperature cools. During the winter months, the horses may be at the pasture gate as soon as it gets cold, wanting the warmth of their stalls. Responding to the horses as individuals is likely to improve the overall wellbeing of each horse and the herd as a whole. Just like people, no one shoe fits all.

Food and Water

Horses in feral or pastured environments spend approximately 70% of their time foraging for food (McGreevy, 2012). They tend to graze in cycles of three or more feeding periods per day, with long breaks between each cycle, and the most grazing occurs in the morning and early evening (Waring, 2007).

Typically, they maintain themselves on a high-fiber, low-protein diet that includes grasses and legumes, but they will resort to eating roots, herbs, shrubs, aquatic plants, or branches and twigs as necessary (Waring, 2007). This is in stark contrast to horses in a controlled human environment who spend approximately 10% of their time foraging (McGreevy, 2012), and are likely to eat a higher-protein diet.

It is important to note that foraging is not the same thing as free-feeding. Foraging requires the horse to move frequently or even constantly while seeking food, sometimes traveling long distances in a day. During this process, the horse may eat a variety of food types, some of which are higher or lower in fiber and protein. Recently, there has been a movement among horse owners or caretakers to provide free-feed for their horses in an attempt to mimic the feeding patterns of horses in the wild. In order for this to work effectively, the horse must have the space, and be motivated to move while eating, and the type and quality of the hay must be carefully considered. If these factors are not attended to, horses are likely to overeat and suffer the physical consequences of obesity and may even develop laminitis, a very painful hoof condition.

Horses digest their food the most effectively when their heads are down at ground level as in a natural setting, and they like to be able to see and hear and move their ears while eating (Waring, 2007). The design of many of the feeders commonly used in the horse industry are contrary to the ethological preferences of horses. If they have to stick their heads into a feeder that is against a wall, or even free standing, they cannot comfortably see and hear and move their ears, and in many cases, their necks are elevated above the ground.

Horses also may like to dunk their feed in water to moisten it, particularly if it is dry forage. Although some caregivers believe water should be separated from feed, thereby motiving the horse to move, others feel water should be provided in close proximately so the horse can dunk its dry forage.

Common horse knowledge suggests that horses drink between 5–10 gallons of water per day. Horses are more likely to drink temperate or warm water over very cold water (Waring, 2007). In cold weather climates, heated water buckets can encourage water consumption, and in hot weather climates having ample access to fresh, clean water is very important.

Horses whose movement and feeding patterns are the farthest from what they would experience in nature may develop a myriad of health and behavioral problems including weight gain or loss, digestive issues, a tendency to colic, wood chewing, eating feces, licking salt, or excessive water consumption (Waring, 2007).

Healthcare

As stated in the beginning of this chapter, one of the Five Freedoms is the freedom from pain, injury, or disease. Horses who work in equine-assisted therapy programs have a right to speedy and effective care, as well as regular and ongoing wellness services.

Horses who are in pain should not be asked to work and the cause of their pain should be identified, remediated, or remedied if possible. All effects should be made to keep horses physically and emotionally healthy and fit.

Veterinary Care

Horses should have routine veterinary care at least once a year (twice for horses over 20 years of age) that consists of a wellness checkup, a dental exam, and any necessary vaccinations.

Wellness checkups usually include checking the horse's vital signs; determining body condition score; assessing movement; checking the condition of the hooves, feet, and legs; looking for abnormal lumps, growths or skin problems; and an appraisal of the nervous system (Loving, 2008). Veterinarians will also frequently inspect the horse's living conditions and discuss diet, nutrition, exercise, and socialization with the owner or caregiver.

Horses are vaccinated annually or biannually for a variety of diseases. Common vaccinations include tetanus, equine encephalomyelitis, influenza, rhinopneumonitis, West Nile virus, strangles, and Potomac Horse Fever (American Association of Equine Practitioners, 2016).

Historically, veterinarians recommended de-worming 4–6 times a year, with seasonal changes. More recently, however, vets are supporting fecal testing to detect for parasites. This approach is far more targeted and specific to each individual horse, and can be significantly less taxing on the horse's system. It is important to discuss these options with a veterinarian to make the best choice given geographical region and the horse's lifestyle. Some horse owners or caretakers who believe in "natural" care choose not to de-worm at all. This is a dangerous mistake. According to the University of Minnesota, studies show that 80% of colic cases are associated with parasites (Wilson, 2016). Beyond colic, parasites can make horses extremely ill, and if untreated can lead to the contamination of other horses.

Dental Care

Just like humans, the health of a horse's mouth is of great importance to their overall health. If a horse is experiencing tooth or mouth pain, he/she may become irritated, aggressive, or withdrawn. All veterinarians are trained in basic dental care, but some have specialized in dentistry, making them a better choice for more serious concerns or procedures.

Horse teeth are different than human teeth. A horse tooth will continue to emerge or "erupt" (commonly misconstrued with growth) until the reserve crown beneath the gum is exhausted. Usually this happens once the horse is around 20–25 years of age (Taylor Veterinary Dentistry, 2016). In the wild, horses forage approximately 70% of the time (McGreevy, 2012), and tooth eruption evolved accordingly. When horses are stalled and don't forage, the erupting teeth cannot be controlled naturally. Thus, horses must have their teeth "floated" (ground down) at least once a year.

Other tooth- and gum-related problems may cause horses pain and suffering, and should be diagnosed and treated as quickly as possible. Signs of tooth or mouth issues can include head tossing, bit-resistant behaviors while riding, a change in food intake, and sensitivity around the head and face.

Hoof Care

Domestication has altered equines in many ways, and the structure and shape of horse hooves is no exception. Each breed of horse and each individual horse within those breeds have different hoof care needs, but all horses rely upon their hooves to exist, and they can experience a great deal of stress if their feet are in pain.

Ideally, horse hooves are balanced in order to work effectively without causing pain and discomfort. In the wild, horses move between 5–18 miles per day (Hampson, et al., 2010) through varied terrain and are not responsible for carrying humans. This, along with their diets, helps to keep their hooves in decent condition. If a horse is unable to keep up with the herd or flee from predators due to a problem with his/her hooves, the horse usually dies. When horses live in captivity, they commonly carry humans, and their lifestyle does not involve moving as many miles a day. Thus, their hoof care needs are different.

As stated previously, no two horses are alike, and thus their hooves should not be treated equally. Some horses may do very well being "barefoot" (without shoes), while others experience ongoing discomfort which can only be mitigated through constant attention to their feet or by shoeing. This can change seasonally, or may be based upon the type of terrain a horse moves across and what he/she is doing. Unfortunately, it is all too common to see horse owners become invested in "natural hoof care" practices, which includes the horse going "barefoot," but not have the knowledge, skill, time, or resources to keep the hooves trimmed in a way that supports comfortable movement. This can lead to the horse suffering for the human's philosophical beliefs. Owners are urged to understand the commitment associated with keeping certain horses "barefoot" and decide if this decision is realistic for their situation. If they realize it isn't possible to invest the time or money needed, and the horse will do well with shoes on, it is recommended the owner choose that option. This is especially important for horses who are asked to work regularly in a therapy program.

As a general rule, horse hooves need to be trimmed every 6–8 weeks and the horse shoes replaced (Boyce, 2016). If the horse is barefoot, the trimming process is different and requires a specific skill set. Hoof walls and the sole of the horse's hoof must also be tended to by applying moisturizer, creating mud holes for horses to stand in to help dry hooves, or removing the horse from moist environments and keeping them in drier areas if their feet are too wet. Diet also plays an important role in hoof health.

Complementary Care

Providers of equine-assisted therapy commonly use alternative forms of healthcare for their horses. Examples include acupuncture, massage, chiropractic, aromatherapy, energy work, or other forms of body work. Herbs and supplements can also be used to help aid in the healing process, or provide daily support for horses.

Even though Dr. Allen Schoen was recognized in 2016 as one of the fifteen most influential veterinarians for his pioneering work in the field of integrative veterinary medicine, in his recent book co-authored with

Susan Gordon (Schoen & Gordon, 2015), he reminds his readers to be wary of anyone who markets their complimentary animal services as the "only" way to treat a problem. Non-veterinarians are not legally allowed to diagnose diseases or conditions, and these authors point out the importance of a collaborative relationship between complementary and conventional care.

As with every other category of horse healthcare, it is essential to remember that each horse is an individual, and will respond differently to healthcare approaches. Careful observation and setting aside personal biases or beliefs can help ensure ongoing equine wellbeing.

Hygiene

The World Horse Welfare (2016) organization states, "One of the most important elements of protecting your horse and yard from disease is good hygiene" (p. 3). Hygiene is critical in maintaining the health and wellbeing of horses kept by humans. In the wild, horses have their own way of dealing with hygiene that cannot be replicated without acres and acres of space to roam. In typical human confinement, horses cannot maintain their own hygiene effectively.

According to the Kentucky Equine Research Group, "Horse farms had markedly fewer biosecurity [procedures designed to protect a specific population against harmful biological or biochemical substances] protocols in place than other animal operations, such as pig and cattle farms" (EquiNews, 2014, para. 3). This group notes that proper hygiene is essential to protect horses from the spread of communicable diseases such as ringworm, salmonellosis, strangles, methicillin-resistant Staphylococcus aureus, and other gastrointestinal and respiratory diseases.

Important steps to take to ensure good hygiene include once or twice daily removal of manure and urine from stalls, paddocks, or smaller enclosures and the addition of clean bedding material, and disinfecting and scrubbing water containers routinely, removing scum or algae buildup (World Horse Welfare, 2016).

Fly and pest control is also essential for the comfort and health of horses. Flies cause physical irritations, annoy horses, and carry bacteria that can lead to disease in horses (Texas A&M, Veterinary Medicine & Biomedical Science, 2012). As Waring (2007) states, horses in the wild will travel many miles to avoid flies and other types of pests. If horses are confined to small areas where they cannot escape to a different type of environment (forested, dry, windy, hilly, etc.), they cannot effectively manage the problem themselves. Fly mitigation strategies include the use of fly masks, fly sprays, and oral fly treatments. During the summer months or whenever flies and other pests are present, caretakers should make sure to protect their horses through the use of these preventive measures.

☐ Conclusion

Although horses and humans have been co-existing for thousands of years, humans still have a great deal to learn (and unlearn) about horses. The study of equine ethology provides probably the most unbiased understanding of equines because it studies horses in the wild, and compares natural behaviors to those observed in human-controlled environments.

The human desire to anthropomorphize—or place values, judgements, and human constructs—onto animals can both help and hurt the animals in question. The most important way to avoid the negative ramifications of anthropomorphism is to use well reputed scientific study of animals in their natural environments to temper the desire for assumptions. Through this process, humans can learn more about horses, and will be able to engage with them in healthier and safer ways, and take better care of them.

Providers of equine-assisted therapy have an ethical responsibility to ensure the welfare of their equine partners. This requires understanding them more fully, being able to objectively assess them, asking for help and support from outside sources, and responding appropriately to their needs.

☐ References

American Association of Equine Practitioners (AAEP). (2016). *Owner Vaccination Guidelines*. Retrieved from: https://aaep.org/horse-owners/owner-guidelines/owner-vaccination-guidelines

American Society for the Prevention of Cruelty to Animals (ASPCA). (2016). *Five Freedoms*. Retrieved from: http://aspcapro.org/resource/shelter-health-animal-care/five-freedoms

Anderson, M.K., Friend, T.H., Evans, W.J., & Bushong, D.M. (1999). Behavioral assessment of horses in therapeutic riding programs. *Applied Animal Behaviour Science*, 63, 11–24.

Ball, C.G., Ball, J.E., Kirkpatrick, A.W., & Mulloy, R.H. (2007). Equestrian injuries: Incidence, injury patterns, and risk factors for 10 years of major traumatic injuries. *American Journal of Surgery*, *193*(5), 636–640.

Boyce, M. (2016). *Hoof Care*. Retrieved from: www.extension.umn.edu/agriculture/horse/care/hoof-care/

Brandt, K. (2004). A language of their own: An interactionalist approach to horse-human communication. *Society & Animals*, *12*(4), 299–316.

Carmichael, S.P., Davenport, D.L., Kearney, P.A., & Bernard, A.C. (2014). On and off the horse: Mechanisms and patterns of injury in mounted and unmounted equestrians. *Injury: International Journal of the Care of the Injured*, *45*(9), 1479–1483.

Ciesla, A. (2007). The characteristic of horses used in hippotherapy in selected horse therapy centres in Poland. *Acta Scientiarum Polonorum Zootechnica*, *6*(1), 3–14.

Cook, R. (2011). Human incidents and injury within the hippotherapy milieu: Four years of safety study data of risk, risk management, and occurrences definition of hippotherapy. *Scientific and Educational Journal of Therapeutic Riding*, 57–66.

Cuenca, A.G., Wiggins, A., Chen, M.K., et al. (2009). Equestrian injuries in children. *Journal of Pediatric Surgery*, *44*(1), 148–150.

Dalla Costa, E., Minero, M., & Lebelt, D. (2014). Development of the Horse Grimace Scale (HGS) as a pain assessment tool in horses undergoing routine castration. *PLoS One*, *9*(3), 1–10.

de Grauw, J.C., & van Loon, J.P.A.M. (2016). Systematic pain assessment in horses. *Veterinary Journal*, *209*, 14–22.

de Oliveira, K., Soutello, R.V.G., da Fonseca, R., et al. (2015). Gymnastic training and dynamic mobilization exercises improve stride quality and increase epaxial muscle size in therapy horses. *Journal of Equine Veterinary Science*, *35*(11–12), 888–893.

EquiNews, Kentucky Equine Research. (August 5, 2014). *Farm Hygiene Important for Horse Biosecurity*. Retrieved from: www.equinews.com/article/farm-hygiene-important-horse-biosecurity

Fazio, E., Medica, P., Cravana, C., & Ferlazzo, A. (2013). Hypothalamic-pituitary-adrenal axis responses of horses to therapeutic riding program: Effects of different riders. *Physiology and Behavior*, *118*, 138–143.

Fureix, C., Beaulieu, C., Argaud, S., et al. (2015). Investigating anhedonia in a nonconventional species: Do some riding horses Equus caballus display symptoms of depression? *Applied Animal Behaviour Science*, *162*, 26–36.

Gehrke, E.K., Baldwin, A., & Schiltz, P.M. (2011). Heart rate variability in horses engaged in equine-assisted activities. *Journal of Equine Veterinary Science*, *31*(2), 78–84.

Goodwin, D. (1999). The importance of ethology in understanding the behaviour of the horse. *Equine Veterinary Journal, Supplement*, *28*, 15–19.

Goodwin, D., McGreevy, P., Waran, N., & McLean, A. (2009). How equitation science can elucidate and refine horsemanship techniques. *Veterinary Journal*, *181*(1), 5–11.

Hampson, B.A., De laat, M.A., Mills, P.C., & Pollitt, C.C. (2010). Distances travelled by feral horses in "outback" Australia. *Equine Veterinary Journal*, *42*(38), 582–586.

Hausberger, M., Gautier, E., Biquand, V., Lunel, C., & Jégo, P. (2009). Could work be a source of behavioural disorders? A study in horses. *PLoS One*, *4*(10), 2–9.

Hausberger, M., Roche, H., Henry, S., & Visser, K.E. (2008). A review of the human-horse relationship. *Applied Animal Behaviour Science*, *109*(1), 1–24.

Hawson, L.A., McLean, A.N., & McGreevy, P.D. (2010). The roles of equine ethology and applied learning theory in horse-related human injuries. *Journal of Veterinary Behavior: Clinical Applications and Research*, *5*(6), 324–338.

Henshall, C., & McGreevy, P.D. (2014). The role of ethology in round pen horse training–A review. *Applied Animal Behaviour Science*, *155*, 1–11.

Hill, C. (2006). *How to think like a horse: Essential insights for understanding equine behavior and building an effective partnership with your horse*. StoreyPublishing.

Kaiser, L., Heleski, C.R., Siegford, J., & Smith, K.A. (2006). Stress-related behaviors among horses used in a therapeutic riding program. *Journal of the American Veterinary Medical Association*, *228*(1), 39–45.

Kaufmann, J.H. (1983). On the definitions and functions of dominance and territoriality. *Biological Reviews*, *58*, 1–20.

Krueger, K. (2007). Behaviour of horses in the "round pen technique." *Applied Animal Behaviour Science*, *104*(1–2), 162–170.

Lesimple, C., Fureix, C., Menguy, H., & Hausberger, M. (2010). Human direct actions may alter animal welfare, a study on horses (Equus caballus). *PLoS One*, *5*(4), 1–8.

Lesimple, C., Hausberger, M., Hommel, B., & Staios, M. (2014). How accurate are we at assessing others' well-being? The example of welfare assessment in horses. *Frontiers in Psychology*, *5*(21), 1–8.

Łojek, J., Pluta, M., Cie, A., et al. (2015). Conformation analysis of horses used in equine-assisted activities at Polish hippotherapeutic centers. *Acta Scientiarum Polonorum Zootechnica, 14*(2), 121–134.

Loving, N.S. (March 1, 2008). *Annual Wellness Exam.* Retrieved from: www.thehorse.com/articles/20641/annual-wellness-exam

Matsuura, A., Ohta, E., Ueda, K., Nakatsuji, H., & Kondo, S. (2008). Influence of equine conformation on rider oscillation and evaluation of horses for therapeutic riding. *Journal of Equine Science, 19*(1), 9–18.

McDonnell, S. (October 5, 2016). *The Science Behind "Licking and Chewing" in Horses.* Retrieved from: www.thehorse.com/articles/38258/the-science-behind-licking-and-chewing-in-horses

McGreevy, P.D. (2012). *Equine behavior: A guide for veterinarians and equine scientists* (2nd edition). Philadelphia, PA: Saunders Ltd.

McGreevy, P.D., Oddie, C., Burton, F.L., & McLean, A.N. (2009). The horse—human dyad: Can we align horse training and handling activities with the equid social ethogram? *The Veterinary Journal, 181*(1), 12–18.

McKinney, C., Mueller, M.K., & Frank, N. (2015). Effects of therapeutic riding on measures of stress in horses. *Journal of Equine Veterinary Science, 35*(11–12), 922–928.

Merkies, K., Sievers, A., Zakrajsek, E., Macgregor, H., et al. (2014). Preliminary results suggest an influence of psychological and physiological stress in humans on horse heart rate and behavior. *Journal of Veterinary Behavior: Clinical Applications and Research, 9*, 242–247.

Moisa, C.M., Barabasi, J., & Papuc, I. (2012). Selection methods for horses used in hippotherapy. *Bulletin of University of Agricultural Sciences and Veterinary Medicine Cluj-Napoca: Veterinary Medicine, 69*(1–2), 156–163.

O'Rourke, K. (2004). Horse-assisted therapy: Good for humans, but how about horses? *Journal of the American Veterinary Medical Association, 225*(6), 817–817.

Pawelec, A., Kubinska, M., Jastrzebska, E., & Wejer, J. (2014). Characteristics of hippotherapeutic horses in Poland. *Annales Universitatis Mariae Curie-Skłodowska Lublin—Polonia, 32*(3), 9–19.

Pluta, M. (2009). Characteristics of the trunks of horses used for classic hippotherapy. *Annales Universitatis Mariae Curie-Skłodowska Lublin—Polonia, 27*(3), 1–16.

Popescu, S., Diugan, E., & Spinu, M. (2014). The interrelations of good welfare indicators assessed in working horses and their relationships with the type of work. *Research in Veterinary Science, 96*, 406–414.

Schoen, A., & Gordon, S. (2015). *The compassionate equestrian: 25 principles to live by when caring for and working with horses.* Trafalgar Square Books.

Starling, M., McLean, A., & McGreevy, P. (2016). The contribution of equitation science to minimising horse-related risks to humans, *Animals, 6*(3), 1–13.

Steward, L. (April 5, 2017). *What Is Your Pet Telling You?* Retrieved from: www.youtube.com/watch?v=oTVlCnenYeE

Taylor Veterinary Dentistry. (2016). *Equine Dentistry, 101.* Retrieved from: www.taylormadeteeth.com/TMVD_eq_dentistry_101.htm

Texas A&M, Veterinary Medicine & Biomedical Science. (2012). *Important to Protect Horses from Increasing Fly Problem.* Retrieved from: http://vetmed.tamu.edu/news/pet-talk/important-to-protect-horses-from-increasing-fly-problem

Waring, G.H. (2007). *Horse behavior* (2nd edition). Norwich, NY: William Andrew.

Warren-Smith, A.K., & McGreevy, P.D. (2008). Preliminary investigations into the ethological relevance of round-pen (round-yard) training of horses. *Journal of Applied Animal Welfare Science, 11,* 285–298.

Wenholz, S.D. (2004). *Understanding Equine Pain.* Retrieved from: www.thehorse.com/articles/11906/understanding-equine-pain

Wilson, J. (2016). *Equine Vaccinations and Deworming.* Retrieved from: www.extension.umn.edu/agriculture/horse/health/equine-vaccinations-and-deworming/

World Horse Welfare. (2016). *Hands on against Disease.* Retrieved from: www.worldhorse welfare.org/Files/f3ba55c2. . ./Keeping-your-horse-healthy-pack.pdf

8   A Vision for the Future

☐ How It All Began

One day, standing in the middle of a dusty arena, I realized the power of horses to change lives. I was 19, a young, up-and-coming hunter/jumper riding instructor and horse trainer, and the idea that riding horses could help people overcome significant physical or emotional obstacles never really crossed my mind.

The woman I was teaching had progressed nicely, and was finally ready to canter for the first time. The horse she was riding was lovely and kind, easy to handle and very responsive. I watched as she got into two-point, picked up the trot, and gently asked the horse to canter. He started off on the correct lead and around they went. After a few moments, I asked her to transition to the trot. Nothing happened. The horse continued to canter, and the woman remained in two-point, never asking the horse to change his gait. I asked repeatedly with no response. Finally, I used voice commands and my body language to slow the horse down. As I caught the reins, I looked up at the woman's face and was shocked to see tears pouring down her cheeks. I helped her dismount and asked another student to cool down the horse. We walked to a bench and sat down. "What's wrong?" I asked. She could not speak. We sat together for a while, as she collected herself. Finally, she was able to tell me that nothing about the lesson had caused her to cry, and that she would be back next week. I got her some water and walked her to the car.

The next week she came back. She seemed collected and focused so I asked if she wanted to try cantering again. She agreed and when the time was right I asked her to transition into the canter. The exact same thing occurred. Around and around they went. I continued to ask her to stop and nothing happened. Just like the week before, I used voice commands and slowed the horse down, and just like the week before she was sobbing. This continued week after week.

Finally, one day in that arena something different happened. Into the canter goes the horse, and I get ready to once again intercede to slow the horse down. Instead, all of a sudden the woman yelled "STOP!" The horse came to a sliding halt. I rushed up to see what was happening. Instead of a sobbing rider I found the woman sitting tall and proud atop her horse. I asked what had happened. And then she told me. For over a year her boss had been raping her. She was terrified to tell him no and even more terrified to report him because she was sure she would lose her job. For the past year, she had lived in fear, knowing that what was happening was not right, but not being able to find a way to stop it. She explained that the day before coming to barn she had found the courage to tell him no. She told me that learning to ride had taught her she could no longer be a bystander observing her own life, and that riding had given her the strength to stand up.

My world changed that day. I realized there was a power in the horse-human relationship that far exceeded my knowledge or understanding. I wanted to know more, and learn how I could support and protect interactions that could cause such profound change. And, I knew then and there it was not about me. It was something that happened between that woman and that horse.

My life's work from that time on has focused on helping to support and protect this industry—the horses, the patients, and the magic that happens when humans and animals connect.

As such, this final chapter offers a vision for the future, in which each and every person interested in equine-assisted therapy will come together to clarify, collaborate, and protect this industry we love, thereby contributing to its healthy growth and long-term sustainability.

☐ Clarify

Although equine-assisted therapy has been provided for over 60 years in many countries around the world as a form of human healthcare, the industry is still very much in a process of establishing its identity and unifying as a professional practice.

Terminology, scope of practice, and competency requirements for those providing the services are significant issues that the industry as a whole has not been able to agree upon. This lack of clarity has led to ethical concerns and challenges with research, and has compromised the ability for patients to access services.

Terminology

At present, the American Hippotherapy Association, Inc. (AHA), the Professional Association of Therapeutic Horsemanship, International (PATH Intl.), the Equine Assisted Growth and Learning Association (EAGALA), the Federation of Horses in Education and Therapy, International (HETI), and the Horses and Humans Research Foundation all use different terms and provide different definitions and descriptions for those terms.

Without well-written, agreed-upon, and properly used terminology, researchers cannot possibly differentiate between services, and thus uniformity between such services cannot be insinuated or assumed. Essentially, without consistent terminology, researchers may be studying apples and trying to compare them to oranges. The outcomes of these studies are thus flawed from the beginning, and results are compromised. This does not go unnoticed by those analyzing the quality of the research, which is an important consideration when deeming a practice "evidence-based" (Bond, 2007; Bachi, 2012; Whalen & Case-Smith, 2012; Tseng, et al., 2012; Selby & Smith-Osborne, 2013; Jenkins & Digennaro Reed, 2013; Anestis, et al., 2014; Kendall, et al., 2015; Angoules, et al., 2015; Lentini & Knox, 2015; Wang, et al., 2015; Lee, et al., 2016).

Although issues with terminology are noted in equine-assisted therapy research and scholarly writing (Debuse, et al., 2005; Angsupaisal, et al., 2015; Lee, et al., 2016), the importance of addressing this issue has yet to reach a critical mass. Providers of non-therapy services continue to offer services that look alarmingly like therapy, and advertise that their services are designed to address serious physical and mental health issues. Licensed therapists commonly reference research conducted using non-therapy services like adaptive riding or equine-assisted learning to support their work, and the research continues to use non-therapy methods to "treat" serious physical and mental health conditions. All of this poses health and safety risks for patients interested in receiving equine-assisted therapy while confounding referents, researchers, scholars, and even the practitioners themselves.

Overwhelmingly, what appears to be missing industry-wide are short, concise, well-crafted, and nationally (if not internationally) agreed-upon definitions of terms followed by a longer description of the service itself. Most organizations and associations seem to confuse defining a term with describing a service. Both are needed, but each serves a different purpose, and the two should be carefully considered and separated accordingly.

Pepper & Driscoll (2015) recommend using the following outline when creating definitions:

- The term (word or phrase) to be defined
- The class of object or concept to which the term belongs
- The differentiating characteristics that distinguish it from all others of its class

For example, the definition for hippotherapy might read,

> "Hippotherapy (term) refers to how occupational, physical, and speech therapists incorporate equine movement and the farm milieu in a patient's treatment plan (class) and utilizes clinical reasoning in the purposeful manipulation of equine movement to engage sensory, neuromotor, and cognitive systems to achieve functional outcomes (differentiating characteristics)."

Following the definition, a brief description could follow, which may include who provides the service or additional details about how it is implemented. For example,

> "Equine-assisted therapy (term) broadly refers to any type of therapy or treatment (class) that includes equine interactions, activities, or treatment strategies, and the equine milieu (differentiating characteristics) [End of definition, beginning of description]. Services are regulated by healthcare laws and provided by appropriately educated, trained and credentialed (licensed or registered) healthcare professionals. These individuals act within their scope of practice, and focus on addressing the patient's clinical treatment goals. Equine-assisted therapy includes equine-assisted physical therapy, equine-assisted occupational therapy, equine-assisted speech therapy, and equine-assisted mental health."

Associations, organizations, and individual providers must come together and set aside their differences to agree upon a system for addressing the issues with terminology.

Scope of Practice

Due to confusions related to terminology, the lack of clarity between therapy and non-therapy services, and the absence of internal regulations, the lines that typically define scope of practice have become blurred in the equine-assisted activities and therapies industry. Patients may not receive the services they actually need (Snider, et al., 2007; Bond, 2007; Ewing, et al., 2007; Jenkins & DiGennaro Reed, 2013), and providers may offer services they are not trained, educated, or licensed to provide.

It will take an effort on the part of membership associations and training organizations to stress the importance of remaining clearly within legal and ethical boundaries. Committing to terminology that clearly separates therapy from non-therapy practices will help the situation, as well as providing education and training about scope of practice boundaries and enforcing regulatory actions. Membership associations and training organizations are urged to choose which group to represent rather than attempting to represent both. If such organizations and associations aren't able or willing to do this, at the least they have a responsibility to understand the distinctly different purposes of both services, and provide separate training and/or support for the two professions.

Non-therapy providers and licensed professionals alike can be helpful in establishing and maintaining appropriate boundaries regarding what services they provide. If both are supportive of the process, and understand the need for clarification and separation between services, the two groups can support each other through a system of referrals.

Competency

In the United States, there is a fairly significant discrepancy between what are considered the core competencies for licensed physical, occupational, speech, and mental health therapists providing equine-assisted therapy.

Many physical, occupational, and speech therapists who provide equine-assisted therapy in the United States are credentialed through the American Hippotherapy Certification Board (AHCB). This process requires professionals to have experience, education, and training in the use of hippotherapy, and the exam evaluates for competency in the areas of theory and application of hippotherapy principles, horsemanship, movement science, and program administration.

Like the AHCB, the Certification Board for Equine Interaction Professionals (CBEIP) requires a specific amount of experience, education, and training, and its exam also evaluates for competency in the areas of assessment, evaluation, and planning, facilitator skills (which includes equine skills and knowledge), and administration and risk management. But most licensed mental health professionals have chosen not to engage in the credentialing process provided by the CBEIP, as demonstrated by the low numbers of individuals certified by the board currently (CBEIP, 2016). Instead, these individuals tend to seek out methodological training options that may not adhere to an industry-wide set of competency requirements or standards, and only provide a certificate of completion in a specific model or method. This leads to a great variation in the knowledge, education, and experience of licensed mental health professionals interested in providing equine-assisted therapy. In order to rectify this situation, licensed mental health professionals are advised to come together and support the process of developing industry-wide core competency, putting energy and financial resources towards the scientific advancement of the competency requirements and the testing process.

Clearly, there are core competencies relevant to *all* professionals providing equine-assisted therapy. It would behoove the industry for credentialing bodies to come together and agree upon a set of core competencies that any professional who wishes to include horses in clinical practice should demonstrate. The American Counseling Association (ACA) has paved the way for this to occur smoothly and effectively, and credentialing bodies are urged to consider the ACA's "Animal-Assisted Therapy in Counseling Competencies" as a potential model for developing competencies. These core competencies can then be taught by training organizations, and thus a baseline of knowledge can be established across all disciplines.

☐ Collaborate

Building consensus, collaborating, and having an open mind are all vital characteristics of healthy industries. As addressed earlier, horse people tend to be more independent and less cooperative than owners of other animal species (Robinson, 1999), but this should only motivate us all to do better. For the industry to grow and flourish, it is time to set aside differences and instead look for similarities.

The field of counseling provides an exceptional model of how to build consensus and collaborate. Delegates from 31 different organizations came together under the "20/20: A Vision for the Future of Counseling" initiative. They established core principles that unified the various membership, certifying, and accrediting groups within the profession of counseling (Kaplan, et al., 2014), and the outcome was a published doctrine entitled *Principles for Unifying and Strengthening the Profession* (Kaplan & Gladding, 2011). This historic event used a consensus-building approach called the Delphi method. This method was developed in the 1940s as a "systematic means for gathering expert opinions about complex issues or problems for which there are no verifiable, evidenced-based solutions" (Kaplan, et al., 2014, p. 376), and is facilitated by professionals non-biased to the outcome. The second step for the "20/20: A Vision for the Future of Counseling" initiative was to develop an agreed-upon definition for the term "counseling." Thirty delegates participated, and the outcome was a mutually agreed-upon definition that is now used across the country and in some cases, internationally.

Collaboration and consensus building is not only for membership associations and training organizations. Individual practitioners have an important role to play in the practice of collaboration. Like the patients they serve, each licensed healthcare professional is different, and brings unique strengths, skills, and abilities to the table. These differences should not be seen as negative characteristics or points of contention, but rather as possible opportunities for collaboration and learning. A critical step in professional development is recognizing which patients one can best serve, and which should be referred to another professional. This relies, in part, upon believing in the abundance of business, rather than being concerned with the potential scarcity of business (Covey, 2004).

Developing a platform to openly discuss industry-wide issues is an important first step for the industry as a whole, while individual providers can seek out opportunities for collaboration, build a solid referral network, and explore ways to support one another.

☐ Protect

Horses are beautiful, magical, wonderful creatures. Having a relationship with one is a gift that will continue giving throughout a lifetime. Sadly, horses are disappearing in greater and greater numbers from the United States. According to the U.S. Department of Agriculture, from 2007–2012 the U.S. horse population decreased approximately 10%, similar to the 12% decline in farms and ranches where they may have lived (Koba, 2014), and the American Veterinary Medical Association reports the populations of pet horses decreased from 7.3 million to 4.9 million between 2006–2011 (Burns, 2013).

James J. Hickey Jr., president of the American Horse Council, stated in 2014, "It's really because of the economy" (Koba, 2014, para. 4), when addressing the decline of horses in the United States. He goes on to note a 300% increase in the costs of hay and feed due to drought conditions (in Koba, 2014). Signs of the decline are evident all around the American West. Horse facilities sit empty or have been replaced by subdivisions and condominiums, and like the American Horse Council, one might ask, "Where have all the horses gone?"

Equine-assisted therapy provides a meaningful way for horses to remain in the lives of humans. However, without careful protection and thoughtful, knowledgeable tending, this industry may go the way of other horse industries, turning into a niche hobby enjoyed by a few and provided only by the most dedicated. Therefore, it is the responsibility of everyone providing equine-assisted therapy to take seriously the issues facing the industry, and work together to identify potential threats, challenges, and opportunities.

☐ Next Steps for the Industry

The growth and success of this industry relies upon the efforts of individual practitioners, the national and international associations and organizations, and everyone who wishes to see it flourish. Each one of these individuals and entities has an important role to play. Having an open mind, and working towards consensus and collaboration, will help the industry face the challenges ahead.

The following recommendations for next steps echo the voices of providers from around the world who contributed to an international professional practice survey (Stroud & Hallberg, 2016), and are supported by extensive study and research conducted for this book.

Accept the Investigational Nature of Equine-Assisted Therapy

Given the various issues inherent in current equine-assisted therapy research, it is obvious there is still much to be learned about equine-assisted therapy. All who provide or support equine-assisted therapy have an ethical responsibility to recognize the investigational nature of this emerging treatment approach, and make choices about widely publicizing complementary findings that may, in fact, be inaccurate.

Wilson & Barker (2003) state:

> Advocates of HAI [human-animal interactions] benefits frequently claim effectiveness based on anecdotal success and/or limited data. It is not uncommon in HAI research to read conclusions implying program effectiveness when no assessment of the efficacy of the

intervention has been conducted or studies implying causation based on results of descriptive or correlational analysis.

(p. 25)

Carlsson (2016) agrees with Wilson & Barker, suggesting, "A reflection on research focusing on effectiveness is that participants and staff perceptions sometimes exceed statistical evidence" (p. 20).

Both Benda, et al. (2003) and Park, et al. (2014) contribute to the discussion. "Little objective research has been offered to document the widespread clinical impression of benefit reported by therapists, parents, and pediatricians, particularly for children with cerebral palsy" (Benda, et al., 2003, p. 818); and Park, et al. (2014) state, "Despite this lack of consistent evidence on the benefit, horseback riding therapy is often recommended by clinicians for children with CP [cerebral palsy] to improve gross motor function" (p. 1737).

Finally, Thompson, et al. (2012) report, "The websites we reviewed led visitors to believe that equine programs provided participants with positive experiences and outcomes. However, the benefit claims . . . were never based on systematic empiricism" (p. 384).

As stated before in this book, it is assumed professionals and organizations making these benefits claims are not doing so maliciously. But, accepting and honoring the investigational nature of equine-assisted therapy can actually help to keep vulnerable populations safer, and will likely lead to higher quality research, promote professionalism and the ethical provision of services, and support scholarly, open-minded curiosity and exploration.

Clarify the Difference Between Therapy and Non-Therapy Services

The equine-assisted activities and therapies industry frequently refers to the "confusion" between therapy services (including equine-assisted psychotherapy and hippotherapy) and non-therapy services (including equine-assisted learning and adaptive riding). In truth, the differences are quite straightforward.

As every recreational equestrian knows, riding is good exercise, as are all the tasks that go along with caring for horses. These horse-related activities are pleasurable and reported to contribute to physical, social, and mental wellbeing (Davis, et al., 2015). Although these activities are beneficial, they should not be confused with therapy used to treat an illness or disability.

It is possible that the primary reason for the confusion is less about people not understanding the differences, and more about the possible outcomes of acknowledging and adhering to those differences. If providers and the industry as a whole committed to clarifying the lines between therapy and non-therapy services, individual providers, programs, and national associations would likely have to adjust terminology, alter their marketing strategies, and change some of the services they offer. In some cases, providers may also have to enhance their professional skills or recruit appropriately qualified personnel to continue offering services.

For example, some adaptive riding programs focus primarily on marketing the physical health benefits of riding for a variety of healthcare conditions, citing research related to treating these conditions with horseback riding. This confuses consumers, causing them to believe adaptive riding will "treat" these conditions. To keep the lines clear, these providers should focus on marketing the importance of adaptive recreation, learning a new skill, getting exercise, and socializing. They should refer participants seeking treatment to qualified and appropriately licensed physical, occupational, or speech therapists.

Providers of equine-assisted learning may also offer services that cross or blur the lines between therapy and non-therapy. Some models of equine-assisted learning use the same activities and processing style as equine-assisted psychotherapy and provide services to the same or similar clientele. Many training programs teach the same curriculum to both licensed mental health professionals and non-licensed people. If a non-licensed provider offers virtually the same service as a licensed professional, it is highly likely the emotional responses and reactions invoked by the activities and the processing style will mirror those that occur in therapy. Just because the service is called something different does not make it different. If equine-assisted learning providers were to rectify this confusion, they would need to use language, activities, and a facilitation style that clearly differentiates their services from therapy, focusing on an educational or coaching approach, goals, and methodology.

Ideally, an observer should be able to watch an equine-assisted therapy session and then watch a non-therapy lesson or service and clearly see the difference. For instance, a riding lesson is wholly different than a therapy session, regardless of the abilities or disabilities the rider might be experiencing. It should be obvious the goal of a riding lesson is to learn to ride. When adaptive riding instructors focus on attempting to address (or treat) physical health conditions with specifically designed activities that are used in therapy, they stop focusing on teaching the student how to ride, and thus contribute to the ongoing confusion. Likewise, picture watching a student in a classroom, or a professional participating in leadership coaching in an office setting. Imagine if that individual was encouraged to discuss deeply personal issues, past traumas, and engage in cathartic activities aimed at exposing unconscious emotions. Clearly this would seem odd, out of place, and verging on unethical.

Obviously, the industry has some work to do before getting to the point where the services and terminology clearly differentiate between therapy and non-therapy services. But, with dedication, education, and training, providers can make a difference by personally committing to keeping the lines clear between therapy and non-therapy services.

Address Confusions Between the Professional
Membership Associations

Professional membership associations and training organizations are urged to step away from a competitive stance and instead identify how they fit into the larger order of the industry. Membership associations, training organizations, and credentialing bodies all serve different purposes and, in theory, should not be in competition with each other.

If one looks to the larger healthcare industry, it is clear there are not multiple professional associations for each licensure type. This sort of duplication naturally creates competition and confusion, and leads to challenges establishing overarching standards, ethics, professional practice guidelines, and terminology.

The Professional Association for Therapeutic Horsemanship, International (PATH, Intl.) and the AHA overlap in membership types and purposes. AHA provides support solely for physical, occupational, and speech therapists or therapy assistants who provide equine-assisted therapy, while PATH Intl. also provides support for these individuals, but includes licensed mental health professionals, educators, and adaptive riding instructors. Although the largest concentration of PATH Intl. members appears to be adaptive riding instructors, PATH Intl. has taken a lead in establishing the standards, ethics, precautions, and contraindications commonly used by licensed therapists. This has the potential to be problematic, as licensed professionals must first adhere to the laws and ethics of their profession. If a PATH Intl. standard comes into conflict with any of these laws or ethics, PATH Intl. certainly cannot require the licensed professional to act in a manner contrary to what is ethical or legal for that profession. Furthermore, PATH Intl. does not provide training or a certificate for any type of licensed healthcare professional. Thus, it seems strange that PATH Intl. would set the standards of practice for these professions.

AHA does offer a set of "Best Practice Guidelines" but defers to the PATH Intl. standards. AHA also provides training for licensed physical, occupational, and speech therapists and offers resources like billing and coding information, recommended terminology, and useful distinctions between therapy and non-therapy services. AHA has an established relationship with the larger professional associations governing the professional practices of physical therapy, occupational therapy, and speech therapy, while PATH Intl. does not seem to have this type of relationship.

The needs of mental health professionals are, by and large, neglected by both PATH Intl. and AHA. In light of this, many of these professionals seek out the EAGALA for support. The issue with this choice is that EAGALA is a model-specific training organization that does not meet the needs of all licensed mental health professionals seeking inclusive and broad-based professional support. Furthermore, EAGALA shows no deference to PATH Intl. or any other industry membership association or credentialing body, and does not require or recommend that its members or trainees use the PATH Intl. standards or code of ethics, or become credentialed through the CBEIP.

All of these associations use different terminology, and the roles these associations play within the industry seem convoluted. This may enhance the feeling that each of these associations is posturing in an attempt to be seen as "the" leader in the industry. This is unnecessary if each association were to have a specific role within the industry.

For example, perhaps the AHA could expand its mission and vision to include mental health professionals, thereby embracing all licensed professions that typically offer equine-assisted therapy. The needs of all licensed professionals are similar, but differ drastically from the needs of non-licensed individuals. Thus, it would make sense for licensed professionals to come together under one membership association and develop standards and ethical guidelines that support the work of equine-assisted therapy. Physical, occupational, and speech therapists would continue to be credentialed through the AHCB, while licensed mental health professionals would be credentialed through the CBEIP. If this occurred, PATH Intl. could transition to supporting only the needs of non-licensed providers like those offering adaptive riding and equine-assisted learning. PATH Intl. could either continue offering its own certification, or support the development of a non-biased credentialing body for adaptive riding and equine-assisted learning. This clear delineation would further support the need to separate therapy and non-therapy services.

Training organizations or other methodologically based associations like EAGALA provide very different services than non-biased professional membership associations, and thus should not be confused in the mix at all. Since there is ample room for many different models or treatment approaches, there is no need for competition between training organizations, or for suggesting one model is "better" than another. All training organizations or methodologically-based entities could guide their members towards the correct professional membership association, and could support the appropriate credentialing bodies.

Advocate

It is all too common to see unethical practices occurring and assume someone else will do something about it, or to leave the development of the industry to someone who might have more time. But, the reality is that each licensed professional who provides equine-assisted therapy has a vital role to play in establishing the safe and ethical growth and development of this industry.

Advocacy means having a voice during important discussions that could shape the direction of the industry. Professionals are urged to answer professional practice surveys even if it takes time, attend national conferences and meetings, and volunteer for committees. Advocacy also means supporting the separation of therapy and non-therapy services by helping to educate others and reporting violations. Finally, advocacy means standing up for wellbeing of all who participate in equine-assisted therapy, very much including the horses.

The more involved licensed professionals become, the greater influence they will have as the industry moves forward.

Develop a Consortium

Consensus building and developing a more collaborative and open-minded mentality can be accomplished by the formation of a national or international delegation of stakeholders including providers, researchers, educators, thought leaders, and the heads of associations and organizations who come together in a professionally-facilitated congress to discuss the state of the industry and outline a plan for addressing the challenges it faces.

One of the primary motivations for creating this type of consortium is to decrease the personalization of equine-assisted therapy, and support the professionalization of the industry. Limited access to research, unsuccessful attempts at collaboration between all types of stakeholders, and the lack of a disciplined, scholarly, and non-biased process used to address industry issues has probably helped to perpetuate some of the challenges the industry faces.

If such a consortium was created, important topics for discussion include:

- Defining the professional practices of equine-assisted physical therapy, equine-assisted occupational therapy, equine-assisted speech therapy, and equine-assisted mental health as distinct from each other and obviously distinct from adaptive riding or equine-assisted learning.
- Building consensus around definitions and terminology.
- Coming to an agreement about the roles and function of the various associations and organizations within equine-assisted therapy.
- Identifying sub-groups to address the development of a body of knowledge and competency recommendations for the distinct professional practices of equine-assisted therapy.
- Addressing issues of research methodology, and developing a plan for an industry-wide research agenda supported by the outcomes of current systematic reviews and a comprehensive literature review.

Establish a Research Agenda and Support Research Funding

A research agenda acts like a road map for identifying, organizing, and prioritizing research initiatives. Effective industry-wide research agendas are typically established through an intensive and inclusive process that includes reviewing current literature, summarizing the results of research findings, identifying gaps in evidence, consulting with experts (both in practice and in academia), and presenting the research agenda to associated broader professional fields for review and commentary (Center for the Advancement of Informal Science Education (CAISE), 2016).

The Horses and Humans Research Foundation seems a likely choice for spearheading the creation of such a research agenda. The Horses and Humans Research Foundation could bring together individual researchers, academic institutes, organizations, and membership associations with research interests in a process that unifies the industry around an informed and educated road map for research. Such an effort could help transition the state of equine-assisted activities and therapies research from responding primarily to current practice trends in the industry to exploring broader, more objective questions that could advance the level of knowledge and understanding across the industry.

As stated earlier in this book, current research agendas seem to focus primarily on research that will "prove" the effectiveness of equine-assisted therapy for specific conditions or populations.

One of the important components to a research agenda is including research targeted at understanding how a treatment strategy works, rather than trying to prove that it does work. Carlsson (2016) supports this approach, stating "The focus on efficacy in this field has led to less knowledge about the process" (p. 20). As such, high quality large scale research projects that investigate the processes associated with change are needed over more poor quality, small scale research projects that focus only on attempting to establish efficacy.

Another important responsibility of those such as the Horses and Humans Research Foundation who set research agendas or help to obtain funding for research agendas, is understanding the difference between therapy and non-therapy approaches. Research focusing on treating physical and mental health conditions shouldn't use non-therapy approaches like adaptive riding and equine-assisted learning. Rather, these research projects should use equine-assisted physical therapy, equine-assisted occupational therapy, equine-assisted speech therapy, or equine-assisted mental health as the treatment intervention. Conversely, if the research project is interested in learning how an equine-assisted activity can improve social skills and quality of life, or enhance educational or recreational experiences, then adaptive riding or equine-assisted learning would be appropriate.

Funding for research is a significant limiting factor in the equine-assisted therapy industry. In many cases, individual practitioners fund their own research, or are supported by small grants. Attracting professional researchers who can conduct long-term, large scale research is an expensive undertaking, and not currently common in the equine-assisted therapy industry. The Horses and Humans Research Foundation is working hard to change this, and ideally, over time a greater emphasis will be placed on these large scale research projects, and major grants or other funding sources can be identified to support this work.

Agree Upon Competency Requirements

Historically, each individual association or training organization has attempted to create its own version of what competency is and how a professional should demonstrate it, but since each of these entities developed this content mostly (or totally, in some cases) in isolation from the other organizations or associations, there is disagreement, and camps have formed based upon personal beliefs. Furthermore, in some cases, training organizations have decided not to support the efforts of national credentialing bodies, therefore impeding the efforts to standardize and unify competency requirements.

Licensed mental health professionals are advised to follow in the footsteps of physical, occupational, and speech therapists who have joined together to support the credentialing process established by the AHCB. Although perhaps not perfect, the CBEIP already exists, and could greatly benefit from increased support from licensed professionals. With such support, the CBEIP could update the exam content using empirical research rather than opionion-based material and establish ties with the ACA, potentially including the ACA's Animal-Assisted Therapy in Counseling Core Competencies into the CBEIP's competency requirements. Collaboration with a major professional association like the ACA could help the CBEIP gain more respect and support throughout the licensed mental health community.

If both of these credentialing bodies could gain traction and become known for setting industry competency standards, training programs would be able to develop curriculum based upon those standards to support the educational and training needs of professionals. This effort would help to standardize the industry, and promote a more comprehensive understanding of equine-assisted therapy.

Attend to the Needs of the Horses

Last, but very much not least, the welfare of horses who work within equine-assisted therapy practices or programs is of the utmost importance. Additional energy and effort is required to better understand how to support and enhance the wellbeing of these animals.

It is clear from the research that carrying unbalanced humans, or dealing with stress, behavioral issues, or other psychological conditions can have an impact on horses (Minero, et al., 2006; Lesimple, et al., 2010; Kaiser, et al., 2006; Fazio, et al., 2013). Therefore, equine-assisted therapy providers have an ethical responsibility to carefully assess their horses and address the physical and emotional needs of these animals so they can best handle the work they are asked to do.

Outside, non-biased evaluation should become a more common, comfortable, and sought-after component to equine-assisted therapy programs. Hiring a consultant or veterinarian to help develop an assessment tool, using the tool internally, and then identifying outside sources to come and use the tool, will improve the quality and reliability of equine evaluations.

At present, an important discussion topic is how to manage the large numbers of donated horses who may be elderly, physically unfit, emotionally traumatized, and sometimes even in pain that are donated and, in many cases, put to work in equine-assisted therapy programs. Another issue for consideration is how to attend to the needs of horses who are either burned out and need a break from equine-assisted therapy, or are aging and need to be retired.

Finally, the equine-assisted therapy industry faces challenges dealing with a dwindling equine population, a decrease in agricultural land that is in close proximity to urban hubs, and the increasing cost of equine care.

Many licensed professionals providing equine-assisted therapy face these challenges and concerns. Finding a way to come together and discuss them in a supportive and open-minded environment could generate new ideas, and help foster a deeper sense of collaboration.

☐ Conclusion

Equine-assisted therapy combines the power of the horse-human relationship with the clinical practices of licensed healthcare professionals. It supports including the wisdom and innate healing abilities of nature and other species in conventional healthcare. This is an amazingly potent, yet complicated, process.

Understanding another species and knowing how to safely, ethically, and effectively involve that species is extremely important. The novel, dynamic, and complex treatment milieu adds another dimension professionals must take into consideration. As such, providers of equine-assisted therapy have an immense amount of knowledge to amass, and a great responsibility to keep both their patients and the horses they work with physically and emotionally safe. This is no simple task, and deserves much attention and thoughtful care.

As a whole, the industry of equine-assisted therapy is poised to position itself as an influential addition to human healthcare. But, it is challenged to come together and grow as one, putting aside personal motivations and embracing the professionalization of the practice. It is hoped this book will aid in that process, and provide food for thought for this generation of practitioners—and those to come.

☐ References

Anestis, M.D., Anestis, J.C., Zawilinski, L.L., Hopkins, T.A., & Lilienfeld, S.O. (2014). Equine-related treatments for mental disorders lack empirical support: A systematic review of empirical investigations. *Journal of Clinical Psychology*, 1–18.

Angoules, A., Koukoulas, D., Balakatounis, K., Kapari, I., & Matsouki, E. (2015). A review of efficacy of hippotherapy for the treatment of musculoskeletal disorders. *British Journal of Medicine and Medical Research*, 8(4), 289–297.

Angsupaisal, M., Visser, B., Alkema, A., Meinsma-van der Tuin, M., Maathuis, C.G.B., Reinders-Messelink, H., & Hadders-Algra, M. (2015). Therapist-designed adaptive riding in children with cerebral palsy: Results of a feasibility study. *Physical Therapy*, 95(8), 1151–1162.

Bachi, K. (2012). Equine-facilitated psychotherapy: The gap between practice and knowledge. *Society & Animals*, 20, 364–380.

Benda, W., McGibbon, N.H., & Grant, K.L. (2003). Improvements in muscle symmetry in children with cerebral palsy after equine-assisted therapy (hippotherapy). *Journal of Alternative and Complementary Medicine*, 9(6), 817–825.

Bond, M. (2007). Horseback riding as therapy for children with cerebral palsy: Is there evidence of its effectiveness? *Physical & Occupational Therapy in Pediatrics*, 27(2), 5–23.

Burns, K. (February 1, 2013). *Vital Statistics*. JAVMA News. Retrieved from: www.avma.org/news/javmanews/pages/130201a.aspx

Carlsson, C. (February 14, 2016). A narrative review of qualitative and quantitative research in equine-assisted social work or therapy—Addressing gaps and contradictory results. *Animalia an Anthrozoology Journal*.

Center for the Advancement of Informational Science Education (CAISE). (2016). *Research Agendas*. Retrieved from: www.informalscience.org/research/research-agendas

Certification Board for Equine Interaction Professionals (CBEIP). (2016). *Certified Professionals*. Retrieved from: www.cbeip.com/certified_professionals.aspx

Covey, S.R. (2004). *The 7 habits of highly effective people: Powerful lessons in personal change*. New York, NY: Free Press.

Davis, D.L., Maurstad, A., & Dean, S. (2015). My horse is my therapist: The medicalization of pleasure among women equestrians. *Medical Anthropology Quarterly*, 29(3), 298–315.

Debuse, D., Chandler, C., & Gibb, C. (2005). An exploration of German and British physiotherapists' views on the effects of hippotherapy and their measurement. *Physiotherapy Theory and Practice*, 21(4), 219–242.

Ewing, C.A., MacDonald, P.M., Taylor, M., & Bowers, M.J. (2007). Equine-facilitated learning for youths with severe emotional disorders: A quantitative and qualitative study. *Child and Youth Care Forum*, 36(1), 59–72.

Fazio, E., Medica, P., Cravana, C., & Ferlazzo, A. (2013). Hypothalamic-pituitary-adrenal axis responses of horses to therapeutic riding program: Effects of different riders. *Physiology and Behavior*, 118, 138–143.

Jenkins, S.R., & Digennaro Reed, F.D. (2013). An experimental analysis of the effects of therapeutic horseback riding on the behavior of children with autism. *Research in Autism Spectrum Disorders*, 7(6), 721–740.

Kaiser, L., Heleski, C.R., Siegford, J., & Smith, K.A. (2006). Stress-related behaviors among horses used in a therapeutic riding program. *Journal of the American Veterinary Medical Association*, 228(1), 39–45.

Kaplan, D.M., & Gladding, S.T. (2011). A vision for the future of counseling: The 20/20 Principles for unifying and strengthening the profession. *Journal of Counseling & Development*, 89, 367–372.

Kaplan, D.M., Tarvydas, V.M., & Gladding, S.T. (2014). 20/20: A vision for the future of counseling: The new consensus definition of counseling. *Journal of Counseling & Development*, *92*, 366–372.

Kendall, E., Maujean, A., Pepping, C.A., et al. (2015). A systematic review of the efficacy of equine-assisted interventions on psychological outcomes. *European Journal of Psychotherapy & Counselling*, *2537*(17), 57–79.

Koba, M. (May 30, 2014). *Where Have All the Horses Gone? Blame the Economy*. Retrieved from: www.nbcnews.com/business/economy/where-have-all-horses-gone-blame-economy-n118646

Lee, P.T., Dakin, E., & Mclure, M. (2016). Narrative synthesis of equine-assisted psychotherapy literature: Current knowledge and future research directions. *Health and Social Care in the Community*, *24*(3), 225–246.

Lentini, J.A., & Knox, M.S. (2015). Equine-facilitated psychotherapy with children and adolescents: An update and literature review. *Journal of Creativity in Mental Health*, *10*(3), 278–305.

Lesimple, C., Fureix, C., Menguy, H., & Hausberger, M. (2010). Human direct actions may alter animal welfare, a study on horses (Equus caballus). *PloS One*, *5*(4), 1–8.

Minero, M., Zucca, D., & Canali, E. (2006). A note on reaction to novel stimulus and restraint by therapeutic riding horses. *Applied Animal Behaviour Science*, *97*(2–4), 335–342.

Park, E.S., Rha, D.W., Shin, J.S., Kim, S., & Jung, S. (2014). Effects of hippotherapy on gross motor function and functional performance of children with cerebral palsy. *Yonsei Medical Journal*, *55*(6), 1736–1742.

Pepper, M., & Driscoll, D.L. (2015). *Writing Definitions*. Retrieved from: https://owl.english.purdue.edu/owl/resource/622/01/

Robinson, I.H.. (1999). The human-horse relationship: How much do we know? *Equine Veterinary Journal Supplement*, *28*, 42–45.

Selby, A., & Smith-Osborne, A. (2013). A systematic review of effectiveness of complementary and adjunct therapies and interventions involving equines. *Health Psychology*, *32*(4), 418–432.

Snider, L., Korner-Bitensky, N., Kammann, C., Warner, S., & Saleh, M. (2007). Horseback riding as therapy for children with cerebral palsy: Is there evidence of its effectiveness? *Physical & Occupational Therapy in Pediatrics*, *27*(2), 5–23.

Stroud, D., & Hallberg, L. (2016). [Horses in healthcare: An international assessment of the professional practice of equine-assisted therapy]. Unpublished raw data.

Thompson, J.R., Iacobucci, V., & Varney, R. (2012). Giddyup! or whoa nelly! Making sense of benefit claims on websites of equine programs for children with disabilities. *Journal of Developmental and Physical Disabilities*, *24*, 373–390.

Tseng, S.-H., Chen, H.-C., & Tam, K.-W. (2012). Systematic review and meta-analysis of the effect of equine assisted activities and therapies on gross motor outcome in children with cerebral palsy. *Disability and Rehabilitation*, *35*, 1–11.

Wang, G., Ma, R., Qiao, G., Wada, K., Aizawa, Y., & Satoh, T. (2015). The effect of riding as an alternative treatment for children with cerebral palsy: A systematic review and meta-analysis. *Integrative Medicine International*, *1*(4), 211–222.

Whalen, C.N., & Case-Smith, J. (2012). Therapeutic effects of horseback riding therapy on gross motor function in children with cerebral palsy: A systematic review. *Physical & Occupational Therapy in Pediatrics*, *32*(3), 229–242.

Wilson, C.C., & Barker, S.B. (2003). Challenges in designing human-animal interaction research. *American Behavioral Scientist*, *47*(1), 16–28.

Index

Lightning Source UK Ltd.
Milton Keynes UK
UKHW020037150421
382016UK00005B/35